DOWN THE JERSEY SHORE

DOWN
T H E
JERSEY SHORE

Russell Roberts and Rich Youmans

RUTGERS UNIVERSITY PRESS, NEW BRUNSWICK, NEW JERSEY

Library of Congress Cataloging-in-Publication Data

Roberts, Russell, 1953–
    Down the Jersey Shore / Russell Roberts and Richard Youmans.
    p.   cm.
    Includes bibliographical references and index.
    ISBN 0-8135-1995-0 (cloth)—ISBN 0-8135-1996-9 (pbk.)
    1. Atlantic Coast (N.J.)—History, Local.   I. Youmans, Richard, 1960–
II. Title.
F134.5.R63   1993
974.9′00946—dc20   92-44337
                                                                          CIP

British Cataloging-in-Publication information available

To Megan and Patti, for their love and understanding, and to my parents, for having the good sense to move to the Jersey Shore when I was just five years old

—RUSS

♦

To my mother and father, who first introduced me to the Jersey Shore, and to Ann, who supported me through this project

—RICH

CONTENTS

ACKNOWLEDGMENTS

No project of this magnitude could have been accomplished without the help and generosity of many, many people. Those that we would like to single out for their kindness on our behalf are Marilyn Kralik, for all the information and also a wonderful meal on a cold winter's night; Tom Hoffman, for giving of his time so freely; Josephine Harron, for opening Lucy the Elephant on a cold day in February; the dedicated members of the Ocean County Historical Society, for never giving up the search to find Joseph Francis's letters to Thomas Bond; Debbie Fimbel, for her patience in answering our questions; Mike Mangum, for his invaluable aid in directing us to those few remaining masters of traditional shore crafts; June LeMunyon, for opening the Tuckerton Historical Museum on a day when the heavens poured; Jerry Woolley, for having so much information right at his fingertips; George Moss, for pointing the way; and Shirley S. Albright, for sending more information than we ever dreamed possible.

Others to whom we owe a debt of gratitude are the Archives of AT&T/Bell Laboratories; the Atlantic County Historical Society; the Cape May County Historical and Genealogical Society; Dorn's Photography Unlimited; Dr. Stewart Farrell; Wendy Gulley of the Nautilus Memorial Submarine Force Library & Museum in Groton, Connecticut; the Keyport Historical Society Steamboat Dock Museum; Tom Laverty; the Miss America Pageant; the Monmouth County Historical Association; the Ocean City Historical Society; the Ocean County Historical Museum; Dr. Norbert P. Psuty, Ph.D.; Richard Steele Photography; Elbert Wilbert; the Wildwood Historical Society, and last, but certainly not least, the wonderful staff members of all the libraries that we haunted during the length of this project. We couldn't have done it without you (nor would we have wanted to try)!

September 1992

DOWN THE JERSEY SHORE

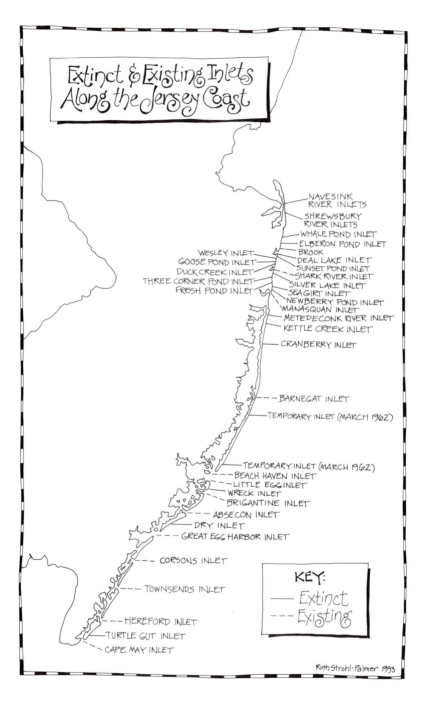

Extinct & Existing Inlets Along the Jersey Coast

NAVESINK RIVER INLETS
SHREWSBURY RIVER INLETS
WHALE POND INLET
ELBERON POND INLET
WESLEY INLET
BROOK
GOOSE POND INLET
DEAL LAKE INLET
DUCK CREEK INLET
SUNSET POND INLET
SHARK RIVER INLET
THREE CORNER POND INLET
SILVER LAKE INLET
FRESH POND INLET
SEA GIRT INLET
NEWBERRY POND INLET
MANASQUAN INLET
METEDECONK RIVER INLET
KETTLE CREEK INLET

CRANBERRY INLET

BARNEGAT INLET

TEMPORARY INLET (MARCH 1962)

TEMPORARY INLET (MARCH 1962)
BEACH HAVEN INLET
LITTLE EGG INLET
WRECK INLET
BRIGANTINE INLET
ABSECON INLET
DRY INLET
GREAT EGG HARBOR INLET

CORSONS INLET

TOWNSENDS INLET

HEREFORD INLET
TURTLE GUT INLET
CAPE MAY INLET

KEY:
——— Extinct
- - - Existing

Ruth Strohl-Palmer 1993

INTRODUCTION

~~~~~~

There's a lot more to the Jersey Shore than first appears. On the surface the Shore seems pretty basic: it has nice beaches, fun-filled boardwalks, and a bunch of restaurants and motels. You spend the day on the beach, lying in the sun, listening to the radio, or just catching up on sleep. You go back to your motel or lodging house, take a shower, eat at a restaurant, and then hit the boardwalk, where you can find even more things to eat, go on a seemingly endless variety of stomach-churning rides (not right after you eat!), or just walk along and soak up the carnival-like atmosphere. Beaches and boardwalks, motels and restaurants— that pretty much sums up the Jersey Shore, right?

Well, not really.

To look at the Shore and see only sun and fun is like looking at the Mona Lisa and noticing only her smile. Sure, that smile catches your eye—but you're missing so much more.

There's no denying that beaches, boardwalks, motels, restaurants, and everything else that visitors enjoy are part of the Jersey

Shore, a very important part. But they're only a small portion of the whole picture. The Shore could well be one of the cultural storehouses of New Jersey. Running through this 127-mile stretch of beachfront is a virtual mother lode of history and tradition. It's a rich vein, full of fascinating stories.

Unfortunately, it's often difficult to find any tangible evidence of the Shore's history. Progress tends to destroy the past, and nowhere is this truer than at the Jersey Shore. Today it's hard to believe that just over one hundred years ago the Shore was a desolate region filled with marshlands and beaches. Except for a few spots like Long Branch and Cape May, no one wanted to go to the Shore for vacation, much less live there. But within the relatively short span of a century, the entire Jersey Shore has been totally transformed. Now bustling towns and busy roads have replaced the windswept wilderness, and vacationers must make reservations months in advance.

As the Shore has changed, so have its needs. Today there is no longer any reason for real estate entrepreneurs to build giant elephants to sell beachfront real estate, or for lifesavers to patrol dark and dreary beaches at night looking for stranded ships, or for railroads and steamships to bring people to areas that had previously been inaccessible. Today there are no large stretches of undeveloped land available for dreamers to found new communities, nor do presidents and society's darlings flock to the Shore in the summertime, sending everyone into a frenzy of excitement by their mere presence. Lighthouses are not needed anymore, and neither, it seems, are traditional crafts. As the reasons for these things fade, so do the stories behind them.

Change, of course, is an inevitable consequence of life. But at the Shore, change has been so extensive and so complete that it has virtually eradicated all evidence of what came before. Many of the people, places, and things that played a major part in the Shore's history are gone now, and we are all the poorer for the loss. Today the only place to find the Jersey Shore's past is in historical museums and societies, where it is nourished by the love of people who refuse to let it die.

To find the past in museums and historical societies, we must make a deliberate effort to seek it out; otherwise it will remain hidden, like the treasure that Captain Kidd is said to have buried somewhere along the Jersey coast. Like Kidd's treasure, the his-

tory and heritage of the Shore contains many a fine gem, its lus-
ter untarnished by the passage of years.

The purpose of this book is to bring these gems into the light, so
they can gain a greater appreciation. In searching for them, we
found so many that not all could be included. But we've tried to
present as many as possible—those that shine the brightest
through the sands of time. To do this, we have sometimes
stretched the boundaries of the Shore a bit, wandering from the
immediate coast to probe a bit farther inland.

Indeed, the Jersey Shore cannot be defined by mere geographic
boundaries. To think of the Shore as just a narrow strip of sand
bordered by the ocean is much too simple. Although it may sound
like leftover hippie philosophy from the peace and love decade of
the 1960s, the Jersey Shore is truly a state of mind. It doesn't
begin when you first hear the roar of the ocean, nor does it end
the minute you cross over the Garden State Parkway. People who
live ten or twenty miles from the beach still think of themselves
as living at the Shore, and it would be hard to argue with them.

For these reasons we have defined the Shore loosely. Places
like Lakewood, Holmdel, and others that don't appear on maps to
be right along the coast but which have played a part in the
Shore's history have been included in this narrative. It may con-
found the mapmakers, but we think it makes for more interesting
reading.

Because we have an elastic definition of the Shore, we have
chosen a different way to present its story. Instead of the standard method, which is to begin at Sandy Hook and work doggedly
south to Cape May, we have divided the book into chapters with
unifying themes. Each chapter looks at a separate aspect of the
Jersey Shore. The information that we have gathered is, as far as
we know, accurate (except in such chapters as the one that re-
lates local ghost stories, where verification will have to come from
a higher authority). In most cases, we steered clear of legends
and hoary tales handed down through generations and relied instead on accounts we perceived as more factual, such as newspaper stories, books, and magazine articles.

We have tried to do several things in this book. The first is to
present the early days of development at various points along the
Jersey Shore without regard to geography or strict chronology.
The chapters on transportation, towns, boardwalks, and famous

visitors and residents are examples; in these glimpses of the past we can discover the reasons for the present. Since this is a book about history and heritage rather than a sociological text, we have not traced the history of Shore development up to today.

We also explored topics that we felt were interesting, yet whose history has long since become obscured. Why is there a giant elephant on the beach in Margate? How did the Miss America Pageant originate in Atlantic City? What are the stories of the lighthouses that dot the coastline? We have tried to answer specific questions like these.

Finally, because writers are readers as well, we picked some topics just because we wanted to read about them. Ghost stories, unknown inventors, the Life-Saving Service—these are subjects about which we have always been interested. We hope you will be too.

Throughout the book we have tried to keep the sense of loss—of time racing by and sweeping the Shore along with it—out of the writing. There are enough things in life whose passing is mourned without this book adding to our collective sense of sadness. However, in two chapters—those on traditional crafts and the changing coastline—a certain sense of loss could not be avoided. It is the nature of these topics, and of the implications they portend for the future.

However, this is not to say that we are discouraged about the Shore's future. The gloom-and-doom scenarios currently popular about the Shore—it's too crowded, it's overdeveloped, it's ripe for devastation by natural forces— are simply not for us. We're bullish on the Jersey Shore. Sure it's not the same as it was years ago, but what in life is?

Often, things that seem simple at first turn out under investigation to be quite complex. Take this trip down the Jersey Shore, and you'll find that there is, indeed, much more than first meets the eye.

CHAPTER

ONE

SHORE TOWN STORIES

~~~~~~

"**I** will take the farmlands, but not those swamps and sand dunes—not at any price! Be reasonable, gentlemen, what will those islands ever be good for—sea gull nests?"

So said Thomas Budd in 1695, protesting a requirement that forced him to buy beachfront land on Absecon Island at four cents an acre before he could buy the more desirable farmland on the mainland for ten times that amount. But his protestations were to no avail; Budd did indeed become the owner of "swamps and sand dunes."

For a long time, Thomas Budd's opinion of shore property was shared by just about everyone. The shore was considered as desirable a place to live as the desert. This view prevailed well into the second half of the nineteenth century. As late as 1865, one person—the Widow Wardell—owned all the property from Long Branch to north of Sea Bright. Her claim came straight from the king-of-the-mountain real estate manual: her boys could beat up anyone else they found on the beach.

5

Gradually, however, things began to change. A few hardy souls ventured down to the shore and discovered that it was not the God-forsaken wilderness they had feared but a quiet, peaceful place with abundant natural advantages. Word spread, and soon others came to see for themselves. Before too long a region whose ownership had once been determined by whoever's sons were the toughest was dotted with towns, railroads, and people.

The story of the development of Jersey Shore towns is one that would horrify any English teacher, because there is no unifying plot, no central theme. Sometimes it is the story of a strong, driven figure, such as Asbury Park's James A. Bradley, marching about with two-foot ruler in hand as he plotted and planned and made his town rise out of the swamp and the briers. Other times it is the story of deeply religious people, like the Lake-family men who founded Ocean City, who knew what they wanted and scouted the coast until they found it. Occasionally a town's real story takes a while to develop, as when John Wanamaker arrived in Island Heights twenty years after it first began and transformed the town with his vision. And sometimes it is the idealistic story of dreamers like those who founded the North American Phalanx, struggling mightily to carve a socialist utopia out of the wilderness.

Each Jersey Shore town is unique. Each has its own story. Here are just some of the many.

◆

"Went to Peck's Beach to see the land that we might learn whether it would do for a camp meeting resort. We had a very pleasant day indeed."

With those words, in the diary of S. Wesley Lake on September 10, 1879, Ocean City was born.

It was not an expected birth. If Lake had been told only a few months before that he'd be a founding father of a town on the Jersey Shore, he might well have laughed uproariously. He was a minister, after all, a distinguished member of the Methodist Episcopal church, not a town father.

But the event that changed Lake's life, as well as the future of the Jersey Shore, occurred on August 22, 1879. On that day Lake, along with a fellow clergyman from Philadelphia, William B. Wood, attended worship service at Ocean Grove. (Ocean Grove, founded in 1869, was the first Methodist camp meeting town on the Jersey Shore, and it spawned many imitations.) Later, in a simple notation for such a momentous day, Lake wrote in his diary: "Attended Camp Meeting at Ocean Grove."

Lake had always been struck by the amazing contrast between the quiet, spiritual life of Ocean Grove and the "debauchery" of the other Jersey Shore, as represented by Atlantic City. He enunciated this quite clearly in 1883 when he wrote about the idea behind Ocean City: "While at Farmingdale [where he served as minister] I made frequent visits to Ocean Grove and there seeing the wonderful difference between Ocean Grove and Atlantic City I could not help but say, Oh! God,! give us as many Ocean Groves as possible. At Atlantic City there is constantly before the eye bar-rooms, lager beer saloons, cigar shops, balls, hops, etc. Oh what a place for a christian [sic] to take his children to spend the summer. I never could think of taking my children to such a place." It was, he wrote, not only the right but the "absolute duty" of ministers to carve out a niche on the Jersey Shore for those who wanted to live according to their religious convictions. "Why should the rum and sabbath desecrating elements possess all of the New Jersey coast?" he asked rhetorically.

After his attendance at Ocean Grove that August day, Lake discussed with Wood the idea of having a Christian resort along the southern Jersey Shore—Ocean Grove being too far north for people from Philadelphia, Wilmington, Baltimore, and other points south. When he returned to his Pleasantville home, he discussed the idea with his brothers Ezra and James as well as with his father, Simon, a wealthy farmer and fruit grower who had served in the state general assembly during the Civil War. The family decided to pursue the project for several reasons, including the excellent real estate prospects that a seaside resort represented.

At first the Lakes looked north of Pleasantville, to the part of Absecon Island that is now Margate. However, the land there was held by an estate with numerous minor heirs, and it would have taken years to untangle the title mess.

Shortly afterward, during a sailing trip to a camp meeting in South Seaville, they saw Peck's Beach, an island known to them since their cousin William had surveyed it five years earlier.

Peck's Beach was a wild, desolate island about two miles from the mainland, a place better suited for Thomas Budd's sea gull

Shore Towns with Religious Roots

Many towns were founded along the Jersey Shore in the later half of the nineteenth century to emulate the life-style of Ocean Grove's Methodist Camp Meeting Association. Today, only Ocean Grove remains as a camp meeting town. Below are the towns that began as camp meeting associations or were founded by other religious organizations.

ATLANTIC HIGHLANDS. This area was known as Bay View until 1881, when the Atlantic Highlands Association was established by, among others, Thomas H. Leonard and the Reverend James Lake. Atlantic Highlands soon became known as a prominent camp meeting resort for Methodist ministers.

BELMAR. This town was founded by summer residents of Ocean Grove, who felt that their old resort was becoming too crowded. They named the new town Ocean Beach and incorporated the Ocean Beach Association in March 1873. The name Belmar did not come into being for another twenty years.

AVON-BY-THE-SEA. Founded in 1883 by Baptist ministers and patterned after Ocean Grove, this resort was originally known as Key East. The American Institute of Christian Philosophy held its annual summer school here, and a school for disabled orphans was run by the Episcopal church. Originally part of Neptune Township, the borough of Avon-by-the-Sea was established in 1900.

SEASIDE PARK. In 1874 the Seaside Park Baptist Association bought much of the land on which today's borough is situated. The association planned to develop exactly what its name implied—a park by the sea—and began to sell lots toward that end. By 1880, however, the planned resort had failed, and the land was auctioned off. The borough of Seaside Park was established in 1898.

CAPE MAY POINT. Originally known as Sea Grove, this town was founded in 1875 by two Philadelphia merchants and devoted Presbyterians—John Wanamaker (yes, *the* John Wanamaker) and Alexander Whilldon—who, seeing the success of such Methodist resorts as Ocean Grove, decided their denomination should have a camp meeting town of its own.

nests than a Christian meeting town. Seven miles long and less than a mile wide, the island contained little more than dunes, woods, meadows, marshland with small creeks and streams, and mud flats. Numerous birds—from orioles and Virginia mockingbirds to bald eagles—rippled their shadows across the sand, and the brush was filled with possums, foxes, and wild cats.

The area was reportedly named for whaleman John Peck, who used the island as a base in the late 1700s and early 1800s to render the blubber of the whales harpooned by his crew. According to records in Burlington City, Peck once legally owned a whale that had been stranded there. By the time the Lakes saw the island, however, there were no more whales and hardly any people, either. It is generally acknowledged that the only permanent residents of the island at that time were Parker Miller and his family, although John Robinson (Miller's right-hand man) and Hannah Kettles were also said to have been living there.

So it seems likely that the Lake party didn't see any people that fateful September 10 when they explored Peck's Beach, but what they did see must have pleased them. After exploring the island, the group knelt under a cedar tree at what is now Sixth Street and Asbury Avenue, on a corner of the Tabernacle grounds, and prayed. If they were praying for guidance, they found it; that day they decided that Peck's Beach was the place they had been looking for.

According to legend, Simon Lake took out a ten-thousand-dollar mortgage on his farm and orchard to finance the new town. However they got the money, the founders bought up all the titles to land on the island, the untangling of which took Ezra Lake a considerable time. But sole ownership was necessary if they were to achieve their plan of a Christian community. Strict rules about Sunday worship and liquor consumption could work only if they were followed by all; one leak—or drink, if you will—and the whole enterprise would go under.

From this point things proceeded rapidly. On October 20, 1879, Wesley Lake recorded the name of the new town in his diary: "The name of the place was . . . New Brighton." But this didn't last long. The November 11 entry in Lake's diary brought the news that "the name was changed from New Brighton to Ocean City." It is believed that the decision to change the name was influenced by the success of Ocean Grove.

But for Wesley Lake, who had yearned for years to "have a little cottage near the sea," possibly the happiest diary entry of all was the one he made on May 26, 1880: "Spent the day on the beach arranging for building a house. Contracted with D. B. Smith to build me a house, my first cottage."

Ocean City grew rapidly. The First Annual Report of the Ocean City Association (the governing body), dated October 26, 1880, listed "35 dwellings, 1 large hotel, 10 private stables, or barns, and 2 public bath-houses, in addition to the 3 Government Life Saving Stations." Not bad for what had been a windswept wilderness just a year before! And to judge by that same report's indication that 508 building lots had already been sold (totaling over eighty-five thousand dollars), the new town was off to a roaring good start.

Ocean City grew rapidly, helped, no doubt, by the increasing popularity of traveling to the Shore for health reasons. Suddenly everyone wanted to escape the dusty and dirty cities for a chance to walk in the sunshine, breathe the fresh air, and swim in the ocean. Naturally, Shore towns missed no chance to promote their climatic benefits, such as Mary Townsend Rush's 1895 *Ocean City Guide Book and Directory*, in which she extols the virtues of swimming with a fervor typical of the time: "Down to its shores flock invalids, worn and weary with the burden of the body; school children, white and wan; and businessmen with nerves unstrung and shattered. Nature lays her hand upon her children and restores the waning strength to the weary body, paints the white face with the ruddy hue of health, looses the tension, and soothes into an indescribable peace and rest the overtaxed nerves. The gratitude beaming through the results of these ministrations arises in the sincerest psalm of praise and adoration ever offered to the Creator."

With public relations like that, it's no wonder that Ocean City quickly became—and still remains—one of the most popular resorts on the Jersey Shore.

◆

Ocean City was founded by a group of idealistic men with strong principles. The North American Phalanx was founded by a similar group of strong-principled men and women. The difference is that while Ocean City went on to become a monument to those who founded it, all traces of the North American Phalanx have vanished like yesterday's dewdrops.

It wasn't supposed to be that way. Located in the vicinity of modern-day Colts Neck, the Phalanx was in the vanguard of the planned utopian communities that were being established in the mid-nineteenth century according to the socialist theories of

François-Marie-Charles Fourier of France. Albert Brisbane, an American traveling in Europe, encountered Fourier's theories of social harmony through cooperation and brought them back to the United States. Among his converts was Horace Greeley, publisher and editor of the influential *New York Daily Tribune.* Greeley frequently published Brisbane's articles, and in the early 1840s he gave Brisbane a twice-weekly column in the paper.

It may well have been through the popular *Tribune* that Charles Sears, a merchant from Albany, New York, learned of Brisbane's ideas, including his call for the formation of a phalanx (derived from the Greek, connoting "firmness of union"). Sears helped organize an Albany branch of the North American Phalanx, which decided to found a community based on the Fourier-Brisbane philosophy. On January 1, 1844, representatives that had been scouting suitable locations for the community bought 673 acres from Hendrick Longstreet and Daniel Holmes of Monmouth County for the price of $14,600. The first settlers arrived soon afterward, and one of the most important social experiments in American history got underway.

Thanks to movies and television, when today we hear the phrase *utopian community* we tend to think of starry-eyed dreamers spouting platitudes about free love and power to the people. But that was hardly the case with the North American Phalanx. From the beginning, the Phalanx was a no-nonsense, hard-working agricultural community whose membership fluctuated between 125 and 150 people. A person's skills were an important part of the "entrance examination" that all applicants had to pass before being admitted into the Phalanx as an "associate." (Other admission criteria included the ability to work with others in an association, good moral character, and the competence to make contracts.)

The associates indeed knew farming. Among the agricultural innovations they utilized was the preservation of produce by canning. Fruits and vegetables grown at the Phalanx were canned, then shipped to major markets such as New York City, where they were sold through a store at 85 Barclay Street. The label on the can read simply: "Packed at Phalanx, Monmouth Co., NJ."

Life at the Phalanx was something that few Americans had ever experienced. Dining, recreation, working—all were meant to be done together. The feeling of community, of everyone working together for the common good, was always the goal. But communal living didn't mean a loss of privacy; each family had a separate apartment (unmarried associates had smaller facilities). The living philosophy was summed up by the triangular symbol on the community's stock certificate, which had "Unity of Man" in the center, surrounded by "With God," "With Nature," and "With Man" on each side.

One of the most interesting aspects of the Phalanx was how labor was divided. Work was organized into six "series" (agriculture, manufacturing, livestock, domestic matters, festal plans, and education), each directed by a chief. Each series was subdivided into groups that were responsible for different functions and had their own elected chiefs. Every evening, the chiefs gathered to plan the next day's work and posted their decisions for the associates to see. Associates signed up at the beginning of the year for participation in one or more groups.

This unique labor organization brought several benefits: a shortened workday, freedom to rotate among various work groups, and a system of wages that had the least desirable jobs earning the highest pay.

Although the Phalanx was a socialist community, money was the major factor that helped it become the most successful of the forty or so planned utopian communities that existed in the United States during this time. New members had to pledge one thousand dollars worth of stock. This provided operating capital and gave associates a financial stake in the success of the community. Unspent profits were returned to the associates each year as dividends. By focusing on profit-making ventures such as canning, rather than just self-sufficiency, the leadership was able to put money back into the community, and the life-style reflected it. In comparison with the rest of the United States, the standard of living at the Phalanx was very high, and this contributed to the associates' contentment. Homes and buildings had central heating, gas lights, and washing machines long before any of these features were common.

Life at the Phalanx had an idyllic quality. The grounds contained a school where children were taught art, music, and drama, in addition to the basic subjects; a day nursery for working mothers; guest cottages; landscaped gardens and paths; and an artificial pond for bathing, boating, and ice harvesting. As one visitor wrote: "After supper the lawn, the gravel walks and little lake-front . . . present an animated and charming scene. . . . Happy papas and mammas draw their baby wagons . . . groups of little girls and boys frolic in the clover under the big walnut trees by the side of the pond. . . . There seems to be a large measure of quiet happiness here."

Socially, the Phalanx was again far ahead of the rest of America. During a time of religious intolerance and rioting against Catholics and others, the Phalanx constitution guaranteed religious freedom. Among the religions represented in the community were those of the Universalists, Unitarians, Baptists, Jews, Quakers, Catholics, Shakers, Episcopalians, Presbyterians, and Swedenborgians. Women participated in many of the work groups along with men and were even able to wear bloomers—a scandalous fashion at this time.

Far from being viewed as weird for their unorthodox life-style, Phalanx residents were considered good neighbors. The school was so widely admired that, in 1847, it became the model for the newly established Atlantic Township elementary school system. Associates participated in local activities and copped several first prizes at the first annual Monmouth County Agricultural Society Fair in September 1854.

But despite all this, by the beginning of 1856 the North American Phalanx had ceased to exist. What went wrong? Although two widely divergent events caused the Phalanx to disintegrate, the root causes seem to bedevil all idealistic societies: divisive disputes over doctrine and power.

In 1849 a man named Marcus Spring, who was the largest Phalanx stockholder with 527 shares, angered many associates by building a private cottage for his family in the midst of communal dwellings. Spring also began to criticize the secular nature of Phalanx life, claiming that it could be strengthened through regular religious services. The majority of associates opposed this and united behind Charles Sears. When Spring realized he was in the minority, he and thirty followers left the Phalanx in 1852. Journeying north, they formed the Raritan Bay Union at Perth Amboy. The venture failed within three years.

While Spring's departure took both money and workers away from the Phalanx, the philosophical aspects of the acrimonious debate took away something even more important: the heart.

Many associates began questioning the validity of what they were attempting to do. On top of this, the question of whether to give women a more equitable role in the community further depleted the associates' morale. (Although they worked at many of the tasks, women were shut out of decision-making roles until 1853.)

Then, on September 10, 1854, a fire destroyed the flour and saw mills, important machinery, and the blacksmith and tin shops. When the community filed a claim for $14,379, its insurer, Mohawk Valley Insurance Company, went bankrupt. Faced with financial losses too great to cover and with their faith rapidly fading, the associates voted to sell their lands at auction in June 1855. The great experiment was over.

◆

Lakewood, ten miles west of the ocean, has a very different origin than most of its Shore-town cousins. Instead of being founded as a summer resort, Lakewood was born with the gleam of icicles, the whisper of falling snow, and the sheen of a frozen lake in mind.

It was in the winter of 1879 that fifty-year-old Henry Kimball decided to head for Atlantic City to try to clear up a weakness in his lungs exacerbated by his position with the New York Stock Exchange. On the way he suddenly decided to visit Sarah A. Bradshaw, an old school friend who lived in what was then known as Bricksburg. It was a fortunate decision.

Apparently the visit worked wonders on Kimball's health, for when he returned to New York he was bubbling over with enthusiasm for the sparsely populated area. As an article in the December 23, 1882, *New York Times* explained: "When he [Kimball] returned to New York, nearly cured, he said to his physician, 'I have found the place of all places, only 50 miles from New York. It has made me a sound man, and I am going to make it my winter home.' He took the physician out with him, and the doctor agreed that it was a fine place for people with lung troubles. There were thousands of acres of pine lands, stretching for miles in every direction. The soil was so loose and light there was no chance for any malaria."

The article went on to say that Kimball was "so delighted with his new-found health he talked the matter over with some of his Stock Exchange friends who were troubled in a similar way, and after examining the place thoroughly they bought . . . more than 19,000 acres, and went out there to spend their winters." Because the name Bricksburg was no longer appropriate (the town had been founded by the Brick family), the new owners initiated a house-to-house survey, conducted by a local newspaper, to choose a new name. The winner was Lakewood—"a very appropriate name, because there is a beautiful lake and the place is in the midst of the pine woods," said the *Times*. Brightwood was the runner-up choice.

The Laurel House was the first hotel built in the new winter resort. It filled with visitors so quickly that it was expanded until it could accommodate more than two hundred guests. As described by the *Times*, the rooms were opulent yet comfortable: "Every chamber has its electric bell, its soft carpets, its abundant closet-room, its cheerful fire, its ample windows, and its sleep-inducing bed." The hotel featured so many open fireplaces that more than thirty chimneys poked up from its roof.

Kimball was the best salesman for his new resort. "This region is the best place in any of the Northern States for anybody with weak lungs," he said in the *Times* article. "We have here the purest of air, filtered through miles of pine forests; the purest of water, and the best possible soil for the purpose, with perfect drainage, and a climate always at least 10 degrees warmer than that of New York." (This was a dubious claim, insofar as the temperature was reportedly obtained from a thermometer mounted on a hotel pillar that contained a steam pipe.)

But while the temperature may have been in doubt, there was no denying the magnificence of the Laurel House cuisine. A peek at a menu from May 1, 1907, reveals a cornucopia of fine food: oysters, broiled shad, boiled leg of mutton, roast chicken, asparagus, roast mallard duck, fried whitebait, braised sweetbreads, coconut custard pudding, sherry wine jelly, ladyfingers, oranges, and sliced apple pie.

Armed with a combination of pine-scented air and enough food to feed a sultan's palace, Lakewood could hardly miss as a winter resort. Before you could say "famous person," the rich and powerful descended on the once-sleepy town. On the roster of Lakewood's visitors were William Cullen Bryant, Oliver Wendell Holmes, Joseph Pulitzer, and Charles Scribner. President-elect Grover Cleveland chose his cabinet in Lakewood in 1893. (Fifteen years later, sick and dying, Cleveland visited Lakewood one last time, celebrating his final birthday in the nearly deserted Lakewood Hotel, which stayed open an extra six weeks after the season ended just to accommodate him.) Rudyard Kipling first came to Lakewood around 1889; he found his visit so enjoyable that he referred to the town as "Peaceful, pleasure-loving Lakewood" in his *American Notes* (1891).

The winter months unfolded at Lakewood like a Currier & Ives picture. The local gentry rode in their carriages through picturesque parks, under pines and over pine needles; attended dancing cotillions; and took quiet strolls around the lake. Weather permitting, there was rowing or skating, often on beautiful Lake Carasaljo—named not for an Indian princess, as legends suggest, but rather for Joseph Brick's three daughters, Caroline, Sarah, and Josephine. Artists and writers flocked to Lakewood, where they could often be found giving or attending lectures on art, literature, history, and contemporary issues such as "Dress Reform for Health and Beauty" and "Slaughtered Armenia."

Two of the town's most famous citizens during this golden era were John D. Rockefeller and George Gould (son of railroad magnate and financier Jay Gould). Rockefeller began buying land in Lakewood in 1901, paying $87,532 for property on four streets. In 1902 he bought the Ocean County Hunt and Country Club on Ocean Avenue for $12,500. The Golf House, remodeled and enlarged, became his stopover home between his winter residence in Florida and his summer home in New York. Gould built a thirty-room mansion called Georgian Court in 1897 at the top of Seventh Street. On the grounds of his 200-plus-acre estate he also constructed an enormous building (275 feet by 200 feet) called the Casino. Built in 1899 because one of his lawn parties had been spoiled by rain, this modest little structure featured a tanbark hippodrome, a gymnasium, a swimming pool, a bowling alley, Turkish and Russian baths, an automobile room, racquet and squash courts, and nearly two dozen guest bedrooms.

Although the Rockefellers have moved on to other resorts and the rich and powerful no longer ride down the streets in their splendid carriages, parts of Lakewood retain their early splendor.

◆

We come now to two Jersey Shore communities that, like the North American Phalanx, are no more. But unlike the Phalanx, these were not the casualties of some great experiment that went awry. Rather, they were simple fishing villages filled with men and women who depended on the sea for their life and livelihood and knew nothing else. As the Shore changed, these uncomplicated people could not. Eventually they just disappeared, like grains of sand blown away by a coming storm. Even the town names have an old-time, almost ghostly ring to them: Nauvoo and Galilee.

In his delightful 1889 book, *The Jersey Coast and Pines*, Gustav Kobbe called Nauvoo, on the Sea Bright beach, and Galilee, on the shoreline of Monmouth Beach, "the only ones of their kind in this country." Of the two, Nauvoo was the more prominent. The name, according to local historian George Moss, comes from the Mormons, not the Hebrews as is commonly believed, and means "beautiful and pleasant place." (It is a matter of historical record that there was a Nauvoo Legion Militia of the Utah Territory, organized by Mormon leader Joseph Smith.)

Although over a century old, Kobbe's description of Nauvoo is still one of the best: "There are about two hundred and fifty boats with crews of two each. . . . The beach is a scene of varied activity. A boat is lying with prow seaward and her little white jib and spritsail hoisted. A fisherman stands at her bow, another near her stern. They shove her through the glistening surf, and, as she rises buoyantly on the incoming billow, leap into her as a

Fishermen making a landing in the surf at Sea Bright, using one of their specially designed surfboats. (Photo courtesy Special Collections and Archives, Rutgers University Libraries)

rider leaps into the saddle. The wind spreads out her sails and she skims over the water like a sea-gull."

Kobbe estimated the daily catch of each of the 250 boats at about 150 pounds of fish per day. The fishing technique he described has not changed much today: "The usual method of fishing is with hook and line from an anchored boat, using menhaden for bait; but there are also pound nets in the vicinity of Nauvoo. Bluefish, bass, weakfish, blackfish—in fact, all kinds of fish inhabiting the waters off this coast are caught in plenty. These, with the crabs and clams abounding in the river, make sea-food abundant and cheap at Seabright and the resorts near it."

One year earlier, in an article for *Harper's Weekly*, Kobbe had provided a rustic description of old Nauvoo: "[It] consists of two streets of huts running through from ocean to river, except for the break made by the railroad. On sand-hills on the bluff back of the dike, or on hummocks between the two streets, are the ice-houses, of which one sees little more than the peaks. The huts are rough two-story shanties, with a room for cooking and eating on the ground-floor, and an attic where the men sleep. Sometimes six or eight men dwell in one hut. Those fishermen who are married and have families live in neater houses, with here and there a garden plot in the rear. On the beach is a platform, around which many of the fishing folk gather on fair Sunday afternoons, during the summer and listen to a simple service."

The work was simple and monotonous. Each day, before the boat landed, the catch would be cleaned on board so that the foul matter discarded from the fish would not be left lying on the beach. Once ashore the catch would be placed in baskets and brought to the ice houses, where the fish were packed between layers of ice. Next the iced fish were placed in boxes and brought to the railroad station, where a train took them to their final destination—usually New York City's Fulton Fish Market.

For decades the fishermen at Nauvoo and Galilee worked the sea in this manner. But nothing stays the same, and neither did Sea Bright and Monmouth Beach. Soon the once-desolate towns were teeming with gleaming new hotels, well-heeled vacationers, and a growing army of full-time residents. Their life-style clashed with that of the Nauvoo and Galilee fishermen living on the beach in their little shacks. In 1928 some disgruntled residents of Monmouth Beach tried legal action to halt the fishing because the fishermen got up too early and their fish—as fish often do—smelled.

As the area built up, the fishermen were forced out. In 1904 the Sea Bright beach was dotted with 280 boats. By 1949 just 6 boats were left.

Sometimes progress is a good thing. Sometimes, however, you don't know what you've lost until it's gone. From the November 7, 1891, issue of *Harper's Weekly*: "A brawl in the settlement [Galilee] is almost unknown, all living closely together on the best terms. [The fishermen] are trusting and trustworthy, for nothing is ever stolen from the boats, left exposed with all the implements of their trade."

◆

The chief claim to fame of Island Heights, located adjacent to Toms River in the central part of the Shore, is that it used to be the home of John Wanamaker and his Commercial Institute Summer Camp. Long before Wanamaker, however, there was the land: lush, hilly, with leafy trees, creeks, and ponds. Possibly it was this breathtaking natural beauty that attracted settlers to the island. Around 1680 it was known as Dr. Johnson's Island. Later it was called Dillon's Island, after another resident, who sided with England during the revolutionary war and helped the British sack Toms River. (The tiny creek that separates Island Heights from the mainland is today called Dillon's Creek. Reportedly it was once big enough for large vessels.)

The area's relative isolation came to an end in 1878, when a group of men, including several ministers, purchased 172 acres— about 25 percent of the island. Like the Lakes, they had been impressed by Ocean Grove and decided to found their own Methodist camp meeting community on the lovely island.

Civilization came with a rush to Island Heights. Within six weeks after the nearly unbroken wilderness was purchased on July 1, trees were leveled, streets cut, and a wharf built. A campground was established on a forty-foot bluff overlooking the Toms River.

Initially things went according to plan. Visitors came to Island Heights in the most picturesque fashion possible, via the ships of local captains sailing up the Toms River who would be waiting at the nearby train station to provide water taxi service. The tents of these faithful campers filled the new Christian community. Three or four camp meetings were held every summer: one for temperance, one for Sunday school, and others as general meetings. To maintain the resort's Christian character, a law was passed forbidding the sale of liquor within one mile of the town.

Even the railroad had a rustic quality. In the early 1880s, after the Pennsylvania Railroad had constructed a line from Whiting to the beach, Island Heights residents raised enough money to build a spur and bridge from what is now Pine Beach into town. Unfortunately, they didn't raise enough money to build a loop for the train to turn around; consequently, the locomotive always had to back out of the station.

What the railroad brought to Island Heights was a vast new influx of people, particularly from the upper crust of Philadelphia. What it took away was the community's Christian flavor. Even though the ministers wanted a religious community, they also wanted to sell real estate, and the best way to do that seemed to be to market Island Heights as a Barnegat Bay resort. Within ten years of its founding, Island Heights was promoting its social attractions and resort aspects and deemphasizing the camp meetings. Eventually the meetings disappeared altogether.

With the arrival of John Wanamaker in 1899, Island Heights underwent yet a third metamorphosis. Wanamaker had been staying in Lakewood when told of Island Heights, and the camp meeting aspect of the community attracted him, even though he was Presbyterian, not Methodist. Calling Island Heights the Pearl of Resorts, Wanamaker bought some land and established the town's most famous institution: The John Wanamaker Commercial Institute Summer Camp.

Wanamaker was an anomaly for his era. He was a man of uncommon ingenuity, and not only for business; during his stint as U.S. Postmaster General he invented postcards, house mailboxes, parcel post, and rural free delivery. In an age of robber barons and the deliberate flaunting of opulence by the rich for their own amusement, Wanamaker cared deeply about the employees of his famous department store chain (the Philadelphia store was the world's biggest retail outlet). He published manuals for employee safety and offered his staff reading rooms, gymnasiums, and health clinics. It was for his youngest employees, however, that he saved his greatest munificence: the Commercial Institute Summer Camp.

The summer camp was an outgrowth of the John Wanamaker Commercial Institute, which offered classes in a variety of academic subjects to store employees. Situated on six and one-half

Female cadets at John Wanamaker Camp, Island Heights, circa 1917.
(Collection of Richard Steele)

gorgeous acres overlooking the water in Island Heights, the camp was a free summer retreat for both male and female Wanamaker employees from Philadelphia and New York. Most of the cadets, as they were called (for reasons that will be apparent shortly), were in their late adolescence, though some were as old as their early twenties. Those who were married could bring their families; single cadets often had summer romances that eventually led to marriage. The average length of stay at the camp was two weeks.

The cadets probably wished that it could have been longer. There in Island Heights, young men and women who often knew no other life than that of the city frolicked in the sunlight, fresh air, and green fields like schoolchildren. They slept in tents, participated in yachting, boating, bathing, and fishing, played football and baseball, and in general had as fine a time as could possibly be imagined.

But it wasn't all fun and games. Besides attending classes in all academic disciplines, the men and women were drilled in military fashion using real guns (hence the term *cadets*). The males wore deep blue dress uniforms with white piping, and the females wore kilts. Although something of a quasi-military operation, with a regular schedule and reveille every day, the camp was not modeled on any particular branch of the service. Wanamaker, as usual, did things his own way.

The cadets also formed a drum and bugle corps, as well as a twenty-five-piece marching band (bagpiper included). Hundreds of local residents would turn out every night to watch and listen as the cadets, in their eye-catching uniforms, would parade up and down the camp performing drills and songs.

Even after Wanamaker's death in 1922 the summer camp continued for many years. The advent of World War II spelled the end of the camp, though, as suddenly young men had a different type of camp to attend—boot camp.

The camp meetings are long gone, and so are John Wanamaker and his cadets. Still, for those who live in the beautiful, rambling old Victorian houses that dot its streets, Island Heights is still the Pearl of Resorts.

♦

The story of Asbury Park's early days is the story of James A. Bradley. Founder, eccentric, friend, pious visionary—Bradley played all these roles and more as he molded Asbury Park out of the wilderness and sent it on its way to being one of the Jersey Shore's premier resorts.

As did many other towns on the Jersey Shore, Asbury Park sprang from the fertile seeds sowed by Ocean Grove. As Bradley himself said, in an article published in the *Asbury Park Journal*: "One afternoon in May, 1870, I was walking along Broadway, New York, and suddenly ran against our friend, David H. Brown, Esq., Treasurer of the Ocean Grove Association.

"'How is Ocean getting on?' [Bradley asked.]

"'Very fairly,' said he, 'why don't you buy a lot? Those who have their names put down now have first choice.'

"'Well, put me down for two.'"

When Bradley and his manservant John Baker journeyed to Ocean Grove a few days later, the region's condition was best summed up by Baker, who despairingly called it "a wilderness." Yet despite the primeval conditions, Bradley clearly enjoyed his time there. One day he decided to explore the large, undeveloped area just north of Ocean Grove, on the other side of a shining lake. As he told the *Journal*: "One day, Rev. Mr. Osborne and myself went over, and, at the risk of having our clothes torn from our bodies, worked our way through the briers, until we came to

Sunset Lake. And . . . we stood on the banks of as beautiful a sheet of water as can be found anywhere." Anxious that someone unsympathetic to the Ocean Grove way of life not buy the land, Bradley bought it himself, paying ninety thousand dollars for five hundred acres and naming it after the first bishop of the Methodist Episcopal church ordained in America: Francis Asbury.

Although he had no formal training as an urban planner, Bradley soon proved himself an expert at laying out a town. He made the house lots large enough to avoid overcrowding and located frequent parks throughout his new town. To further emphasize the feeling of spaciousness, the streets were made wider than in any other resort town (a feature that still startles first-time visitors). Although the boardwalk had several beach pavilions, the carny-style amusements common at Atlantic City were strictly forbidden. Bradley insisted that the sea and its healthy breezes be unencumbered.

In *Jersey Coast and Pines*, Kobbe praised the physical appearance of Asbury Park: "The place has been laid out with good taste, many natural features of beauty having been skillfully utilized. The streets are of ample dimensions, lined with shade trees. . . . Along the beach there is a well-kept plank walk one mile long, with seats and pavilions, at intervals."

People flocked to Bradley's town. By 1872 the first school was opened; five years later a new school was needed. Churches, a post office, and hotels were built in short order. During the 1883 season, 600,000 people came in three months to what had been, just a few years before, a howling wilderness. Six years later there were almost two hundred hotels and boarding houses and nearly eight hundred private homes in town.

For over three decades, Bradley *was* Asbury Park. He seemed to be everywhere at once, giving orders, checking work, moving on to the next project, swinging a two-foot folding rule all the while. He was called simply The Founder.

One nice thing about running your own town is that you can do things your own way, and Bradley took full advantage of this. He covered the beach with old boats, animal cages, funny benches and seesaws, old stones, and pieces of statuary, calling them "playthings for children." He built a high, rustic pavilion called Crow's Nest overlooking Deal Lake for use by picnickers and sightseers. He had sheds placed throughout the town for horses to stand under during inclement weather (on the beach he erected large wooden parasols for this purpose); inside the sheds he put up the following sign: "Up the hill, urge me not, Down the hill speed me not, On the plain spare me not, And to the hostler trust me not."

But if there was one issue that energized Bradley more than anything else, it was morality. With a zeal that would have warmed an old Puritan's heart he waged unrelenting war against anything and everything that he considered immoral—a difficult task at best in a resort town that was rapidly maturing and testing society's limits, just as any growing child does.

Typical of his attitude were the "Bradley bags" that women were forced to wear while bathing. The suits, made of heavy blue flannel, were high in the neck, with puckered sleeves that came down to the wrist. They had a skirt and pants that came down to the ankles, with stockings underneath. A big, floppy straw hat, tied under the chin with tape, was the required headgear. Canvas shoes completed the outfit. The only skin showing on a woman's body was on her hands and possibly her chin and nose. (When wet, the entire ensemble had to weigh a good twenty

Ocean Avenue on Baby Parade Day in Asbury Park, 1907. At one time this was the premier event along the Jersey Shore—what the organizers of the new Miss America Pageant in Atlantic City hoped to emulate. (Photo courtesy Special Collections and Archives, Rutgers University Libraries)

pounds or more; either the women were extremely strong back then, or they never went swimming.)

When something annoyed Bradley, or when he just wanted to impart some pearls of wisdom, he took out small ads in the local newspapers. One that appeared in the August 14, 1916, edition of the *Asbury Park Evening Press* was vintage Bradley. It complained about "rascals who have automobiles and nod to girls" for the purpose of asking them if they wanted a ride. Bradley's solution: "if you are a father punch them, and if after a few hours ride you should catch them, shoot them."

Eventually Bradley's interest in Asbury Park waned. Maybe it was because, despite his efforts, society's morals were changing too fast for him, or maybe he was just tired after single-handedly carrying the town on his back for so many years, but gradually The Founder was seen less and less in the town he had created. In 1897 he founded another town just to the south of Asbury Park and called it Bradley Beach. On April 15, 1903, he sold the beachfront to the city of Asbury Park for $100,000 and the entire sewer system for $50,000.

On June 7, 1921, at ninety-one years of age, James A. Bradley died. He lived to see the city he had created out of swamps and briers become the "Atlantic City of the North," but whether this made him happy was another matter. Bradley once said in an interview that "I want to look down from Heaven on Asbury Park, and I want to be pleased with the view." Knowing Bradley, heaven undoubtedly got an earful on June 7, 1921.

♦

The story of Jersey Shore towns doesn't end here, of course. There are as many stories as there are towns. Although others may lack the color of a Bradley, the determination of the Lakes, or the tragedy of the North American Phalanx, virtually every Shore town story has something in it that helps us understand the town's present and, possibly, its future.

TWO

BY RAIL
OR BY SEA

~~~~~~

Even after the rest of New Jersey began to bloom with cities, towns, and villages in the late eighteenth and early nineteenth centuries, the Jersey Shore remained undeveloped and almost primitive; it was not uncommon for miles of coastal land to be inhabited by just a handful of people. The reason for this was quite simple: traveling to the Shore was arduous—and often painful.

"There was more penance than joy in a trip to the seashore," wrote a woman about journeying (most likely by stagecoach or wagon) to the Shore in the 1840s. "A few sturdy people went. . . . Their pilgrimage was as weary as that of the Mohammedans to Mecca."

A more vivid account was provided by a man who had the distinct misfortune of traveling to the Shore in what was called a "Jersey wagon" (a highly uncomfortable freight-hauling wagon) in the 1830s and 1840s: "It [the wagon] seemed to have been designed by the Shakers in protest against every semblance of luxury or even comfort." Its back and sides were square, straight, and "as free from graceful lines as those of a ready-made coffin." Adding to the displeasure, nasty green-headed flies plagued these early travelers throughout their trip, making "one continuous meal" of them. By the end of the journey, said the man, "the more robust were generally able to climb out [of the wagon] but the feebler ones . . . had to be lifted out."

Since arriving half-dead wasn't exactly a ringing endorsement of traveling to the Jersey Shore, much of the coast remained sparsely populated and little-visited for decades. The only exceptions were Long Branch and northern Monmouth County as well as Cape May in the southern part of the state. Steamships began serving these locations about 1820, but the rest of the Shore was basically unaffected. It would remain that way until the railroad arrived in the middle of the nineteenth century. The iron horse cut through the Shore like a sharp knife through ripe fruit, extending a network of tracks up and down the coast and making the entire region truly accessible for the first time. The railroad transformed the Shore overnight, and it was largely responsible for the explosion of development that occurred along the coast in the second half of the nineteenth century.

This chapter describes how steamships and trains enabled the Shore to grow. It is not our intent to provide an exhaustive chronology of the various steamboat routes and rail lines that served the Shore (whole books have been written about those subjects), but rather to illustrate the amazing changes brought by these two methods of travel. Although it may be hard to imagine today in this automobile-oriented age, practically every town along the Jersey Shore stands as a monument to the power of the steamship and the train.

◆

June 21, 1809, was a big day in Cape May, although none of the town's residents probably realized it at the time. On that day, in a heavy fog, the steamship *Phoenix* anchored inside the cape for the evening. The one-hundred-foot ship had been cruising down the Jersey Coast, intending to drop anchor in Hereford Inlet, but the foul weather forced a rerouting to Cape May. The *Phoenix* didn't stay long, leaving the next day to complete its trip to

Philadelphia, but it had been the first ship propelled by the recently invented steam engine ever to reach Cape May. Most residents probably hoped it would not be the last.

Cape May had been a resort town even before the *Phoenix* wandered into its harbor. In 1801 Cape May Postmaster Ellis Hughes had advertised in the *Philadelphia Daily Aurora* that the town was "the most delightful spot that citizens can go in the hot season." Travelers who got there found Hughes's words to be true, but it was the getting there that was the problem; mindful of the torture that a trip to the Shore by wagon or coach entailed, most people simply stayed away.

That's why the dawn of steamship travel held such promise for Cape May. Here, finally, was a way for people to travel that didn't require them to have the endurance of an Olympic athlete. Cape May held its breath and hoped.

On June 18, 1816, the town's hopes were realized. An advertisement in the Philadelphia-based *American Daily Advertiser* announced what was probably the first regular steamboat service transporting visitors from the City of Brotherly Love at least part of the way to Cape May during the summer:

> It is announced with great satisfaction that the Steam boat and Packet Line, is now extended to CAPE MAY. The facility with which Passengers can now be forwarded during the ensuing BATHING SEASON; the great additional accommodation and comfort which will be experienced, and the variety and novelty of the route, will no doubt be suitably appreciated by the citizens of Philadelphia. Passengers will embark on board the Steam boat Delaware, Wilmon Whilldin, master, every Friday at one o'clock, and proceed for New-Castle, where the elegant packet Morning Star, Jeremiah Bennett, master, will be ready to receive them on board, and proceed immediately for Cape May. The whole route will thus be accomplished in a few hours.

Of course, while the *Delaware* was a major improvement over the Jersey wagon and stagecoach, it didn't exactly skim over the waves on gossamer wings. Passengers were at the mercy of the wind and tide as well as the mechanical gremlins that haunted the early wood-burning, side-wheel steamboats. Still, riding a steamer was better than being bounced back and forth in a Jersey wagon while fending off hungry green-headed flies. Cape May began to catch on.

In 1819 the one-hundred-foot *Vesta* became the first steamship to provide regular service from Philadelphia all the way to Cape May, making the trip twice a week during the bathing season. The captain was J. H. Burns, and the cost was five dollars.

This route must have been successful, because the following year the *Vesta* resumed its summer trips to the town, leaving Philadelphia every Monday and Thursday at two in the afternoon and departing from Cape May at six the next morning. Stage fare from the steamship landing on Delaware Bay to the growing number of boardinghouses at Cape May was fifty cents (servants were half price).

In 1821 two steamships, the *Superior* (replacing the *Vesta)* and the *Delaware*, began serving Cape May. Although it began the run first, the *Superior* soon withdrew, most likely because the owners knew that the route, while popular, could not support two ships.

One passage from the *Delaware*'s advertisement is revealing: "No passengers will be landed or taken on board the way, except at New Castle, where the boat will be detained not to exceed 15 minutes." This brief stop accommodated the growing number of southerners who were traveling to New Castle, Delaware, and boarding ships there for the trip to Cape May. The town at the tip of New Jersey was becoming one of the most popular watering holes for wealthy ladies and gentlemen from the South.

A passenger on the *Delaware*, writing about the trip in the summer of 1823, evokes images that make one yearn for those carefree, unhurried days: "Before us nothing was to be seen but the boundless water, sky and distant sails of inward or outward bound vessels, whilst what land could be seen behind was merely an indistinct spot. Ever and anon, the steady eye could discern a little speck in the remote horizon, either the next moment disappearing or gradually devolving into the topmast, then sails and lastly the hull of some approaching vessel. Once or twice we enjoyed the beautiful sight of a ship passing us in full sail, bearing off with a strong wind inflating all its canvas."

The steamship landing was located approximately two miles above the tip of the cape, on the part of the bay called the Cove (just south of what is now the mouth of the Cape May Canal). Rhoda Forest and her husband, Thomas, ran a tavern at this spot, which was known as "Aunt Rhody's" or "Rhoda's Hole." In 1823 Joseph Higbee bought the property, which became then, as it is now, Higbee Beach.

Initially steamship passengers had to be brought by whaleboat from ship to shore. Progress triumphed in 1826 when a wharf was built at the landing. Of course there was still the matter of getting from the wharf to a boardinghouse. However, the great motivator known as the free enterprise system quickly solved that problem. By the 1840s many area farmers were forsaking their plows for the easier—and more profitable—work of trans-porting passengers to and from the steamship landing. Report-edly, as many as one hundred farmers would converge on the landing with their wagons. Some were there hoping to pick up what taxi drivers would call "fares," while others had filled their wagons with people already at Cape May, who were coming to the landing either to see if anyone else they knew had arrived or just to gossip and buy some of the newspapers brought down by the boats.

This, then, is how the years passed at Cape May. Gradually the town grew into a mighty resort, a place where both northern-ers and southerners enjoyed the cool sea breezes during the sticky summer months. As the passengers became wealthier, the boats became ritzier. There was the *Franklin*, which had a full band on board; the *New Philadelphia*, with polished mahogany and panels around the main cabin depicting twelve views of Ameri-can scenery; and the *Commerce*, whose ad noted that "the bar [is] supplied with choicest liquors and refreshments." On the other hand there was the *Ohio*, whose owners could take pride in the fact that, according to an 1832 newspaper article, "no ardent spir-its whatever [were] used at the yard during her construction."

The rich, the powerful, and those who wanted to be either or both—all came to Cape May, and many by steamship. From humble beginnings the town had become, by midcentury, one of the premier resorts in the United States, and the residents could be excused for thinking that the band would play on forever.

But in April 1861 the music stopped abruptly. The cannons that fired on Fort Sumter signaled not only the start of the Civil War but also the end of the southern traffic so vital to Cape May.

After the war, with the Confederate states' economy shattered and bitterness rife between North and South, few southerners returned to Cape May. Meanwhile, the railroad was spreading across the Jersey Shore, ushering in a new era of transportation. The day of the elegant steamships and their passengers coming to Cape May was over, and with it the town's place as the dominant Jersey Shore resort. The rise of Long Branch and Atlantic City meant that Cape May no longer had sole claim to society's movers and shakers.

◆

Even as the steamships' influence was waning at one end of the Shore, it was gaining in popularity at the other. The steamship era in northern Monmouth County, although it began in 1819, hit its peak in the second half of the nineteenth century and continued into the twentieth. For decades the sight of steamboats in this area was common; people would gather on shore and watch the great boats sweep by, their large stacks billowing huge clouds of smoke, their paddles hitting the water with a rhythmic chunk-chunk-chunk, and the piercing shriek of their powerful whistles echoing across the water.

"It was fun to watch," recalls Monmouth Beach resident Virginia Hammond of the days when, as a child in the early 1920s, she would be fascinated by sight of the mighty ships on the Navesink River. "Every afternoon we used to watch the steamboats go by."

Although the first steamship to ply the waters of the Navesink and Shrewsbury rivers was the *Franklin* in 1819, it was James P. Allaire of the Howell Works (and namesake of Allaire State Park) who first demonstrated the steamboat potential of both rivers. To transport the goods made at his ironworks to the New York markets, Allaire set up docks and warehouses at Red Bank on the Navesink River and at Eatontown Landing (now Oceanport) on the Shrewsbury River. Allaire's goods were taken by wagon to the docks, where they were placed aboard steamships en route to New York. Local farmers and fishermen also found the docks a convenient way to ship their products to the city.

Encouraged by the success of these boats, the Eatontown Steamboat Company was founded in 1843. Its first boat was the *Shrewsbury*, a 126-foot vessel that took four hours to make the trip between Eatontown Landing and New York City, with several stops along the way.

Often the steamboats were able to shorten their trips considerably by using Shrewsbury Inlet, located near the base of Sandy Hook. The inlet had closed in 1810, then reopened twenty years later. Periodically thereafter the inlet would open and close; when open, it afforded ships from the ocean direct access to both the Navesink and the Shrewsbury rivers. Finally, in 1847 the inlet closed for good, blocked by sand collecting around the steamboat *Cricket*, which had become stranded there.

Although passenger traffic was a prime concern, equally important to the financial success of the steamships was the highly profitable shipment to New York City of Monmouth County's renowned produce. Fruits and vegetables grown in Shrewsbury Township on the south side of the Navesink were shipped from the Red Bank docks. Produce from Middletown Township on the north side of the river was picked up at both Brown's Dock (opposite Fair Haven) and Mount's Dock at Locust Point (opposite Port Washington, which is today part of Rumson). Few passengers were taken on at these locations; the steamship captain stopped only when he spied produce stacked up on the docks.

In 1852 two more steamship companies entered the picture: the Red Bank Steamboat Company and the Middletown and Shrewsbury Steamboat and Transportation Company. The intense rivalry between these two lines would result in both going out of business within four years.

Keyport was another Monmouth County town that played an important role in the steamboat era, although in a much different way from other communities. Beginning in 1841 with the *Rainbow*, the tiny village (its population was less than two hundred at this point) built approximately sixty steam vessels over the next several decades.

Possibly the most notable of all the Jersey Shore steamboat builders was Keyport resident Benjamin C. Terry. From his Terry Yards came some of the most durable and well-known vessels on the water. During the Civil War, a boat built by Terry towed the Union army's famous ironclad *Monitor* from New York to Hampton Roads, Virginia, just before it engaged the Confederate ship *Virginia* (more popularly known by its original name, *Merrimac*) in the first-ever battle between ironclads. By the time the war had ended, approximately thirty of Terry's boats had seen Civil War service, including the historic *River Queen*.

One of Terry's most famous steamships—and one of the first examples of how steamboats combined with railroads to build up the Shore—was the *Jesse Hoyt*. This ship was one of the largest ever built by the Terry Yards, measuring 217 feet long and weighing an enormous 487 tons. In 1862 the *Jesse Hoyt* began transporting passengers and cargo to and from New York City via a

Notable Steamships and Trains

Of the many steamships and trains that served the Jersey Shore, some were so special that they deserve to be singled out. **RIVER QUEEN.** Built in Keyport's famed Terry Yards in 1864 and launched on March 31 of that year, this 181-foot steamship wound up in the service of the Union army, where it became the dispatch boat of General Ulysses S. Grant. It was on this ship, early in February 1865, that three Confederate peace commissioners met with Abraham Lincoln to negotiate an end to the bloody war, only to fail. Seven weeks later Lincoln, Grant, General William T. Sherman, and Admiral David Porter met on board the *River Queen* to discuss the impending surrender of the South and the subsequent peace. A famous painting of this conference by G.P.A. Healy, titled *The Peacemakers*, shows the four leaders sitting in a luxuriant drawing room on the ship, with the soon-to-be murdered Lincoln leaning forward, hand on his chin, listening intently as Sherman makes a point. After the war the *River Queen* was a connecting boat for the Long Branch and Sea Shore Railroad between Spermacetti Cove, Sandy Hook, and New York.

GENERAL MCDONALD. The next time someone is complaining about having a bad day, tell him or her the sad saga of the steamship *General McDonald*. On July 14, 1852, the *McDonald*—filled with passengers from Philadelphia—was tied to the wharf at Higbee's Landing at Cape May. Unfortunately, the weight of all the people on board and the swells of a rough sea caused the ship's mooring ropes to become so taut that they ripped away fifty feet of the wharf. The ship had to land its passengers at another wharf nearby. Just to make this a really memorable voyage, the next day while on the way home the *General McDonald* smashed into the schooner *War Eagle*.

(continued)

Notable Steamships and Trains *(continued)*

BLUE COMET. This was one of the first deluxe coach trains in the United States. Put into operation by the Jersey Central Railroad in October 1928 as a way to increase passenger volume between Jersey City and Atlantic City, the Blue Comet was the last word in luxurious train travel. The train featured a color motif of blue (naturally), including blue- and cream-colored cars, blue mohair coach seats, blue carpets, and blue paint throughout the interior. The menu contained a blue plate special—what else?—and a porter (who was reportedly not painted blue) looked after passenger needs. Although at first a big success—in 1930 the train carried over fifty-six thousand passengers—by 1940 ridership had dropped dramatically, and the Blue Comet was discontinued the next year.

RAINBOW. This 220-foot steamboat, built at Keyport in 1841, was the first to come out of Monmouth County. An experimental vessel built for speed, the *Rainbow* was made of light cedar and locust wood and had a sharp stem and a narrow beam (less than seventeen feet). Its career included serving as a day boat along the Hudson River between New York and Albany, carrying visitors from Philadelphia to Cape May, and, in its last years, towing canal boats and barges on the Delaware River.

OWL. In 1912 this Jersey Central train had the honor of making the first stop in Asbury Park on the Sabbath, after more than fifteen years of bitter feuding between Asbury Park officials and Ocean Grove ministers. Since 1875, when the railroad first came to Asbury Park, trains could not arrive in town on a Sunday; the community had been founded on the strict religious principles of neighboring Ocean Grove. As a result, those weekend visitors so necessary to Asbury's financial health had to return home by crossing Deal Lake to the north and boarding a train at Interlaken Station. A tug-of-war for the soul of Asbury Park followed as newspaper editorials and local officials decried the ban on Sunday stops and ministers screamed damnation if the Sabbath was desecrated. Finally, after years of bitter controversy, the city appealed to the Public Utilities Commission, which decreed that Sunday stops must be permitted. Thus it was that on March 3, 1912, the Owl left Jersey City at eleven minutes past midnight and, a few hours later, pulled into Asbury Park, where it was greeted by a jubilant crowd and a twenty-six-piece band.

COFFEE. This was the first Terry Yards steamboat to become a fighting ship in the Civil War. It was bought by North Carolina in May 1861, renamed the *Winslow*, and took several Union ships as prizes during its tenure in the Confederate navy.

five-thousand-foot-long pier built by the Raritan and Delaware Bay Railroad at Port Monmouth. Railroad tracks connected the pier with Eatontown and also Long Branch. The contrast between taking a ship and then a train to the Shore as compared with bumping along in a coach or wagon was like day and night, and a growing number of people began taking advantage of these new modes of traveling to the New Jersey coast.

For the *Jesse Hoyt*, this Port Monmouth service marked the beginning of a long acquaintance with the Jersey Shore. For a while in the late 1860s the ship had competition from steamers using a new terminal built at Spermacetti Cove on Sandy Hook by the Long Branch & Sea Shore (LB&SS) Railroad. But by 1870 shoaling at Spermacetti Cove forced the LB&SS to build a new steamship terminal several miles north on Sandy Hook at Horseshoe Cove.

The *Jesse Hoyt* and the 330-foot *Plymouth Rock* were the first steamers to call at the new Horseshoe Cove terminal. On July 30, 1870, the two vessels carried hundreds of people (among them the tycoons Jim Fisk and Jay Gould, as well as Boss Tweed of Tammany Hall fame) from New York City to Sandy Hook, where they took the train to Long Branch for the gala opening of the Monmouth Park racetrack. The *Jesse Hoyt* became the best-known ship serving the Sandy Hook route. By the time it was retired in 1887, the ship had established a longevity record on this route that would remain unbroken.

By the mid-1870s Long Branch was well on its way to becoming America's most famous resort, rivaling even Saratoga and Newport as the place where the rich and famous went to escape the "rigors" of being rich and famous. (See chapter 3 for more information on this era in Long Branch history.) In addition to docking at Horseshoe Cove, steamships also made the short "outside run" from New York City down the Atlantic coast, docking at a Long Branch pier and thus eliminating the train ride.

Illustrations of the mammoth Long Branch ocean piers from this era have to be seen to be believed. There were five piers altogether, though only one existed at any given time. The two most famous were Ocean Pier (1879–1881) and Iron Pier (1881–1908). Looking like the beginnings of giant highways that were intended to stretch across the Atlantic (Ocean Pier was 872 feet long), adorned with flags, benches, and gas lamps, these piers were focal points of social activity during Long Branch's golden era.

Artist's depiction of the new Iron Pier in Long Branch, showing the scope and size of the steamship pier. (Photo courtesy Special Collections and Archives, Rutgers University Libraries)

The cream of society, dressed to the nines, would gather there either to greet an acquaintance embarking from a steamship or just to be seen. With a steamship puffing away at the end of the pier and gentlemen tipping their top hats to promenading ladies wearing fine silk dresses with matching hats and parasols, this must have been a magical time indeed.

But sometimes the magic failed. Storms washed out several of the piers, including one built in 1872 by Jay Gould and Jim Fisk that lasted a grand total of one week. At other times rough seas prevented steamships from docking at the pier, and people who went there hoping to meet a loved one or friend coming off the ship found out precisely what "so near, yet so far" meant.

Nearby towns, seeing the benefits that regular steamship service brought to Long Branch, began wanting a piece of the pie for themselves. Such was the case in Bay View (soon to become Atlantic Highlands), where, by 1877, residents anxious for town growth were agitating for direct steamer service with New York. In that year Thomas H. Leonard, who aided in the founding of Atlantic Highlands, built a freight pier 450 feet long into the bay.

Two years later he bought the steamship *Thomas Collier* (sometimes erroneously spelled *Collyer*) in Baltimore for sixteen thousand dollars and enrolled it in the recently established Bay View Transportation Company to transport farm produce into New York during the summer. In his 1923 book, *From Indian Trail to Electric Rail*, Leonard described the *Collier* as "an able little boat, but small, and when she lay at the face side of the bulkhead, from the shore she looked to one, by the motion of the waves, as if she was trying a game of 'Hide and Seek.'"

Besides cargo, the *Thomas Collier* also carried passengers between Bay View and New York for fifty cents round trip. As Leonard related in his book, the new town was advertising for "excursion parties" (tourists) to come by boat from the city. One of the first who answered the ad was "an old gentleman and lady, with an umbrella and an old-fashioned market-basket." When the elderly couple found that the entire town consisted of just a few buildings, the man, according to Leonard, "increased the temperature of that noonday hour by a flow of English elocution that would have done credit to Patrick Henry."

The Sea Bird *steamship at the dock in Atlantic Highlands in 1886. (Photo courtesy Special Collections and Archives, Rutgers University Libraries)*

With the founding of the Atlantic Highlands Association in 1881, demand steadily grew for more reliable steamer service than the *Collier* could provide. In that same year, the old steamer and twenty thousand dollars were exchanged for the *Marion.* Despite getting stranded on its first trip when a crew member dropped a hawser (rope) line into its wheel, the ship made up to three "excursion trips" per day during the busy season. Later, in conjunction with the railroad, other steamships (including the *Jesse Hoyt*) came to Atlantic Highlands as the new town grew.

In 1891 the U.S. Army decided to reclaim the Horseshoe Cove portion of Sandy Hook, thus prompting the building of a new steamship/railroad terminal at Atlantic Highlands. Just prior to the terminal's opening on May 30, 1892, the *New York World* called the new, 2,400-foot-long pier "the finest deep-water terminal in the State." The days of visitors being unpleasantly surprised at the desolation of the area were long gone, largely because of the steamship. As James H. Leonard (brother of Thomas) said when he addressed the large crowd celebrating the opening of the terminal, steamship service "insured the success of the town."

Atlantic Highlands illustrates how the steamship helped bring more people to the northern Jersey Shore and opened that entire region to development. Thanks to steamships, people could now easily reach towns like Long Branch, Sea Bright, Monmouth Beach, and Atlantic Highlands, which had been well off the beaten path. Once at the Shore, many people decided to stay, while others went back home determined to move to this young, vital area with its untapped potential and abundant natural advantages.

Ironically, while the railroad helped to kill off steamship travel to Cape May, it seems to have worked in concert with the ships along the northern Shore. After trains took over much of the cargo business, the steamships turned to passenger travel, and the early decades of the twentieth century were boom years for steamers in northern Monmouth County. In 1926 more than one million people made the trip from New York to New Jersey—and that was on the boats of just two companies. To improve the passengers' comfort, the boats became fancier; the *City of Richmond,* for example, offered watermelon, Shrewsbury oysters, steamed

Steamship Albertina *plying the waters of northern Monmouth County. The* Albertina *ran from the late nineteenth century through the early twentieth century. (Photo courtesy of the Doran Collection)*

clams, ale, and lager. This could be enjoyed in one of the opulently decorated saloons or while listening to either the melodic sounds of a band or hundreds of singing birds.

But lurking in the background was the eventual destroyer of steamship travel in the north—the automobile. By the mid-1930s, everyone seemed to have a car; the steamship suddenly looked slow and impractical. (Trains hung on awhile longer, but eventually cars and trucks took away most of their influence too.) The sound of slapping paddles and the blasts of mighty whistles slowly faded away as steamships became relics of a bygone age. The last vestige of the great steamboat era at the northern Jersey Shore was swept away on May 6, 1966, when a fire destroyed the pier at Atlantic Highlands.

◆

As remarkable as the influence of steamships was on Shore development, it paled in light of the amazing changes wrought by the railroad. No single force was more responsible for transforming the Shore from a sleepy, largely uninhabited backwater to a string of thriving, vibrant communities than the iron horse. In 1878, after taking a train from Camden to Atlantic City, Walt Whitman wrote: "The whole route . . . has been literally made and opened up to growth by the . . . railroad. The railroad thaws, ploughs up, prepares and even fructifies the fallows of unnumbered counties and towns. . . . It sets in motion every indirect and many direct means of making a really substantial community, beginning at the bottom, subsoiling as it were, bringing information and light into dark places, opening up trade, markets, purchases, newspapers, fashions, visitors, etc."

Trains blazed trails for people to follow, and follow they did. In 1850, at the dawn of the railroad era, the population of the four coastal counties (Cape May, Atlantic, Ocean, and Monmouth) was a meager 55,700. By 1885, with trains chugging up and down the coast, the population had jumped nearly 100 percent, to 111,000. In Atlantic City the population grew at an astonishing rate of 425 percent between 1870 and 1880—all thanks to the railroad.

Indeed, among Jersey Shore towns it is Atlantic City that probably owes the most to the iron horse. Not just the community's success but its formation and very survival were due to the railroad. Without trains funneling a steady stream of people into the one-time windswept wilderness, Atlantic City might never have become the Playground of the World. The impact of the railroad on Atlantic City's growth can be applied, on a lesser scale, to every town along the Jersey Shore.

Although the changes were swift, the railroad didn't transform Atlantic City overnight. In fact, it was only through the stubborn, determined efforts of one man that the first train ever steamed into the town at all.

Dr. Jonathan Pitney was just twenty-two years old when he first set eyes on the area he would eventually alter to such an extraordinary extent. In 1820, when Pitney first arrived on Absecon Island, it was nothing more than sand dunes and scrub brush. Yet something about the area appealed to the young doctor, and so he settled down on Shore Road in the mainland town of Absecon. Quickly plunging into the affairs of his new community, Pitney served as postmaster, notary public, and recorder of shipwrecks.

But Pitney's attention kept returning to deserted Absecon Island, which had already impressed him because of its mild, salubrious climate—including the apparent lack of malaria that plagued many swampy areas. (Science had yet to link the disease to mosquitoes, but it was known that constantly moving tidal water helped to prevent it.) Taking long walks along the lonely beach, with the long cloak he typically wore flapping about his lanky body, the doctor would exult at the healthy climate of the area and dream of how much people would enjoy it—if only they could get to it.

Pitney often stated that "only a railroad is needed to make the island blossom as the rose," and by the winter of 1851 he had convinced his friend, General Enoch Doughty, of the soundness of his vision for a "bathing village" on the desolate land. Doughty's conversion was undoubtedly helped by the knowledge of how valuable his own twenty-five thousand acres of Atlantic County land would become if Pitney's dreams came true. On February 11, 1851, Pitney and Doughty drafted a charter for a proposed railroad from Philadelphia to Absecon Island. Soon after, Pitney traveled to Trenton to ask the state legislature for the needed franchise.

His proposal was greeted with waves of skepticism (A railroad to where? A deserted island? It's a "railroad to nowhere!" his critics cried), and he returned to Absecon rebuffed. But Doughty, working behind the scenes, convinced several influential South Jersey industrialists that a railroad would be good for their glass- and iron-making businesses. With their help, Pitney's request for a railroad charter was granted on March 19, 1852. The mighty Camden & Amboy Railroad, which could have blocked the charter through its friends in the legislature, made a colossal miscalculation by haughtily waiving its objections to the new line on the grounds that it seemed certain to fail.

The new railroad—named the Camden & Atlantic—then had the good luck to obtain the services of Richard Osborne, a young engineer. Not only was Osborne's technical knowledge critical in assuring skeptical investors that the spongy salt marsh could safely support a train's weight (thus short-circuiting a move to halt the railroad before it reached the site of Pitney's proposed city), he also devised a sensible and workable route for the trains. According to Osborne, the railroad would enter the island at the south end of Pitney's "bathing village" and run to a central point where the depot would be located. The tracks would run along the middle of the new town's main thoroughfare, a one-hundred-foot-wide boulevard named Atlantic Avenue. From there the train would travel north to Absecon Inlet. While there was literally nothing at the inlet when Osborne drafted his plan, this was a stroke of genius on his part. He reasoned that the new resort town could become an alternative port of entry for Philadelphia-bound cargo during the winter, when ice often rendered the Delaware River unnavigable. Thus not only would the railroad be busy in both summer and winter, it would also spur the new town's growth in two directions: tourism and freight.

Osborne's most important service was yet to come. The directors, greatly impressed by his plan, voted to accept it without change. But there was a hitch: what would Dr. Pitney's new town be called? Names were kicked around—Surfside, Ocean City, Strand, Seabeach, and Bath, among others—but none seemed quite right. Then, according to an account later related by Osborne: "I unrolled a great and well-finished map of the bathing place and they saw in large letters of gold stretching over the waves, the words *Atlantic City*. This title was greeted with enthusiasm by the board. The name was unanimously adopted and that day, Atlantic City came into existence on paper."

After the necessary land was bought for the railroad at a cost of $17.50 per acre, track began to be laid from Cooper's Point in Camden. By late June 1854, just before the opening ceremonies were scheduled to begin, the entire line was completed and ready except for a drawbridge over the Beach Thorofare waterway outside Atlantic City. But this was the new town's crowning moment; everyone had worked hard to reach this point, and a little thing like an unfinished drawbridge wasn't about to spoil it. On July 1, 1854, the wood-burning Atsion pulled out of Camden carrying a load of six hundred officials, guests, and newspapermen. Its destination: Atlantic City.

This was no luxury train. Its seats were nonupholstered boards, and both engine smoke and the ubiquitous New Jersey mosquito made the trip something less than memorable. There was also that unfinished drawbridge to contend with; passengers had to disembark when they reached it and be ferried to another train, the Roanoke, which brought them the rest of the way to the United States Hotel in Atlantic City, where a celebration awaited.

But all these obstacles and inconveniences seemed like trifles. The railroad had arrived in Atlantic City; the impossible had been accomplished. Supposedly the first train whistled as it passed Dr. Pitney's house. Whether that's true or not, the doctor was undoubtedly pleased that his dogged determination had brought the dawn of a new day to his "bathing village."

Three days later, on the seventy-eighth birthday of the United States, regular train service to Atlantic City began. The town's first railroad station was a large shed between South Carolina and North Carolina avenues; the train ran through it onto Atlantic Avenue.

But the *arrival* of the railroad and the *success* of the railroad (and the town, for that matter) were not one and the same thing. The train made just one trip per day, and interest in Atlantic City continued to simmer well below the boiling point. Typical of the skepticism about the fledgling town's future was this comment by a Philadelphia businessman: "Call it a sand patch, a desolation, a mosquito territory, but do not talk to me about a city. You could not build a city there in the first place. And if you could, you could not get anyone to go there."

The Camden & Atlantic struggled for survival during the remaining years of the 1850s and the 1860s. In the spring of 1870 the C&A decided to offer special excursion group rates to civic, religious, and other organizations. The more tickets these groups sold, the greater the discount. As an added incentive, the sponsoring organization received a portion of the gross receipts, with a minimum guarantee of fifty cents per passenger. This popular program increased summer tourist traffic by thirty-five thousand during the first season.

Gradually, more and more people came to Dr. Pitney's town. (Pitney died in 1869, before the boom years really took hold.) In 1871 Atlantic City had 1,043 permanent residents and about 10,000 guest rooms. New attractions like the unique Boardwalk helped to draw visitors, although the accommodations were hardly palatial. (One guidebook advised guests to bring a strong length of rope to escape in case of fire!)

But Atlantic City now offered something that other resorts, such as Cape May, could not: the day trip. People could zip to

Atlantic City by train in a few hours, enjoy the cool sea breezes, and then return home as the sun was setting. The long boat ride to and from Cape May made a day trip there virtually impossible. Slowly the upstart little town on Absecon Island grew. Before the railroad arrived, a local resident had been lucky to earn a few dollars a week hauling oysters sixty miles to Camden. But by the late 1860s, thanks to the tourists brought by train, that same resident could earn twice as much per *day* raising chickens for the local hotels.

Of course, when there's money to be made, everybody wants to get into the act. In 1877 a rival railroad, the famed Philadelphia & Atlantic City Narrow Gauge (so called because its rails were laid forty-two inches apart instead of the standard fifty-six and a half inches) was built. By offering excursion fares for a dollar, it set off a price war that doubled Atlantic City's population in four years (from three thousand in 1877 to over six thousand in 1881). However, the Narrow Gauge's less than sterling construction— its fifty-four miles of track were laid in a mind-boggling ninety-eight days—caused it to be a money-loser from the start. It was eventually bought out in 1883 by the powerful Philadelphia & Reading Railroad. In 1880 another titan, the Pennsylvania Railroad, entered the Atlantic City fray with its West Jersey & Atlantic line.

By this time the future of Atlantic City was no longer in doubt. Drawn by the Boardwalk, the opulent hotels, and the refreshing climate, people flocked to the city of Dr. Pitney's dreams, and the way they inevitably traveled there was by train. Rails offered a more direct route to the beach—one that working-class families could easily afford. Until the automobile replaced it, the iron horse was the strong foundation upon which Atlantic City rested.

◆

Of course, Atlantic City was not the only Shore town that a railroad could make or break. Attracting a railroad was like discovering gold; a line's arrival meant the end of gut-wrenching struggles to survive. In their Fifth Annual Report (1884), the founders of Ocean City might well have been speaking for the entire Jersey Shore when they summed up the railroad's significance to their town: "We have realized that all-rail communication was of the first importance, and absolutely necessary to the prosperity and development of the place."

Quite likely these lines were penned with the memory fresh in the writer's mind of how difficult travel to Ocean City had been without the railroad. The first attempts to get to what had been Peck's Beach were tortuous; the traveler was required to take a stagecoach from Camden to Beesley's Point on Great Egg Harbor and then hop into a sailboat for the two-mile trip to the beach. When the iron horse arrived at South Seaville in the early 1860s, visitors to Peck's Beach had it a little easier—but not by much. After taking the train to South Seaville they had a twelve-mile stagecoach ride to face, with all the dust, mosquitoes, and back-breaking jolts that such a trip entailed. Even when steamboat service, in the form of *The Mizpah*, in 1880 began ferrying people from Somers Point to a new wharf at the foot of Fourth Street in Ocean City, it still didn't give the town the boost it needed. As the town's Third Annual Report put it so bluntly: "we are looking forward, anxiously, to the time when we can dispense with steamboat travel." Clearly the railroad was the answer. (And population figures proved it; helped considerably by the railroad, Ocean City's resident population almost tripled in the 1890s, jumping from 452 in 1890 to 1,307 in 1900.)

But this answer didn't always come easy. The railroad companies were sitting in the catbird seat; with Shore communities knocking down their doors for service, the companies could afford to dictate terms. Again, from Ocean City's Fifth Annual Report: "we have sometimes been almost staggered by the expense involved [in securing a rail line]. The right of way granted . . . the land donated for the several stations and sidings, and for terminal uses . . . the actual cash outlay for surveys, grading, bridge-building . . . [make] a total gross cost to us of about $70,000, for which we receive no stock or compensation whatever, except the general advantages in which all participate."

In addition to the staggering cost, the effort required to get a rail line built was often herculean. Such was the case with Cape May. While the town was quite happy with its steamship service, the disadvantages were illustrated clearly in the winter of 1851. Very cold and snowy weather virtually marooned the town's permanent residents, making ship and even stage service impossible for several months.

By the time normal travel could be resumed, in April of 1852, representatives of counties bordering the Delaware River met at Elwell's Hotel in Camden to discuss the possibility of building a railroad linking that city and Cape May. They were helped immensely by having two influential directors of the powerful Camden & Amboy Railroad living along the proposed routes. Three routes, each passing through Woodbury and Glassboro before separating, were planned: one would go to Salem and then Cape May, while the other two would go to Millville and then split, one branch heading directly to Cape May, the other going to Bridgeton before continuing to the cape.

Not faced with Dr. Pitney's problem of trying to get a charter for a town that didn't exist yet, this plan found smooth sailing in the state legislature. The charter for the new West Jersey Railroad (WJRR) was granted on February 5, 1853.

But complications set in. The Camden-Woodbury segment began operations on April 15, 1857, while work continued on the remaining extensions. But a little over a year later, one of the lines to Cape May was deferred in favor of a new branch from Glassboro to Bridgeton. Shortly thereafter a group of Millville businessmen decided to build a part of the deferred route anyway (incorporating it as the Millville & Glassboro Railroad on March 9, 1859), and off they went. During the summer of 1860 the M&G decided to build a rail line to Cape May, but financial problems quickly forced them to abandon the idea.

So while the Camden & Atlantic, though not exactly prospering, was at least serving Atlantic City, Cape May languished. Each time it seemed as if the railroad was coming, something happened to stop it. It might well have seemed that the only train whistle Cape May would ever hear would be a distant echo from another town.

(There may also have been other factors working against Cape May. Daniel Taggart, editor of the *Atlantic Journal*, wrote in 1860 that "the reason why a road has not been built to Cape May . . . is because a certain clique has been opposed to it unless they could have the whole control of it and when there was a fair prospect for accomplishing the object, would go to work against it.")

Finally things turned around. A group of Cape May County investors decided to complete the line begun by the M&G Railroad; they incorporated the Cape May & Millville Railroad and began working on the abandoned line in April 1863. Work progressed so quickly that service was able to begin in August of that year, although track surfacing and other work wasn't ultimately completed until four years later. But at least Cape May had finally joined the railroad age.

Eventually both the Cape May & Millville and the Millville & Glassboro lines came under the control of the West Jersey Railroad, which itself became part of the Pennsylvania Railroad. The Pennsylvania had the money and power to extend railroad service along the Shore, and this it did, using the Cape May line as the anchor. After establishing the Sea Isle City junction near South Seaville in 1881, the Pennsylvania (or, more properly, the West Jersey & Atlantic Railroad, which was the Pennsylvania's seashore service along the southern coast) built lines over the next ten years to Sea Isle City, Ocean City, Townsend's Inlet, Avalon, and finally Stone Harbor.

◆

Normally the coming of the railroad meant prosperity and progress, as was the case for Atlantic City and the other southern Shore towns. But the iron horse could work the other way too, dooming an area that it bypassed. Such was the case on Tucker's Island.

Tucker's Island was one of the earliest Jersey Shore resorts. Located off the southern end of Long Beach Island, this small spit of land (approximately five miles long and a mile wide) had been hosting sportsmen and other visitors for many decades when the railroad began exerting its influence on this part of the Shore during the 1870s and 1880s. But Tucker's Island, as well as neighboring Long Beach Island, was ignored by the railroad for some time. Until steamboat service to and from Tuckerton was established in 1872, the only way to reach Long Beach and Tucker's islands was by sailing or rowing.

But, having seen the positive effect of the train on other Jersey Shore areas, people who had development on their minds knew the precise recipe for success for Long Beach Island. In 1885 the Pennsylvania Railroad began building a wooden trestle bridge across the bay, their appetite for the project no doubt whetted by $43,800 of front money proffered by entrepreneur William Hewitt.

Work on the bridge moved swiftly, and tracks were rapidly laid on the eighteen-mile-long island. (Ironically, ragweed and goldenrod seeds, brought over from the mainland in carloads of gravel, destroyed one of Long Beach Island's most attractive natural advantages—pollen-free air.) In one of those typically confusing chains of command that railroads seemed to love, the new transportation system was called the Long Beach Railroad, was managed by the Tuckerton Railroad, and was owned by the Pennsylvania Railroad. (Got that?)

In the early summer of 1886 all was in readiness. Train service began in Barnegat City (now Barnegat Light) on June 28, and the first engine chugged into Beach Haven at the southern part of the island on July 24. At long last, the railroad had come to Long Beach Island, and everyone was happy—everyone, that is, except the folks on Tucker's Island. Having the train stop at Beach Haven meant that the people stopped there too; few visitors wanted to bother finding a way to Tucker's Island. As the rest of Long Beach Island grew, Tucker's Island slowly withered, a once-healthy bud now cut off from the rest of the vine. The railroad had given, and the railroad had taken away.

◆

On the northern Jersey Shore, the beginnings of the railroad involved Abraham Lincoln. After several years of trying to obtain authorization from the federal government for a railroad right-of-

One of the early locomotives as it traveled into Island Heights, circa 1900. (Collection of Richard Steele)

Early train travel wasn't always so great. This wreck, at an unknown Shore location, took place on September 10, 1889. (Photo courtesy Special Collections and Archives, Rutgers University Libraries)

way onto Sandy Hook (much of the Hook being a military reservation), the Long Branch and Sea Shore Railroad Company (LB&SS) was finally granted permission by President Lincoln on July 21, 1864.

On July 31, 1865, the new railroad began operations. It linked up at Spermacetti Cove on Sandy Hook with the steamship *Neversink*. Less than five years later the new terminal was built at Horseshoe Cove. In the 1870s the LB&SS became part of the short-lived Southern Railroad, formed by one of the Gilded Age's leading financiers, Jay Gould.

But the real mover and shaker for this part of the Shore was the Jersey Central Railroad. From Sandy Hook all the way down past Bay Head, this train line did the most to spark development of the entire northern Shore. By 1875 the Jersey Central was running trains on its New York and Long Branch line. The line was later described as being "so close to the Ocean beach in some places that the surf blends with the rattle of the cars and the shriek of the locomotive whistle; and at times in high tides, the waves have washed over the track."

Shortly thereafter the Jersey Central extended its line to Sea Girt and then Manasquan. As the tracks stretched down the coast, the towns along the way—Asbury Park, Ocean Grove, Spring Lake—benefited from the iron horse just as the towns along the southern Shore had. The Jersey Central soon became an extremely popular mode of travel for people from New York, and down the Shore they spilled in ever-growing numbers.

Concurrently with the Jersey Central, the Pennsylvania Railroad was also busy extending its feelers into the rich mother lode of the Jersey Shore. In 1883 the rail line expanded its Pemberton Branch to the south bank of Toms River and then to Seaside Park. This sparked development of a whole string of resorts along what is today called Barnegat Beach Island, including Lavallette, Normandy Beach, and Mantoloking.

In the early 1880s, when both Point Pleasant and Bayhead Junction (today known simply as Bay Head) were included in the Jersey Central Railroad's growing orbit, the new train service made such a difference that an Ocean County history written in 1889 stated: "Some 18 or 20 years ago Point Pleasant was an unimproved, undeveloped tract . . . where formerly rabbits and reptiles were wont to burrow. At that time its population did not exceed 12 families who had houses fit to live in, and ingress from or egress to either Philadelphia or New York implied forty miles by stage and the loss of a whole day for the single journey. . . . Now it . . . is reached from New York by the New Jersey Central Railroad and . . . from Philadelphia by the Philadelphia and Long Branch Railroad." The railroad so influenced Point Pleasant that, by 1899, what had been a refuge primarily for "rabbits and reptiles" now boasted trolleys, electric lights, a newspaper, five churches, and four large hotels.

What happened in Point Pleasant was typical of what happened along the entire Jersey Shore when the railroad arrived. For approximately fifty years, throughout the United States, the railroad sparked one of the greatest mass migrations in history, with the Jersey Shore as a chief beneficiary. By 1900 it was over; most Shore towns had been established and, thanks to a steady stream of train passengers, were maturing rapidly. Growth in the twentieth century came primarily from the increased population of existing communities, not from the foundation of new towns.

CHAPTER THREE

FAMOUS VISITORS AND RESIDENTS

It was a nice summer's day in Long Branch, and Ulysses S. Grant, eighteenth president of the United States, was being driven down Broadway in his coach. When Grant's coachman reached the tollhouse at the intersection of Morris Avenue, he blithely drove right past without stopping. After all, this was the president.

But no sooner had the coach rumbled past than the gatekeeper, an old man, bolted out of his tiny gatehouse and shouted for the coach to stop. Grant, realizing the problem, stuck his head out the coach window.

"Maybe you don't know who I am," Grant said, eyeing the tolltaker. "I'm president of the United States."

"I don't care who you are," snapped the man. "If you're president of *hell* it's your business to pay two cents toll, and my business to collect it."

Finding it hard to argue with logic like that, Grant paid the toll. Always an admirer of fighting spirit, he soon became fast friends with the gatekeeper. The two of them would sometimes pass the time of day sitting outside the tollhouse.

Ulysses S. Grant was the first president to visit Long Branch. Six other American presidents (Rutherford B. Hayes, James A. Garfield, Chester A. Arthur, Benjamin Harrison, William McKinley, and Woodrow Wilson) would follow Grant's lead—and in so doing turn the pleasant town on the northern Jersey Shore into the nation's "summer capital."

Long Branch (which, according to the November 19, 1926, issue of the *Long Branch Daily Record*, "gets its name from the longest branch of the South Shrewsbury River") had been entertaining visitors a long time before Grant showed up. In 1778 a boarding-house for stagecoach travelers—possibly located on a farm owned by a man named Philip White—opened in the town.

By the first half of the nineteenth century, Long Branch was a popular health resort. People came to partake of the invigorating climate in much the same way they would travel to the fashionable spas of Europe. But, hampered by the arduous stagecoach trip required to get there, the town did not grow with wild abandon. *Gordon's Gazeteer* of 1834 noted that "Long Branch is a small village of twelve or fifteen houses, one tavern and two stores." Even so, it was still well enough known to host such political notables as Henry Clay, who came to Long Branch to rest in the summer of 1850. (Possibly he was resting from his previous summers in Cape May, where his popularity caused female admirers to chase him along the beach and try to snip off locks of his hair as souvenirs.)

The beginning of Long Branch's rise to international prominence, as well as its "presidential tradition," can be dated from August 1861, when Mary Todd Lincoln, wife of the president, arrived in town. "There will be quite a furore [*sic*] at this fashionable watering place when the President's lady arrives," said the *New York Herald*, and it wasn't mistaken. A throng of people greeted Mrs. Lincoln, including a reception line of twenty-seven young girls dressed in white. Among the events arranged for the president's wife was a demonstration of lifesaving equipment by former New Jersey Governor William A. Newell, founder of the Life-Saving Service.

Mrs. Lincoln apparently enjoyed her stay at Long Branch. Several years later, during a conversation with Grant, she mentioned the resort town. The hero of the Civil War apparently kept those words in mind, because in the summer of 1868 he paid a visit to Long Branch. He liked it as well as, if not more than, Mrs. Lincoln had, because after he was elected president in the fall of 1868 he decided to spend his summers in the town. (In those days even more than now, government officials were expected to abandon the hot, humid summer weather of Washington, D.C., for more temperate climates.)

It is hard for us today to imagine the adulation that much of the country felt for Ulysses S. Grant at this time. We view him through the prism of history, which paints him as a lackadaisical president with corrupt friends. But in the late 1860s he was widely considered the savior of the Union, and treated with great respect.

Accordingly, Grant's first arrival at Long Branch in the summer of 1869 had the town in a frenzy of anticipation. The nine members of the town council eagerly assembled at the train station to greet the president and welcome him to their fair city. However, when they were all lined up and waiting for the train to arrive, these gentlemen looked so undistinguished that a local hotel owner, who was serving as the master of ceremonies, sent them home. In their place he substituted nine of the best-looking and best-dressed guests from his hotel. Posing as the town council, these impostors greeted the president when he arrived, feted him about town, and even presided at a splendid banquet that evening in Grant's honor, while the real town council stayed far away. Grant never knew the difference.

Grant quickly found that Long Branch was everything Mrs. Lincoln had said it was (although he must have wondered exactly who was running things in town if he ever met any real members of the council). "In all my travels I have never seen a place better suited for a summer residence than Long Branch," the president declared. Recognizing the value of such an endorsement, some of the town's notable citizens arranged to give Grant a "cottage" at 987 Ocean Avenue. (In the lexicon of the day, a house was considered a cottage if it needed to be maintained by only three or four servants.) The president gratefully accepted the gift, and a new era was underway in Long Branch.

Of all the presidents who would follow him to Long Branch, Grant was the one most closely identified with the town. This

President Ulysses Grant and his family vacationing in Long Branch, 1872. (Photo courtesy National Archives, photo no. 26-G-3422)

was a different age, when presidents were not insulated from the public with layers of Secret Service agents, and so Grant was able to move easily about the bustling community. Drawings of him bathing in the surf and attending formal parties surrounded by legions of admirers show just how much freedom presidents had at this time.

Since he was both president and a famous war hero, Grant attracted a plethora of rich and powerful visitors when he was in residence at his summer home. One of his lesser-known guests was a French sculptor named Frédéric Bartholdi, who was nurturing a dream to build a monument to American freedom—a monument that would one day be called the Statue of Liberty. In 1871 Bartholdi came to America and met with Grant at his cottage. Whether the two talked about the Frenchman's still-forma-

54

tive ideas for a monument is unknown. What is known, however, is that they did speak of military matters. Bartholdi told Grant how, during the Franco-Prussian War, he had led a group of fifteen men out to repulse a German attack. When he learned that his tiny band was opposed by a force of five thousand men, he immediately retreated. Gazing at the young sculptor, Grant remarked laconically: "Practical . . . but hardly heroic."

Another thing that Grant liked to do when at Long Branch was attend the races at Monmouth Park. Until its demise in 1893, this racetrack attracted the crème de la crème of international society. President Grover Cleveland, Henry M. Stanley (of "Dr. Livingston, I presume?" fame), Bret Harte, American tycoon Jim Fisk, British actress Lily Langtry, boxer James Corbett, and Alfred, Lord Tennyson, were just some of the rich and powerful who watched the horses run at Monmouth Park.

But the racetrack wasn't the only place where the movers and shakers hung out. Lily Langtry, for example, liked to go ocean bathing in the Long Branch surf. In 1883 she stunned the locals with her new bathing suit. In an era when women were wrapped like mummies before they were allowed even to put a toe into the water, Langtry appeared in a one-piece blue and red bathing suit

A Winslow Homer rendition of the famous bluffs at Long Branch, illustrating how steep the approach to the beach was at one time. (Photo courtesy Special Collections and Archives, Rutgers University Libraries)

that would fit right in with today's beach fashions. An obviously overheated reporter for the *New York Herald* wrote that "the full perfection of Mrs. Langtry's figure was seen at its best in the new role she assumed as one of the goddesses of the sea."

Another good place to catch a glimpse of the rich and famous was, oddly enough, at church. Saint James Chapel on Ocean Avenue was later dubbed the Church of the Seven Presidents because of the number of chief executives who worshiped there. In 1886 the aggregate wealth of the congregation was a cool $120 million.

At any time during Long Branch's golden age you might have been able to see, among the cavalcade of notable figures, Buffalo Bill and Annie Oakley; Diamond Jim Brady calling for Lillian Russell at the Cliff Cottage and then taking her for a ride along Ocean Avenue in a custom-built electric automobile; either Ethel, John, or Lionel Barrymore; Oscar Wilde being showered with pink roses by admiring women; and Horace Greeley (who obviously advocated going west for everything but vacations). It was a crazy, magical, exciting time in the history of both Long Branch and the Jersey Shore.

James A. Garfield was another president who is linked to Long Branch—specifically the Elberon area. Before he became the nation's chief executive he too enjoyed the races at Monmouth Park. However, it is tragedy, not pleasure, that ties Garfield inexorably to the Jersey Shore.

On July 2 Garfield had been shot by a disappointed office seeker while waiting for a train in Washington, D.C. Over the next two months, the wounded president's condition steadily deteriorated. Finally his doctors decided that his last, best hope lay in the healthy climate of the Jersey Shore.

Thus began one of the most extraordinary chapters in New Jersey history. In order to take Garfield by train to the beachfront cottage owned by steamship magnate Charles G. Francklyn, it was necessary to build a new railroad spur six-tenths of a mile long—and do it overnight! Thus, during the afternoon and evening of September 5, 1881, more than two thousand workers—regular railroad employees as well as local townspeople—labored feverishly to build the spur. Women gave out sandwiches and cool drinks, while young children handed spikes to workers and held torches. Bakeshops remained open to provide food. The entire community rallied around their fallen leader.

In his 1881 book, *Our Martyred President*, James D. McCabe described what Long Branch awoke to the next day: "When the cottagers awoke in the morning they found a railroad at their doors, running through what was an orchard the night before. The locomotives were drawing armed soldiers over the flower-bordered lawns where ladies in white flannel suits were playing the previous afternoon."

Sadly, however, this mighty effort went for naught. Garfield rallied slightly after arriving at the Jersey Shore but soon suffered a relapse. Then, according to McCabe, on the night of September 19, 1881, "A few minutes after ten o'clock, Garfield awoke. When General Swaim took hold of his wasted hand, he moaned, 'Oh, Swaim, this terrible pain,' and placed the General's hand over his heart. In a desperate gesture, he [Garfield] flung his hands up and cried, 'Oh, Swaim, can't you stop this?' Those were his last words, except for an agonized, 'Oh, Swaim.'"

◆

The rich and powerful were not the only ones drawn to the Jersey Shore. Writers also seemed to have a fondness for the peace and solitude that could frequently be found along the coast. One of these was the great playwright Eugene O'Neill, although greatness was still in the future when the writer lived at the Shore from November 1918 to May 1919. The family of O'Neill's second wife, Agnes Boulton, had what they called the Old House on Herbertsville Road in West Point Pleasant (now Point Pleasant). O'Neill and his wife decided to go down to the house while rehearsals were in progress for his play *Where the Cross Is Made*. But due to a mix-up in communications, Agnes and her parents had both decided to live in the Old House at the same time—along with three younger sisters, a grandmother, three cats, and a dog. Obviously, wall-to-wall people would not have been a good environment for writing, so the Boulton family decided to rent a small cottage by the ocean, leaving O'Neill in the Old House, where he could enjoy the solitude and work in peace.

Despite this seemingly ideal situation, O'Neill was edgy when he and Agnes took the dusty, two-hour train trip from New York to the Jersey Shore. This was not a particularly easy time for the moody, hard-drinking playwright. He was trying to work on *Chris Christopherson* as well as *The Straw* but achieving only limited success. Rehearsals for another play, *The Moon of the*

Caribbees, were taking place in New York City, requiring O'Neill to travel there frequently. He was also worried about the success of still another play, *In the Zone*, a wartime story that was playing on vaudeville. Then, in early December, his father was hit by an automobile in New York, and though he was not injured seriously, his condition added to O'Neill's burdens.

One of the first things the playwright did on arriving at the Old House was choose which room he would use to write. (Apparently the home's many stoves dismayed him; just about every room had one, and each had to be shaken down every day, the ashes taken out, and coal brought in—a lot of work for a playwright struggling to concentrate!) Eventually O'Neill picked the dining room, which had a fireplace as well as a big table on which he could do his writing. Out of the dining room closet came the dishes and glasses; into it were stuffed scripts, books, and other tools of O'Neill's trade.

The couple had problems with the local residents during their time in the Old House, undoubtedly exacerbated by O'Neill's sullen, withdrawn demeanor. The playwright would sometimes feel hard stares from the mailman and the neighbors, and once the couple found a dead dog on their lawn, its throat slit. Agnes concluded that the locals—many of whom she had known since childhood—were displeased that she and her husband had taken over the large home while the rest of the Boulton family had to manage in a smaller place.

Unfortunately, work did not go smoothly for O'Neill, and the Christmas season, far from being joyous, was gloomy. The holiday itself usually depressed O'Neill anyway, and New Year's Eve was not much better; the playwright spent the last night of 1918 with the *Saturday Evening Post* and a bottle.

The new year did not bring a new start for O'Neill. He continued to have problems in following his old work habits, which included sitting down to write following breakfast. Instead of working in the afternoon, he would often take long walks—a neighboring woman thought his solitary strolls so strange that she asked Agnes if her husband took drugs. He also spent many hours bouncing tennis balls against the side of a weathered, two-story building known as the "barn," located behind the Old House. He would throw a ball against the barn's side for half an hour at a time, running to catch it as it bounced back before hurling it again with even greater force. (He didn't spend all his time

58

so idly; Agnes became pregnant during the couple's stay at the Old House.)

One sunny afternoon O'Neill and his wife took a long walk down a road that the playwright had not explored before. Soon they came to a ramshackle house with a sandy yard full of trash; dirty babies maneuvered around old kerosene stoves and broken chairs, and a red-faced man lay supine in a hammock. Hanging quilts on a clothesline to dry was the mother, while nearby stood three blonde young girls—all pregnant.

O'Neill was fascinated by the family. Agnes explained that no one knew where they had come from; one day they had simply appeared at the house, which had been empty and in disrepair for some time. The mother took in washing to make a living; the father apparently spent his time drinking cheap whiskey.

As Agnes Boulton wrote in her memoirs, *Part of a Long Story*: "After supper that night, which he ate in silence, apparently very absorbed, Gene went into the bedroom and lay down on the bed. Then he came back, and took paper, pencils and his writing board from the closet. 'I've thought of a one-act play—a peach! I'm going to outline it now and go ahead with it tomorrow. I should be able to finish it before I have to go to New York.'"

O'Neill started the play the next morning and quickly became immersed in it, finishing within several days. It was his first extended work at the Old House. Unfortunately, this play, which might have told us much about the Shore during this time as viewed through the eyes of Eugene O'Neill, is today listed among his lost plays; no copy is known to exist.

◆

Another leading writer who lived at the Jersey Shore for a time during the early part of this century was Timothy Thomas Fortune, a pioneering black journalist who filled the gap in African-American history between the decline of Frederick Douglass and the rise of Booker T. Washington. Fortune's tenure at the Jersey Shore, like O'Neill's, was not a happy one. But whereas O'Neill was on the brink of producing some of the greatest plays in American history, Fortune's years at the Jersey Shore precipitated his decline into poverty and despair.

Born the son of slaves in 1856, Fortune became one of his era's most distinguished journalists. He wrote numerous articles on race violations in the country, including *Black and White* (1884), in which he explored southern society. Besides founding the National Afro-American League and the Afro-American Council (the platforms of both organizations helped to shape the goals of the National Association for the Advancement of Colored People), Fortune also established the nation's leading black newspaper, the *New York Age*. The paper's reputation rested largely on Fortune's hard-hitting editorials denouncing racial discrimination and demanding equal rights for all blacks. By the turn of the century, Fortune was one of the best-known spokesmen in the North for black Americans.

During the summer of 1901, Fortune made arrangements for his entire family—his wife, Carrie, and his two children, son Fred and daughter Jessie—to go to Red Bank. There the whole family fell in love with a twelve-room house situated on more than an acre of ground that included fruit trees, a grape arbor, and shade trees that often kept the property delightfully cool. Fortune decided to buy the house, which due to the legal entanglements of an estate was being sold for the unbelievably low price of four thousand dollars. Scraping together every cent he could find, including a small inheritance from his father, Fortune bought the home, which he called Maple Hill.

From the start, Fortune found life at the Jersey Shore both physically and psychologically invigorating. Whenever possible he limited his trips into New York City to once or twice a week; he preferred to do his writing and editing at home, where he could also tend to his beloved garden and fruit trees. Fortune was especially proud of the fruit he grew, even offering to send some as far as Alabama to Booker T. Washington, for whom Fortune acted as confidant, adviser, publicist, and ghostwriter. Washington countered by offering Fortune a horse from the Tuskegee farms. (Fortune declined because of the care and expense this would have involved.) Washington visited his friend at Maple Hill in the spring of 1902, an event that drew Fortune's many friends and political acquaintances to his home.

But the bucolic life in Red Bank was not enough to exorcise the demons that tormented Fortune. His weakness for alcohol undoubtedly aggravated the despair to which he would frequently fall victim. In 1905 he wrote to his friend Emmett Scott at Tuskegee, "I have reached the conclusion that the Fates have the cards stacked against me. . . . All the way I have shaken the trees and others have gathered the fruit." Adding to his anxieties was the financial burden of Maple Hill. Fortune worried that, after his death, all he would leave to his family would be debts.

Fortune's troubles mounted in October 1906 when he and his wife separated. (He later stated, in a letter to his daughter, Jessie, that the separation was simply the result of differences in temperament that had caused friction for years.) Carrie and Fred left Maple Hill and moved into a Harlem apartment that Fortune agreed to pay for. Though the couple saw each other again in December, Fortune refused Carrie's pleas for a reconciliation.

Fortune's letters at this time suggest he was in the throes of acute depression and possibly contemplating suicide. The specter of aging—he was just shy of fifty when he and Carrie separated— also weighed heavily on his overburdened mind.

Perhaps inevitably, in 1907 Fortune suffered a mental breakdown. That year he sold the *New York Age* and subsequently had a falling-out with Washington, contending that the Wizard of Tuskegee had no further use for him after he sold the newspaper. By 1908 Fortune had moved out of Maple Hill and Carrie had moved back in. She continued to live there until 1910.

For Fortune, the next several years brought only more misery. The once-proud and strong voice of an entire race was reduced to sitting in parks and begging acquaintances for money to buy food. Finally, in 1919 Fortune regained his health and began writing editorials and columns for the *Norfolk Journal and Guide*. In 1923 he became editor of the *Negro World*, a publication of Marcus Garvey's Universal Negro Improvement Association.

Timothy Thomas Fortune's death on June 2, 1928, brought forth a flood of eulogies in the black press. Kelly Miller, dean of Howard University, called him "the best developed journalist that the Negro race has produced in the Western World."

Today the Fortune house in Red Bank is a National Historic Landmark, a testimony to the important role that Fortune played in history. It is regrettable that while at the Jersey Shore this fiery and eloquent man could not find the peace he so desperately needed.

◆

During the late 1880s and early 1890s the town of Asbury Park was rapidly becoming one of the Jersey Shore's premier resorts.

As the town was maturing, so was a young resident who was destined to write one of the seminal American books of the late nineteenth century—Stephen Crane.

Crane was just twelve years old in 1883 when his mother moved the family to 508 Fourth Avenue in Asbury Park. Crane's brother Townley was working in Asbury Park as well, as the Jersey Shore correspondent for the *New York Tribune*. Young Stephen proved himself a good student in the local school, with a tendency to remember such words as *irascible, pyrotechnic,* and *impartial,* and a fondness for baseball. However, his life's work was foreshadowed when, between two baseball games, he dashed off an essay that later won a prize of twenty-five cents.

In the summer of 1888 Crane began working for Townley. He would bicycle around Asbury Park, collecting news and gossip and making observations that he turned over to his brother, who would send them along to the *Tribune*. Three years later Crane became a full-fledged reporter, covering the busy Asbury Park beat for his brother and the *Tribune*. Many of Crane's articles were satirical sketches of the rich, pompous gentry who poured into town during the summer.

Crane was just warming up. By the end of the following summer of 1892, before leaving the Jersey Shore ultimately to find his destiny as the author of *The Red Badge of Courage*, Crane had written a series of articles ridiculing a variety of Asbury Park and Ocean Grove people, places, and institutions. The targets of his satire were high-mindedness, egotism, and the lack of social and moral sensibility among the often self-important vacationers. Crane let fly at them with every verbal arrow in his quiver.

One of Crane's favorite whipping boys was Asbury Park founder James A. Bradley, whose rigid morality made him an irresistible target for the young writer. Typical of his thinly veiled attacks on Bradley was the following: "He [Bradley] usually starts off with an abstract truth, an axiom not foreign nor irrelevant, but bearing somewhat upon a hidden meaning in the sign— 'Keep off the grass,' or something of that sort. Occasionally he waxes sarcastic; at other times, historical. He may devote four lines to telling the public what happened in 1869 and draw from that a one-line lesson as to what they may not do at the moment. He has made sign-painting a fine art, and he is a master."

To Crane, Asbury Park and Ocean Grove were perpetual paradoxes: hordes of vacationers frantically indulging in every type of pleasure under the sun, reformers like Bradley and those who founded Ocean Grove trying just as frantically to keep everyone's enjoyment within a strict moral framework. His satirical needle pricked every target in sight, including women ("Her ball dress is evidently cut lower in the neck than her bathing suit, which makes her look like a doll with a bronze head on a porcelain body"), Methodists ("They greet each other with quiet enthusiasm and immediately set about holding meetings"), and rich men ("He enjoys himself in a very mild way, and dribbles out a lot of money under the impression that he is proceeding cheaply").

Finally, Crane's biting wit did him in. On August 21, 1892, an article by Crane appeared in the *Tribune* that mocked the Junior Order of United American Mechanics, which had held a massive parade in Asbury Park. *Tribune* publisher Whitelaw Reid was Benjamin Harrison's running mate in the fall presidential election, and the article was seen as an attack on American workers and, more important, potential voters. Both Crane and his brother Townley were summarily fired. (Harrison and Reid lost in November to Grover Cleveland.)

Even if Crane hadn't been bounced out of a job, it is likely that he would have soon left Asbury Park anyway. Each day found the young writer growing more and more confident in his abilities, and he most likely felt the need to broaden his horizons.

More than two years later, while working for the *New York Press*, Crane wrote several pieces about ghosts along the Jersey Shore. In 1894 the publication of *The Red Badge of Courage* catapulted him to instant fame. Unfortunately, he had little time left to enjoy it. Stephen Crane died on June 5, 1900, five months short of his thirtieth birthday.

◆

From Asbury Park it's only a short distance to Lakewood, and it is to this town, which gained its fame as a winter resort, that we next go to meet another of the famous visitors to the Jersey Shore—the immortal heavyweight champion Joe Louis. For Louis, the visit to the Shore was brief—maybe too brief.

The year 1936 was a pivotal one for Joe Louis. It was, as the saying goes, the best of times and the worst of times. During the first half of the year he was undefeated, steamrolling through opponents and being hailed as one of the greatest boxers ever. He had a beautiful wife, a lot of money, and enough friends to keep the champagne and laughter flowing forever. The second half of the year, however, would be a much different story.

Louis's next opponent was a German boxer named Max Schmeling. Nobody was giving Schmeling much of a chance against the great Brown Bomber, and Louis took the same view. His fight team decided to train him for the bout in Lakewood.

Louis, who would have preferred the peace and quiet of Pompton Lakes, came into camp in Lakewood with a chip on his shoulder the size of New Jersey. Feeling that there was no need to indulge in hard hours of training for such an easy fight, Louis would frequently cut his workouts short to play golf or otherwise indulge himself.

One of the most enjoyable ways that Louis passed the time was with his new wife, Marva. She stayed at the Stanley Hotel, which was just about two blocks from the Alpert Mansion where Louis was living. They had been married only two months, and the pair acted like the newlyweds they were.

Eventually the fighter's handlers saw the light and sent Marva back to New York. But other women were flocking around training camp, anxious to get a glimpse of the Brown Bomber, and Louis often gave them more than a glimpse. The combination of his extracurricular activities and playing golf under the hot sun took eighteen pounds off Louis in five weeks. It is an unwritten law of the ring that sex weakens a fighter, and Max Schmeling proved the old saw with great finality in Yankee Stadium on June 19, when he treated Louis like some punch-drunk palooka, pounding the champion repeatedly before knocking him out in the twelfth round. It was the Brown Bomber's first defeat.

Maybe Louis should have gone to Pompton Lakes after all.

◆

The automobile age brought a new crowd of sports enthusiasts to the Shore. In the early part of the twentieth century, the sands at Cape May offered automobile racers one of the best courses available on which to test their newfangled machines. The sand was as hard and smooth as the famous beach course at Ormond-Daytona in Florida. In July 1905 the local newspaper *Star of the Cape* reported that "men, who were recognized all over the country, as being eminently qualified to pass upon such matters, have declared it the finest speeding ground in the country for the distance."

Heavyweight champion Joe Louis during training in Lakewood before his fight with Max Schmeling, 1936. (Collection of Richard Steele)

The Cape May course ran directly along the sand from the life-saving station east of Madison Avenue to Sewell's Point at Cold Spring Inlet, a span that for many years was called Poverty Beach. Only its short, two-mile distance kept this stretch of beach from becoming a serious threat to the popular Ormond-Daytona speedway.

The year 1905 was probably the zenith of automobile racing at Cape May. Some of the best drivers in the world came to the town to prove their machines' mettle. The July 15 *Star of the Cape* reported that Walter Christie, fresh from competition at Ormond-Daytona, would come to Cape May and attempt to establish new world records for both the mile and the kilometer beach runs. The paper also announced that Christie had issued a challenge to Henry Ford and that "a race between them for the cup at Cape May is a possibility of the near future."

One month later the paper reported that Louis Chevrolet planned to come to Cape May for the next set of races. "[He] will have a try at the mile and kilometre [*sic*] records, recently established on this beach, by Walter Christie, with his 120-horsepower 'Blue Flyer.'" Thus it was that four of the most well-known of all the early auto pioneers—Ford, Chevrolet, Christie, and A. L. Campbell, another racer—gathered on the beach at Cape May on August 25. Christie drove his Blue Flyer, Ford the newly built Beach Skimmer, Chevrolet a Fiat, and Campbell his Red Flyer. In a drizzling rain, with a crowd estimated at twenty thousand looking on, the four men took off down Poverty Beach.

Ford quickly took the lead, but then Fate intervened. A huge wave rolled in off the ocean and hit the Beach Skimmer, knocking Ford out of the lead. Chevrolet roared past him, turned to see what had happened, and hit a soft spot in the sand, ending his hopes for victory as well. The win went to Campbell, with a time of 38 seconds. Chevrolet came in second at 39.4 seconds.

Finishing dead last with a time of 40 seconds wasn't Ford's only problem. He had depended on winning the race and using the prize money to settle his bill at the Stockton Hotel. Suddenly in dire need of cash, Ford hurried around town trying to sell the touring car he had used to tow the Beach Skimmer to Cape May. Finally he found a Reading Railroad engineer named Dan Focer, who unfortunately was just pulling out of the station on his train when Ford caught up to him. As the train gathered speed, Ford ran alongside, trying to conclude the urgent (for him) transaction. Focer finally agreed to buy the car for four hundred dollars and said his brother-in-law would write Ford a check immediately. (Focer wound up with far more than a touring car. Thanks to this meeting, Ford made the engineer the first of his auto dealers in America.)

But Ford's troubles were not over yet. Check in hand he raced to the bank, only to be told that someone would have to identify him before the check would be cashed. (Obviously it is not easy to recognize those who will revolutionize life.) The Stockton Hotel manager supplied the necessary identification, Ford finally got his money, and the Jersey Shore added another interesting footnote to its history.

◆

To many Americans, the name Grace Kelly means different things. To some she is the beautiful, stylish actress who starred in numerous films in the 1940s and 1950s. To others she is the regal Princess Grace of Monaco, elegant spokeswoman for the tiny country. To longtime Ocean City residents, however, the name Grace Kelly means simply "friend."

Kelly, the movie star whose real life turned to fantasy when she married Prince Rainier of Monaco, had been coming to Ocean City ever since she was a child. Her family came to Ocean City for many years during the summer, maintaining a house at Twenty-sixth Street and Wesley Avenue. The Kelly family was to Ocean City and Philadelphia what the Kennedys were to Hyannis Port and Boston.

Given her father's affinity for rowing (he had been an Olympic champion), Grace and the entire Kelly clan were on good terms with the local lifeguard patrol. Years afterward, those who protected the beach at Twenty-sixth Street still remembered how a teenage Grace would bring them sandwiches, milk, and soda. Ocean City was where she learned how to surf and also where she brought her new husband, Prince Rainier, after they were married in 1956.

But even though Princess Grace was an international celebrity and the people of Ocean City were devoted to her, she was afforded no special treatment. In 1980 she was asked to leave the beach for not having a beach tag.

Grace Kelly and her family on the beach at Ocean City (clockwise, from lower left: Grace, her mother Margaret Majer Kelly, brother Jack, sister Peggy, father John B. Kelly, Sr., and sister Lizanne). (Photo courtesy Urban Archives, Temple University, Philadelphia, Pa. / the Philadelphia Evening Bulletin)

When Princess Grace died in an automobile accident on September 14, 1982, it could be honestly said that no one felt the loss more deeply than the residents of Ocean City. Whether movie star, actress, or carefree teenager romping in the surf, Grace Kelly had been one of their own.

◆

We began this look at famous visitors and residents of the Jersey Shore with a story about a president, and it seems only fitting to end it the same way. Long Branch wasn't the only Shore town to play presidential host. Cape May was no slouch in the chief executive department either; five presidents—Franklin Pierce, James Buchanan, Abraham Lincoln, Ulysses Grant, and Benjamin Harrison—visited the area at some point.

One of the founders of Sea Grove (later to become Cape May Point) was the Philadelphia department store magnate John Wanamaker. While involved in establishing Sea Grove, Wanamaker was also the nation's postmaster general. In 1889 he invited the president—his friend Benjamin Harrison—and Harrison's wife to visit the Wanamaker "cottage" by the sea.

Born at the Jersey Shore

Artists have long been attracted to the coast for the inspiration and tranquillity in the rush of the waves, the blue horizon, and the white sweep of a gull's wing. Thus it should come as no surprise that a number of well-known writers, musicians, actors, and other artists were born at the Jersey Shore, including:

ALEXANDER WOOLLCOTT. Critic and actor—born January 19, 1887, in the North American Phalanx (see chapter 2 for the Phalanx)

DOROTHY PARKER. Author—born August 22, 1893, in West End (near Long Branch)

EDMUND WILSON. Literary critic and journalist—born May 8, 1895, in Red Bank

WILLIAM "BUD" ABBOTT. Comedian—born October 2, 1895, in Asbury Park

WILLIAM "COUNT" BASIE. Jazz musician—born August 21, 1904, in Red Bank

NORMAN MAILER. Author—born January 31, 1923, in Long Branch

GAY TALESE. Author—born February 7, 1932, in Ocean City

JACK NICHOLSON. Actor—born April 28, 1937, in Neptune

DANNY DEVITO. Actor—born November 17, 1944, in Neptune

BRUCE SPRINGSTEEN. Rock musician—born September 23, 1949, in Freehold

The Harrisons apparently had such a good time that Wanamaker had a large cottage built in Sea Grove, at a cost of ten thousand dollars, specifically for the president. Harrison graciously declined the offer, indicating that such a large gift from such a prominent businessman might be misconstrued by the public. However, he saw nothing wrong with Mrs. Harrison accepting the present. So, during a ceremony at the White House, Wanamaker handed the president's wife the keys to "her" new seaside cottage.

But the presidential life is a busy one. Neither Harrison nor his wife ever spent much time at the house in Sea Grove, so eventually Wanamaker took back his gift. After all, a businessman likes to see an investment yield dividends.

CHAPTER
FOUR

THERE SHE WAS...
MISS AMERICA?

They come back every year, as certain a sign of the season as the swallows returning to Capistrano every spring. Except that they aren't swallows, they're women. And it's not the spring their return heralds, it's the fall. And they're not returning to some California town but to the Graceful Dowager of the Jersey Shore, Atlantic City. And—well, never mind. Maybe that was a bad example. Let's try again.

Each September, just after Labor Day, when another frantic summer season has ended and a soothing quiet begins to steal over the beaches, bays, and boardwalks, one place on the Jersey Shore erupts into a frenzy of feverish excitement. For one fast-paced week, which culminates in one breathtaking night, Atlantic City is the toast of the entire nation. All eyes are cast toward the Jersey Shore's most celebrated town; reporters, television crews, and celebrities descend on the Gay Lady, eager to answer that one burning question that keeps millions of Americans glued to their television sets until well past their bedtime on

71

a mid-September Saturday night: Who will be the next Miss America?

This question has been on the minds of more and more people recently, as the Miss America Pageant has steadily grown in stature over the past few decades. The pageant has now become a national institution, like barbecues on the Fourth of July, and although some may criticize it for what they perceive as its simple-minded exploitation of the female form, most people treat it like an aunt who comes to visit once a year: for a few days they'll put up with her. Besides—but don't spread this around or they'll deny every word—they really like seeing her again anyway.

People love tradition, and Miss America oozes tradition from every pore. But the greatest tradition of all is not about the people but the place: each and every year, without fail, the pageant returns to Atlantic City. Even though there are dozens of other cities around the country that would probably mortgage their mayor's house for the honor of letting a beautiful young woman cry and lug an armful of roses down the middle of their convention center, while a massive television audience cries along with her, Miss America has kept both high-heeled feet firmly in place in Atlantic City since the first contest in 1921.

Why is that? The answer is partly in the roots of the Miss America Pageant, those zany, crazy, hazy early days of the contest, when anything could happen—and usually did—in the choosing of the "world's most beautiful girl." Unlike today's steamroller-smooth pageant, when every hair is tucked firmly into place both onstage and off, the early Miss America contests were disheveled affairs. Rules were made up on the fly (or, even better, after the fact), contestants sometimes had rather curious backgrounds, and the atmosphere was more sideshow carnival than it was refined and elegant. In fact, after the first seven years the whole thing ground to a halt, like a badly wheezing engine, and it took eight long years afterward to get everything tuned up and running right.

To understand where Miss America is coming from, it's important to know where else she's been, and the answer to that is simple: nowhere. Miss America is strictly an Atlantic City invention, from the top of her glittering crown to the tips of her painted toenails. Born and nurtured in the salt air of Atlantic City, the pageant has never known another home. To leave the friendly confines of the Queen of the Resorts would be tantamount to the New York Yankees abandoning Yankee Stadium—the legendary House That Ruth Built—for one of those domed monstrosities that pretend to be real baseball parks. Cultural icons can't be uprooted as casually as pulling a weed out of the backyard.

However, it's a safe bet that creating a cultural icon was the last thing H. Conrad Eckholm had in mind in 1920 when he proposed to the Business Men's League in Atlantic City that they sponsor a "Fall Frolic" for the end of September. Eckholm owned the Monticello Hotel in Atlantic City, and it distressed his spirit—not to mention his wallet—that all the tourists turned tail and headed home right after Labor Day, thereby missing some of the best weather the Jersey Shore has to offer. September at the Shore usually means comfortable, nonhumid days and the warmest water of the season, but the only ones around to enjoy it were the year-round residents, who obviously didn't have much use for hotels.

The Business Men's League (which, along with the Hotelmen's Association, dominated affairs in Atlantic City) initially endorsed Eckholm's idea for a late September "frolic" complete with marathon race, parade, and boxing match. But in August, possibly concerned about the capricious nature of it all (after all, this *was* Atlantic City), the Business Men's League trimmed the whole event down to an "International Rolling Chair Pageant" to be held on Saturday, September 25. Reportedly, the late date was a compromise to the big hotels, which did not suffer the severe business drop-off right after Labor Day that the smaller establishments did.

Led by Miss Ernestine Cremona, who was dressed in flowing white robes and called Peace, the parade was a success. Three hundred and fifty rolling chairs rumbled along, each with a beautiful woman sitting in it. That, however, was as close as these Miss America ancestors came to the limelight. Paradoxically, Peace had to share top billing with War. Ranks of fighting men—described as "tin-hatted . . . olive drabbed fighters of the World War" by a local newspaper—marched to the cadence of fourteen bands. A tank was in the procession as well, although far enough away from the rolling chairs to prevent a catastrophe in the case of failing brakes.

The newspapers of that era, which never met an adjective they didn't like, were at their hyperbolic best in describing the event. "Glittering Spectacle as Gorgeous Pageant Sweeps Through Admiring Throng" gushed one press account, which later noted the "Riots of Colors, Beautiful Women, Pretty Girls, Gallantly Caparisoned Youths, and Original Costumes and Decorations."

City officials were pleasantly surprised by the success of the parade. Some even dared to dream that someday it might be the equivalent of the wildly popular baby parade that the Atlantic City of the North, Asbury Park, held every year. A committee was formed to investigate the possibility of holding the event again.

No one seems to know who came up with the idea of adding a beauty contest to the list of festivities. It must have already been included by the time Herb Test, a reporter for the *Atlantic City Daily Press*, was hired for publicity purposes. At the conclusion of one memorable meeting about the contest, Test cried out, in a singular burst of inspiration: "And we'll call her Miss America." Thus was a new American tradition born.

But like all good traditions, this one took a little time to get it right. This first pageant, far from spotlighting the contestants as is done today, was largely viewed as a way to help newspapers that covered Atlantic City increase their circulation. The papers ran a contest, asking readers to send them pictures of beautiful girls. Then each paper chose a winner from among the photos submitted and sent her to Atlantic City to compete against the others.

So it was that the entries in the very first Miss America contest did not come bearing the familiar titles of states but rather of cities: Miss Washington (D.C.), Miss Camden, Miss Pittsburgh, Miss Ocean City, Miss Harrisburg, Miss Philadelphia, Miss Newark, and (naturally) Miss Atlantic City. Possibly concerned about hometown favoritism, Miss Atlantic City did the sporting thing and dropped out, leaving the remaining seven to compete.

And what a competition it was! The women were divided into several classes: Professional (meaning actresses, models, etc.), Civic, and Inter-City. The "beauties" were judged in numerous events, including the Rolling Chair Parade and the Bather's Revue, before the winners went head-to-head.

But even though attractive women were undoubtedly the reason why most people were in town (although they might well have

The contestants for the first Miss America Pageant in 1921. Ultimate winner Margaret Gorman is third from left. (Photo courtesy Miss America Organization)

been disappointed that the "thousands" of beautiful women promised by advertisements were in reality just eight), the real star of this first pageant was that ancient, bearded, and hardly beautiful relic of the deep, King Neptune. "Neptune to Make Spectacular Landing on Beach Near Million Dollar Pier" trumpeted a typical headline on September 7, 1921. His arrival was given only slightly less play than the assassination of a head of state.

"Neptune Arrives, Waves Magic Trident, and Super-Carnival Grips the Resort," blared another headline. "Emerging from his marine Kingdom here yesterday morning," said the story, "Neptune, Ruler of the Seas, with one majestic sweep of his trident, relegated business and other earthly cares to the background for the next two days, turning Atlantic City into a super-carnival center." The battle for silliest superlatives reached new heights in describing the sea king; he was variously referred to as "His Bosship of the Briny," "His Majesty of the Waves," and "Blueblood of the Breakers."

As befits a ruler of such magnitude, King Neptune floated to shore on a "shell barge" with a "court of mermaids." Alighting on dry land, his seaweed robe and long white beard flowing in the wind, the King of the Fishes was greeted by "thousands of sea nymphs in last-minute editions of the 1921 surf apparel—solo attire with nude limbs beneath, that made the lifeguards, pinch-hitting as beach censors, blink, gasp. . . ." As if all this wasn't enough, the water just offshore was jammed with giant yachts packed with spectators. "Booming deck guns flashed their tribute in a royal salute, while whistles, sirens, church bells, and other noise-makers chorused in a bedlam of greeting from every part of the resort." (Who said Atlantic City doesn't know how to throw a party?)

The object of this sight-and-sound orgy, King Neptune, was portrayed by octogenarian Hudson Maxim, a local celebrity whose primary claim to fame was his invention of smokeless gunpowder. Unfortunately, he was also highly sensitive to smells. "While I am exceedingly strong and rugged," the king assured reporters, "if I were placed next to someone smelling to high heaven with perfume, I'd collapse and fall in a heap."

And with those comforting words the first Miss America Pageant was underway. For two days the Fragrance-Free King held sway over a party the likes of which hadn't been seen since Rome was in its prime. "A spectacle of beauty and originality unrivaled in the history of celebrations along the Atlantic seaboard," said one news account immodestly, and it was all that and more. There were boat races by lifeguards, a vaudeville show put on by the Dancing Dolls (juvenile performers ranging in age from three to sixteen), an aerial fireworks display that reportedly included a miniature of Niagara Falls, a colossal Mardi Gras–style romp known as Neptune's Frolique, and the Bather's Revue in which, the newspapers assured us, "nude limbs were in evidence everywhere."

The grand finale was, of course, the selection of the beauty contest winner on Thursday night. Curiously, Herb Test's ideal moniker—Miss America—was not used at first. The winner was to be bestowed—burdened would be more like it—with the absolutely awful title of Inter-City Beauty Contest Winner. With the Big Cheese of the Seas looking on, the contest boiled down to two contestants: Virginia Lee, who had won the professional division, and sixteen-year-old Margaret Gorman (Miss Washington). According to press accounts, the contest was judged 50 percent by applause and 50 percent by the judges. The upset win-

Sixteen-year-old Margaret Gorman, the first Miss America, 1921. (Photo courtesy Miss America Organization)

ner was Margaret Gorman. Standing just one inch over five feet tall, weighing 108 pounds, and with a bust smaller than Twiggy's, she was—and still is—the smallest Miss America ever. Like Joe DiMaggio's fifty-six-game hitting streak, this is a record that will probably stand forever.

She had been selected from among fifteen hundred photos sent to the *Washington Herald.* When two *Herald* reporters went to tell Gorman the news, they found her in a park, playing marbles in the dirt. "I wasn't a tomboy, you know," she would say about the incident. "I loved all the boys."

As the "most beautiful girl in America," Gorman won the Golden Mermaid trophy, which was a gilded mermaid reclining on top of a teakwood base. The trophy, reportedly made of real gold, has been variously valued at anywhere from fifty to five thousand dollars. Today it is worth nothing, since it long ago disappeared. According to the rules at the time, a contestant had to win the competition three times in order to keep the Golden Mermaid.

In a newspaper interview from Saturday, September 10, 1921, Gorman said that her prizes (which included a two-foot-tall silver urn) were "very beautiful" and she was "very proud of them." She said, "When I arrive in Washington I am going to carry them under my arms and let the people there see them."

Unfortunately, somewhere over the years her feelings about the experience changed greatly. In a 1980 interview she said, "I never cared to be Miss America. It wasn't my idea. I am so bored by it all. I really want to forget the whole thing." Her husband, she said, "hated" the notoriety of it all. "I did, too, after a while," she added.

But what had been unleashed in the late summer air of Atlantic City wasn't boredom but excitement. The crowds had been large—one paper called them "hardly less in numbers than that of August"—and it was clear that the perfect way to extend the season beyond Labor Day's swan song had been found.

♦

Following an old tourism maxim—If you've got a good thing, run with it until the legs give out—pageant organizers immediately expanded both the length and the scope of the event in 1922. Fifty-seven beauties from as far away as Toronto, San Francisco, Seattle, Birmingham, and Los Angeles came to Atlantic City to compete in the now three-day-long event. Included among them was Miss Alaska, Helmar Liederman, who, according to one newspaper account, came to Atlantic City "from the snowclad fields of Alaska after traveling by dog-sled, aeroplane, train, and boat." Since Liederman really lived in New York City, this must have been an interesting trip indeed. When pageant officials found out that they were the only ones getting snowed, they barred her from competing for the crown. She responded

Margaret Gorman (right) congratulates Mary Katherine Campbell on her victory in the 1922 pageant as Hudson Maxim—a.k.a. King Neptune—looks on. (Photo courtesy Miss America Organization)

with a $150,000 lawsuit. It was the first of several embarrassing incidents that eventually contributed to the pageant's cancellation after 1927.

But fun, not failure, was what was on the minds of the thousands of revelers who poured into Atlantic City for the 1922 event. Included among them was Norman Rockwell, who was one of the judges. Making a return appearance as King Neptune was the Smell-less One, Hudson Maxim. Leading a flotilla of local dignitaries, he floated to shore on a barge camouflaged as a reef; surrounding him were twenty beauties in Asian costumes. He barely had time to get his land legs when the welcoming celebration/explosion was unleashed: "The bands blared forth into the rollicking tunes of 'Atlantic City All the Time,' the gay cadence of the syncopation mingling with the shrill blasts from the whistles aboard the several hundred pleasure craft that dotted the wide expanse of water as far as the eye could see . . . aeroplanes overhead [dodged] bombs flung from a battery of cannon to release parachutes from which were suspended Old Glory in miniature."

So overwhelming was this gaudy spectacle that the city's safety director, William Cuthbert, slipped while stepping onto the dock from one of the escort boats and fell into the water. Cuthbert (who was rescued) had started a trend; later that day, during a group picture, the chairs the contestants were standing on collapsed, knocking Miss Philadelphia cold.

Meanwhile, back at the site of Neptune's arrival, things were heating up in a big way. Next to greet His Royal Fishiness was Miss New Haven, who wore "white linen trouserettes, henna-hued jacket, glinting white silk hosiery and pumps. . . . The ultramodern costume halted Father Neptune and he colored to the rim of his stiffly starched collar that showed above the top of his sea robes."

This was the 1920s, remember, when the female form was just beginning to emerge from years of hibernation behind bolts and bolts of fabric and lace. Further evidence of the changing times occurred during the Bather's Revue, when some of the contestants appeared not in the traditional wool suits with skirts but in "one-piece bathing suits that revealed the form." Several of the contestants who had appeared in the traditional swimwear were furious, claiming they didn't know that "form was to be considered in selecting America's most beautiful bathing girl." Before someone could gently explain that "form" was really the whole point of the thing, these incensed contestants had staged a "beauty strike." The judges, however, dealt with the crisis by ordering everyone to be rejudged wearing a one-piece suit.

The winner of the second Miss America title was sixteen-year-old Mary Katherine Campbell of Columbus, Ohio, who had to defeat not only the winners of the various other "beauty divisions" but also the previous year's winner, perky Margaret Gorman. The crowning took place before twelve thousand people in a ballroom on the Million Dollar Pier (Convention Hall was not yet built). As the decision was announced, the massive crowd went wild; the auburn-haired winner was hoisted onto the shoulders of King Neptune's court and carried around the boisterous room like a conquering hero. Finally she was plopped onto a throne next to poor Hudson Maxim, who was probably sorry by this time that he had ever invented smokeless gunpowder in the first place.

The next day artist Coles Philips, who was one of the judges, extolled the selection of Campbell as heralding the inauguration

Mary Katherine Campbell, the only Miss America to win the crown twice, in 1922 and 1923. (Photo courtesy Miss America Organization)

of a new type of American girl. "Their type is the rather tall girl, with rather straight lines, fairly athletic, broad shoulders for swimming, a clear eye and clean intelligent face. Measurements really mean nothing." (Campbell's measurements were 35-25-36; they must have meant something!)

Mary Katherine Campbell is unique in the annals of Miss Americadom for having been the only entrant ever to win the title twice. In 1923, with the pageant roaring nonstop for a full three days, the returning queen bested seventy-four rivals from thirty-six states to win the crown an unprecedented second time. Like Gorman, however, Campbell soon tired of the unrelenting glare of the Miss America spotlight. "I got so tired of the publicity," she said in a 1958 interview. "I didn't ever want to hear about 'Miss America' again."

Campbell's toughest adversary in the 1923 event was Ethelda Kenvin, Miss Brooklyn—who was subsequently discovered to be "Mrs." Brooklyn when it was revealed that she was married to a Pittsburgh Pirates baseball player. Pageant officials had omitted the teeny-weeny detail of barring married women from the contest.

◆

Although errors like this were starting to form thunderclouds over the pageant, the storm was still a few years off. From a simple contest involving a few local newspapers, the Miss America Pageant had grown in a few short years into a gargantuan, nationwide affair. It was, as the president of the Atlantic City Chamber of Commerce noted, "priceless propaganda."

Thus it should come as no surprise that the following year, 1924, the pageant was expanded to a full five days: September 2 through September 6. Eighty-three beauties—the largest field ever—strutted their stuff through a whirlwind series of events including an American Beauty Ball, a Masked Night Carnival, and a Mardi Gras.

Unfortunately, our old friend King Neptune was ill-treated by the weather gods that year. Hudson Maxim and his sensitive nose were gone from the scene, replaced by Jack de Lange of Philadelphia. But nature showed its displeasure at the new Big Boss of the Waves by hitting the city with a fierce storm at the start of the festivities. It was a very wet monarch who arrived on the pier, wearing oilskins and undoubtedly a soggy scowl. Even the normally exuberant *Atlantic City Daily Press* seemed waterlogged as it described the dreary scene: "A bedraggled, dispirited and very ungodly Neptune it was that stepped out of a swanlike craft yesterday afternoon and implanted his trident in the water-soaked pier at the Atlantic City Yacht Club."

Some of the floats and rolling chairs in this year's Rolling Chair Parade seemed to have reached Thanksgiving Day proportions.

Five theaters in Ocean City cosponsored a twenty-five-foot gondola with clusters of flowers along its sides, four beauties seated in its center, and a red-and-white-draped satin canopy in the rear that sheltered three Latin musicians. The Third Ward Republican Club contributed a huge replica of the GOP elephant standing in the center of a twenty-foot float, surrounded by palms and other foliage. The Atlantic City Chamber of Commerce had a huge male bather measuring eight feet at the waist, sprawled on a miniature beach. On top of the bather was a girl in a swimsuit and a teasing smile who tickled the bather's nose with a long-stemmed rose. "The Playground of the World Welcomes You" read the sign on the side.

The big question at this pageant was whether anyone could beat twice-crowned Mary Katherine Campbell. Some thought they could—particularly eighteen-year-old Ruth Malcolmson (Miss Philadelphia), who had won a silver seashell as the best in the amateur division in the 1923 pageant. But when Malcolmson saw the plain float she was to ride on in the Rolling Chair Parade, she cried. As she explained in a newspaper interview fifty years later: "It was a bare flat-bed truck—with a fake fireplace. But it had a spinning wheel. I was in a black taffeta dress. . . . Betsy Ross, you know." Yet, in a "revolutionary" upset, the young Philadelphian with the curly brown hair won that event. When she won the Bather's Revue too, the stage was set for an epic confrontation between her and the mighty Mary.

It was a night more befitting a prize fight than a beauty contest. The judges deliberated endlessly among the five finalists, while the heat grew more intense on the Million Dollar Pier. Four women fainted; the mayor of Philadelphia, Freeland Jendrick, finally ducked out and went to a Boardwalk theater, leaving word that someone should tell him if Malcolmson won. At last a decision was reached, and when Campbell was first told to step forward the crowd gasped in amazement; the beautiful Ohioan had done the impossible and won the crown a third time! But then a voice boomed out "Philadelphia wins the prize," and it was clear that Malcolmson had dethroned the champ. Someone ran for the mayor.

A half-century later, Malcolmson recalled how different the pageant was in the early days. "It was absolutely uncommercial in those days. I didn't go into show business or get paid for

Ruth Malcolmson, Miss America 1924. (Photo courtesy Miss America Organization)

appearances. It was all so casual then. I remember having dinner with Jack Dempsey. We would sit at lunch with the judges and carry on friendly conversations." But, unlike some other early winners, her memories remained fond ones. When asked if she'd do it again, she replied, "Oh yes, of course. Of course. I was a long shot. I made it. It was glamorous."

Though the new Miss America was as pretty as they come, talk persisted that her win was really a bone thrown to Philadelphia to make up for the fact that no contestant from the City of Brotherly Love had done well up to that point in the pageant. Philadelphia tourism had always been the lifeblood of Atlantic City; some people figured this was the resort's way of saying thanks.

The pageant was hit with another black eye that year when Miss Boston showed up with the usual assortment of clothes and bathing suits—and a seven-month-old baby! Since single mothers hadn't been invented yet, pageant officials investigated and found that the Miss was actually a Mrs. The rules were quickly (and finally) changed to bar married women, but another hole had been pricked in the cloth of the pageant's reputation.

◆

The cloth was shredded beyond recognition the following year. Two serious scandals hit Miss America like a runaway rolling chair, probably making pageant officials long for the good old days when all they had to worry about was Hudson Maxim's sensitive nose.

The first involved the ultimate winner, Fay Lanphier, who as Miss California was the first Miss America to represent an entire state and not just a city. Two months after she won the title, the notorious newspaper *New York Graphic*, which spelled yellow journalism with a capital Y, began running a splashy series of articles claiming the contest had been fixed for Lanphier because she had been signed to appear in a Paramount Pictures film entitled *The American Venus*, a movie about a beauty contest winner. Since accuracy had never been one of the *Graphic*'s major concerns, it wasn't surprising that these charges were later retracted by the newspaper. Yet the damage had been done.

There was a little more fire underneath the smoke of the second incident. It all began when Ruth Malcolmson refused to return as

Fay Lanphier, Miss America 1925. (Photo courtesy Miss America Organization)

a participant in 1925 to defend her crown, claiming that "professionals" had sullied the supposedly all-amateur ranks of the Inter-City beauties. It turned out she was correct. One ringer was a Broadway showgirl named Kathryn Ray, whose boss, Broadway showman Earl Carroll, had been a judge in the Miss Coney Island Pageant, which Ray had won in order to advance to Atlantic City. More funny business was afoot when another showgirl, Dorothy Knapp, conveniently appeared in Atlantic City to take up the torch from the original Miss Manhattan, who suddenly got "sick."

All this overshadowed poor Fay Lanphier's victory. Unlike the first three Miss Americas, who went back and lived quiet lives after their victories, Lanphier tried to parlay her title into a movie career. She did appear in *The American Venus*, as well as a Laurel and Hardy vehicle, but by then someone had discovered that her acting ability was a sure cure for insomnia, and she vanished from the Hollywood scene.

The year 1925 marked several changes in the pageant's rules. In early September officials decided that a Golden Mermaid would go to each year's winner, rather than only to three-time champions. Trophies were presented that year to all the previous Miss Americas.

Malcolmson's decision to stay in Philadelphia brought about further changes in the pageant. As the *Atlantic City Daily Press* reported on September 8, 1925: "The refusal of Miss Ruth Malcolmson, of Philadelphia, to appear this year in defense of the title she won last September has brought about a progressive step by the directors. . . . [T]he winner of this year's title will not be called upon next year to defend her crown, but will be invited to be a guest of honor together with previous Misses America."

While this was a step in the right direction, it didn't stop the hemorrhaging of good faith that the pageant was experiencing. As with an aging beauty queen, each year brought more worry lines, and no amount of makeup—in the form of new rules or procedures—could stem the erosion. Taking pageant potshots seemed to be the new American pastime. A typical broadside came from the YWCA in Trenton, New Jersey, which worried about the pageant's effect on the contestants: "the outlook in life of girls who participated was completely changed. Before the competition they were splendid examples of innocent and pure womanhood. Afterwards their heads were filled with vicious ideas."

In 1926 there were fifty-five contestants (compared with almost seventy the previous year). The event was scaled back to four days, and the only thing happening on the final day, September 11, was an ocean swim. That year, with the female flapper raising eyebrows all across the country, the judges rhapsodized at length on the type of young woman that Miss America should be.

Not surprisingly, the supposedly risqué flapper found little sympathy. The next Miss America "will be a girl of balance and mentality, who has ambitions to marry and have a flock of kids," said painter William G. Kreighoff. "Wouldn't it be a tragedy if we picked as the model of a beauty a flighty little thing with not much heart and less brains, who, as soon as she opened her mouth, put her foot in it?" Magazine cover designer Haskell Coffin chimed in with: "Not a large girl, but well proportioned. A dainty girl of temperament, delicacy and charm—a home-loving, modest, effeminate, but healthy girl."

Norma Smallwood is crowned Miss America 1926 by King Neptune. (Photo courtesy Miss America Organization)

The girl they selected to embody this living example of saint-hood and sexiness rolled into one was Norma Smallwood, Miss Tulsa, who was crowned Miss America 1926 on the night of September 10. One of the contestants she beat was a fifteen-year-old from Dallas named Rosebud Blondell, who, by her own words years later, had "a good, big chest, the kind garbagemen whistle at." She is better known today as actress Joan Blondell, the only Miss America contestant to realize fully the often-elusive dream of silver screen stardom.

Smallwood took the title and ran with it all the way to the bank. (She made, in one estimation, $100,000 from her new notoriety.) Her fondness for greenbacks was brought home during the 1927 pageant. Although she had a role in the pageant as the reigning Miss America, Smallwood vanished from Atlantic City on opening night. Speculation on her whereabouts rocked the resort until it was revealed that both she and her mother had hot-footed it down to Walnut Grove, North Carolina. Smallwood's manager had signed a contract for her to judge a country fair beauty contest, and when the choice was between being onstage for free with glamorous beauties from all over the country and picking up a few bucks in Walnut Grove, Norma went with the money.

Reduced to scrambling once again, pageant officials substituted Alice Garry for Smallwood. The new Miss America was seventeen-year-old Miss Illinois, Lois Delander. After the difficulties of the last two years with winners who had stars in their eyes, pageant officials probably breathed a sigh of relief when the new Miss America announced that she had never considered either the movies or the stage as a career. "I've always dreamed of being a successful artist," she said.

But by this time not even the wholesomeness of a Real American Girl could save the pageant. It had become, in many eyes, an embarrassment, like the unwanted relative at a picnic who spills food and tells off-color jokes. The chief critics were the most powerful: the hotel owners, who had originally embraced the idea, now deplored it as a scandalous, bawdy blight on their town. Julian Hillman, president of the Hotelmen's Association, said: "There has been an epidemic recently of women who seek personal aggrandizement and publicity by participating in various stunts throughout the world, and the hotelmen feel that in

Lois Delander, Miss America 1927. (Photo courtesy Miss America Organization)

recent years that type of woman has been attracted to the pageant in ever-increasing numbers." Others complained about "an air of secrecy" that showed "poor judgement."

If some stories could be believed, poor judgment was probably one of the lesser sins committed in picking the most beautiful girl in the world. In a later interview, Lois Delander said that contestants were physically tape-measured by the judges in 1927. While there is no hard evidence to support such a charge

Memorable Moments of the Miss America Pageant

While it may seem that nothing could compare to the pageants of the 1920s, the Miss America Pageant continued to have its share of goofs, scandals, quirky episodes, and memorable contestants after it was revived in the 1930s. Here are just a few instances.

Long before Vanessa Williams and her infamous appearance in *Penthouse*, the pageant had to deal with another Miss America who had "shown it all." After Henrietta Leaver, Miss Pittsburgh, was crowned queen in 1935, a Pittsburgh sculptor named Frank Vittor unveiled a nude statue of her that he had completed just a few months before. A mortified Miss Leaver first claimed that she had actually posed in a bathing suit and her grandmother had been present all during the session, then finally gave up and eloped to Oklahoma with her high school sweetheart.

Two years later, in 1937, another Miss America abdicated the throne when seventeen-year-old Bette Cooper, a New Jersey native who entered the contest as Miss Bertrand Island, won the crown and took off before her first scheduled appearance the next day. Shortly afterward Walter Winchell reported that Cooper and her chauffeur for the event, Lou Off, had been secretly married. In reality Off had merely helped Cooper—who, after winning, had decided all she really wanted was to go home and return to school—secretly flee Atlantic City. While a romance between the two did blossom, they were never married.

One of the most notorious Miss America contestants was Janice Hansen, Miss New Jersey 1944. In the years following her moment in the pageant, Hansen was questioned by law officials about her suspected involvement with the Mafia, including the alleged smuggling of narcotics and the deaths of several prominent mobsters (she had dinner with mob boss Albert Anastasia on the night before he was killed). Hansen met her end when she and a companion, Anthony "Little Augie" Pisano, were gunned down while sitting in a car in the East Elmhurst section of Queens.

Judges of the 1947 pageant undoubtedly experienced a case of déjà vu when they saw Miss Chattanooga and Miss Tennessee. The Cunnningham sisters—Jane and Jean—were identical twins from Chattanooga. The blonde, blue-eyed beauties each stood 5'6¾", weighed 118 pounds, and had measurements of 35½-25-36. Together they had won the title of Miss Chattanooga

(*continued*)

Memorable Moments of the Miss America Pageant (continued)

before going on to share the state title. Pageant officials, however, ignoring the old maxim of share and share alike, ruled that the nineteen-year-olds would have to compete for the Miss America crown individually. A coin toss settled the matter: Jean became Miss Chattanooga, and Jane was Miss Tennessee.

Bert Parks became a pageant institution during his seventeen-year reign as emcee. Parks and the pageant's theme song, "There She Is," became as closely associated as salt and pepper. However, in 1967, when performing one of his exuberant renditions of the song, Parks yanked out his microphone cable. While the enthusiastic audience in Convention Hall never noticed the gaffe, millions of television viewers were treated to what was probably the only mime performance Parks ever gave.

---

in this or any other year, the rumors alone probably added to the weight of bad feeling that was about to topple Miss America.

With its most powerful allies now turned against it, the pageant was doomed. In March 1928 the hotel operators voted to cancel the Miss America Pageant. In September of that same year, with the pageant, King Neptune, and all the beauties just a memory, a newspaper article claimed that the crowds on the Boardwalk exceeded those of 1927, the last year of the pageant.

"Speaking for my own hotel," said one operator, "business last week was better than during pageant week last year."

It may well have been better, but without the Master of the Oceanic Universe stalking about, trident in hand, surrounded by a court of nubile young sea nymphs while a bevy of bathing beauties strutted around the Playground of the World, it just wasn't the same.

◆

The ban remained in effect for six long years. Then, in 1933, the pageant returned and showed that its hiatus had changed nothing. The list of disasters in the 1933 pageant reads like a primer on how to make a Keystone Kops comedy: Miss New York State collapsed on stage due to an abscessed tooth, Miss Oklahoma was rushed to the hospital to have her appendix removed,

Miss New York City simply dropped out, Miss Arkansas was discovered to be Mrs. Arkansas, and three contestants from the West were disqualified for residing in states other than those claimed. After this fiasco the pageant went into hibernation for two years. When it awoke, in 1935, new blood had taken control, and the pageant began the climb to respectability that has culminated in today's sleek, stylish institution. Through it all the pageant has remained as much a part of Atlantic City as saltwater taffy and the Boardwalk.

But despite the glamour and sophistication of the modern Miss America, those with a yen for daring and adventure know that there will never be another time like those unpredictable, uncontrollable, hedonistic early years in the 1920s—a fact that probably helps those who run today's pageant sleep a whole lot better.

FIVE

WOODEN WALKWAYS ALONG THE SAND

A t first, a boardwalk seems to be such a curious thing. After all, it's not as if it's chiseled in stone somewhere that there must be a walkway made of boards running parallel to Jersey Shore beaches. Indeed, if you stop to think about it, the whole notion of a pedestrian thoroughfare made of wood is rather odd. It reminds one of the western towns portrayed in movies and on television, where everybody clomps along a wooden sidewalk and says "Howdy, Marshall." Wood has many drawbacks: It tends to rot, crack, and dry out. Isn't there a better choice for supporting the weight of thousands of people and buildings? And last but certainly not least, wood gives you splinters. Given all these negatives, what's the big deal about a boardwalk anyway?

As it turns out, wooden boardwalks are as logical as waves in an ocean. Tradition seldom follows a straight line; like running water, the heritage of an area must find its own way. This is what happened with boardwalks, which have come to epitomize something deep and ingrained about the Jersey Shore. There may be other materials that would be better for boardwalks, but as far as the culture and heritage of the Jersey Shore is concerned, a wooden boardwalk makes all the sense in the world.

It has often been said that necessity is the mother of invention, and this is the case with boardwalks. The inspiration behind the birth of the boardwalk was a simple need—how to stop people from tracking beach sand into hotels. Little did anyone realize that the solution to this seemingly minor problem would revolutionize the entire Jersey Shore.

♦

Tradition holds that the boardwalk was conceived in Atlantic City in 1870. As a matter of historical record, however, Cape May seems to have had something called a "flirtation walk" in 1868, which might well have been exactly the same as what was built in Atlantic City two years later. But Atlantic City took the idea and ran with it, and even formally adopted the word *boardwalk* as a proper name (hence the use of the capital B when writing about that town's wooden walkway, while the lowercase b is used for all the others). Today the Boardwalk is as much a part of Atlantic City lore as the Miss America Pageant.

Most sources hold that the first boardwalk resulted from a meeting in an Atlantic City hotel in the spring of 1870. While this meeting did indeed take place, the idea of a boardwalk might have been discussed even earlier. According to *Butler's Book of the Boardwalk*, the notion of a footpath across the beach was advocated by Alexander Boardman (his surname has nothing to do with the origin of the word *boardwalk*). He was both a conductor on the Camden & Atlantic Railroad, which served Atlantic City, and the owner of the Ocean House hotel in town.

Boardman had a problem that anyone who has ever had a house down the Shore can sympathize with: people tracking beach sand all over the place. Obviously tired of cleaning up sand scattered throughout both his train and his hotel by the shoes of people returning from the Atlantic City beaches, Boardman suggested to Henry L. Bonsall, editor of the *Camden Republic* newspaper, that a footpath be built on the beach. Bonsall liked the idea and wrote an editorial about it, which helped spread the notion of a boardwalk. (Although it was not called that yet, we will use the term from now on for the sake of clarity.)

It might well have been through the *Republic* that Jacob Keim heard about this strange new thing—a boardwalk. Keim, who owned Atlantic City's Chester County House hotel, was apparently also having problems with sand in his establishment, and so Boardman's idea made sense. According to *Butler's Book of the Boardwalk*, Keim and Boardman talked the matter over and decided to call a meeting to discuss the pros and cons.

The meeting, held in the spring of 1870 at the Chester House, was attended by eight people (presumably hotel owners). Boardman told the group that, to satisfy visitors, the hotels in town had to provide "fine carpets, good furniture, and other luxuries." Then Boardman said: "Our carpets and even stuffed chairs are being ruined by the sand tracked into our places from the beach. Walking on the beach is a favorite pastime. We can't stop this. We do propose to give the beach strollers a walkway of boards on the sand which we believe will overcome our sand problems."

Impressed by the idea, those at the meeting agreed to petition the city council to build the proposed footpath. Boardman and Keim did a preliminary cost estimate for building the walkway and came up with a total of five thousand dollars. The petitions that were circulated about town advocating a boardwalk were generally met with enthusiasm, although those who owned hotels on Atlantic Avenue were afraid that the boardwalk would draw people to the beachfront and away from their establishments (it did).

On April 25, 1870, the city council received the petition. The minutes of that meeting said, in part: "A petition from property owners of Atlantic City was presented to Council, asking Council to have a board or plank walk erected along the beachfront from Massachusetts Ave., to the Excursion House."

The idea met so little opposition that on Monday, May 9, the council adopted the following resolution:

That the city build a board walk along the beach from Congress Hall (Massachusetts and Pacific) to the Excursion House (between Missouri and Mississippi). That said walk be 10 feet wide; that the boards be laid lengthwise; that the Committee [on Property Protection and Improvement] be instructed to proceed with the erection of the walk immediately.

An early Atlantic City Boardwalk. (Photo courtesy Atlantic County His-torical Society)

Ironically, the resolution also prohibited any buildings within thirty feet of the Boardwalk, which meant that the first Board-walk was completely noncommercial!

No sooner had the resolution passed than a serious problem arose. Tax collections for the previous year (1869) had totaled $9,172.15. If the city spent $5,000 of that money on building this gimmicky new beach walk, it would leave precious little money in the treasury. At this point *Butler's Book of the Boardwalk* claims that Mayor John J. Gardner pulled $1,080 out of his wallet to get the project started. However, the city decided to fund the project by issuing script, which was redeemable the next year. A short time later $5,000 worth of bonds were sold, and with this money the script was retired.

But no matter how it was financed, the Boardwalk was built, and built quickly. By June 26, 1870, the new walkway along the beach was dedicated with parades and celebrations in numerous hotels. The city's newest attraction was constructed of boards one-and-one-half inches thick, nailed to joists set crosswise under the Boardwalk every two feet. Each twelve-foot section was laid on a row of posts sticking up about eighteen inches from the sand.

(There were no handrails as found on today's boardwalks.) At the end of each season the sections were picked up and stored, safe from winter's damaging effects; the next season they were put back onto the sand. (This is the main reason why the walk was made of wood; bricks or concrete could not have been moved so easily.)

The first Boardwalk was an instant success. With the novel attraction acting as a magnet, the city's population took a mighty leap; over the next five years the number of new residents moving into Atlantic City exceeded the total population that had been reached during the city's first sixteen years!

One of the high points for the Boardwalk came on April 16, 1876, when it was the site of Atlantic City's first Easter Parade. The event had been heavily promoted by the railroads, and the wooden walkway was jammed with people decked out in their Easter finery. (Occasionally just a little too jammed; many of the smartly dressed men and women were forced off the narrow Boardwalk and went tumbling onto the sand.)

By the close of the 1879 season, the first Boardwalk was showing the effects of all those thousands of feet that had been happily walking over it. A new Boardwalk, the same height as the first but fourteen feet wide instead of ten, was built in the spring of 1880. (Like its predecessor, the planks in this Boardwalk ran lengthwise; after this they would run crosswise.) By this time the rule against businesses near the Boardwalk had been relaxed, and scores of commercial establishments rushed to position themselves the required ten feet from the walkway (bathhouses had to remain fifteen feet away). Ramps connected the businesses to the popular Boardwalk. The exodus from the city's main business area along Atlantic Avenue that some merchants had warned about in the beginning was now in full swing; the 1883 city directory listed nearly one hundred commercial establishments near the Boardwalk.

Although this second Boardwalk was built to be portable, the third, constructed in 1884 and now twenty feet wide, was the first permanent structure. Because it was now five feet high but still had no railings, the problem of people falling off—and getting hurt—was accelerating. On August 15, 1885, the newspaper *Atlantic Review* reported that "nearly every day somebody falls off the Boardwalk. In nearly every instance, the parties have been flirting."

The Atlantic City Boardwalk on Easter Sunday, 1905, showing how incredibly crowded the walkway could get. (Photo courtesy Special Collections and Archives, Rutgers University Libraries)

By now businesses were frantically building on both sides of the Boardwalk, cutting off the ocean view. Some establishments even roofed over the walkway, completely closing off the sun, sky, and ocean! Nature would have none of this, however, and on September 9, 1889, a hurricane hurtled into Atlantic City, ripping apart much of this Boardwalk and forcing yet another to be built.

The new—or fourth—Boardwalk opened on May 10, 1890, with a ban on building along the ocean side. This twenty-four-foot-wide structure finally had railings. However, that didn't stop twenty-five people from toppling onto the sand one day while they were watching "beer garden waitresses and female performers bathe."

The fifth and final Boardwalk, the one that thousands still use, was opened on July 8, 1896. This version was built on steel girders attached to steel pilings—a far cry from the days when lightweight wooden sections were picked up and stored for the winter. To celebrate the structure's completion, Mrs. Franklin P. Stoy, the wife of Atlantic City's mayor, drove home a golden spike, which was promptly stolen. (The joke was on the thief, because the spike was actually iron covered with shiny yellow paint.) On August 17, 1896, Atlantic City assured itself of the capital B when it officially adopted the name Boardwalk for the "walkway of boards on the sand" that had been suggested simply as a way to keep sand out of hotels.

Throughout the years, the Atlantic City Boardwalk has had some strange attractions on it—things that seem more appropriate for a carnival than a boardwalk. It has played host to the odd (a two-headed woman), the unusual (a gigantic, fourteen-ton Underwood typewriter that was operated via a normal-size typewriter), and the merely famous (performers like John Philip Sousa, Abbott and Costello, and Bob Hope have all "played" the Boardwalk).

Animal acts have been legion along the boards, with trained lions, "educated" horses, and "learned" pigs among the members of the animal kingdom that have strutted their stuff on the Boardwalk. None of them, however, topped the Steel Pier's legendary High-Diving Horse, who plunged sixty feet into a pool every day for decades before throngs of amazed spectators.

Amusement piers are as much a part of boardwalks as wooden planks. They were first conceived in Atlantic City in 1882, with the debut of "Howard's Folly," a 650-foot-long amusement pier built by Colonel George Howard at the foot of Kentucky Avenue on the

Bizarre Attractions of the Atlantic City Boardwalk

Maybe there's something in the salt air—or maybe in the salt-water taffy—but the history of Atlantic City's Boardwalk is filled with bizarre attractions. From the epic jumps of the famous diving horse to Alvin "Shipwreck" Kelly's record-breaking sit (forty-nine days and one hour) atop the Steel Pier flagpole, Atlantic City had it all. Below are some of the more unusual attractions.

EPICYCLOIDAL DIVERSION. Erected by Isaac N. Forrester on the beach in front of the Seaview Excursion (at Mississippi Avenue), this contraption was a forerunner to the modern Ferris wheel. Four large wheels containing passenger cars (up to sixty-four people could ride at once) were mounted on a revolving circular platform; the effect was like riding a ferris wheel on top of a merry-go-round.

THE HAUNTED SWING. Located on States Avenue, this early thrill ride was a large platform swing that could fit twenty people and was set inside a cozy Victorian living room. The swing would seemingly swing back and forth, gaining more and more momentum until it flipped over 360 degrees (definitely not a ride for those with weak stomachs or toupees). But the whole thing was an illusion; the room, with furniture and paintings securely fixed, actually turned around while the swing remained stationary.

THE WILD MAN OF BORNEO. Around the turn of the century, this manacled "wild man" could be found in a caged pit under the Boardwalk. He snarled, screamed, wore animal skins, chewed on raw bones, and generally behaved like the savage everyone thought he was. But in 1901, when he was arrested for performing on a Sunday, it was finally revealed that the Wild Man was simply one of the Boardwalk's rolling chair operators, and he was meekly led away.

#1 ATLANTIC OCEAN. When Million Dollar Pier opened on the Boardwalk in 1906, its main attraction was a Moorish estate owned by one of the pier's founders, Captain John Young. Awash in pastel lights and surrounded by an elegant garden (complete with various sculptures), the house stood right up against the ocean, and Young reportedly enjoyed fishing out of his bedroom window. The house was finally torn down in 1953.

THE INDIAN WHO BURIED HIMSELF. In 1952 Ronald Harrison, a fifty-year-old Sioux, set a unique world record at Steel Pier when he buried himself for six weeks in a concrete box. (The box came complete with a glass top for easy viewing by the curious.) During that time Harrison nourished himself solely with liquids, which he consumed through a tube.

Boardwalk. For generations thereafter, the Iron Pier, the Million Dollar Pier, Steeplechase Pier, and others offered dazzling displays of music, entertainment, and amusement to millions of people. Among the other firsts that the Boardwalk is credited with are the rolling chairs (1884), American picture postcards (1895—the idea was imported from Germany), and saltwater taffy.

Today, with the Miss America Pageant, the casinos, and a variety of other attractions, the venerable Boardwalk is still going strong. There are some things that time can't change, and the instant identification of the Boardwalk with Atlantic City will always be one of them.

◆

Although few would dispute Atlantic City's right to claim the King of the Boardwalk crown, in the late nineteenth and early twentieth centuries the Asbury Park boardwalk was a delightful amusement excursion all its own and was probably Atlantic City's most formidable rival.

The Weekly Journal and Monmouth Republican of April 15, 1903, explained how the Asbury Park boardwalk began: "It was some years after Asbury Park was first settled before the need of a walk on the ocean front was appreciated. As the number of visitors increased greater interest was taken in bathing and finally the custom of a promenade on the beach became the proper thing. In 1877 a narrow boardwalk, similar to those which are now and then seen in rural districts answering as sidewalks, was laid from Wesley Lake to Deal Lake. It was laid flat on the sand and was just wide enough for two to stroll along. In the spring of 1879 a second walk of the same width was laid nearer the surf, but did not extend to Deal Lake."

In 1880 these two boardwalks were replaced by what the newspaper called "the first promenade boardwalk." This was over two thousand feet long and ranged in width from sixteen feet at its narrowest point to thirty-two feet at the widest. Benches were situated every ten feet. The first boardwalk pavilion was also constructed in 1880. Located at Asbury Avenue, the pavilion hosted band concerts, which were, the paper assured us, "attended by thousands." Since the band and a candy stand took up virtually all the room, the pavilion was enlarged the next year.

Another local newspaper, the *Shore Press*, in its May 14, 1880, edition described a typical scene on this new beachfront walkway

The Epicycloidal Diversion on the Atlantic City Boardwalk, the forerunner to the Ferris wheel, circa 1870s. (Photo courtesy Atlantic County Historical Society)

Watching a chicken hit a home run was just one of the many strange amusements on the Atlantic City Boardwalk. (Photo courtesy Special Collections and Archives, Rutgers University Libraries)

A rolling chair on the Atlantic City Boardwalk, circa 1910. (Collection of Richard Steele)

that makes one ache for the ability to turn back the clock, at least momentarily, to those gay and carefree times: "The new walk along the shore, and the other improvements . . . are fully proven as appreciated, by the fact of their being thronged these pleasant evenings by scores who love the sad song of the restless ocean

A typically crowded Atlantic City Boardwalk in 1905. (Photo courtesy Atlantic County Historical Society)

Although casinos have replaced the unusual attractions of yesteryear, the Atlantic City Boardwalk today still draws a crowd. (Photo courtesy Greater Atlantic City Convention and Visitors Bureau)

and the comfortable opportunity afforded to be fanned by health-giving breezes. . . . The band is nightly applauded in the selections, and although the numbers of the programme are not many, the selections and time amply repay the listener to tarry until the close."

As they did everywhere along the Jersey Shore, storms took their toll on the Asbury Park boardwalk. As the *Journal* put it, in the flowery language so typical of newspapers from a century ago: "The original boardwalk was laid in a straight line. On several occasions during the past twenty years old Neptune while in a rage bit huge slices out of the promenade and left it a useless wreck. These portions were rebuilt at a cost of many thousands of dollars and were seldom replaced in their original positions, which accounts for the present irregularities in the walk." [The boardwalk apparently did not run in a straight line, nor was it all one height.]

Despite these quirks, by the early years of the twentieth century the Asbury Park boardwalk was the premier pedestrian pathway along the northern Jersey Shore. The town was at the peak of its popularity, and photos from that era show the broad boardwalk filled with people dressed in all their finery, either promenading proudly or sitting on one of the many benches and staring out at the wide beach.

In 1903 James A. Bradley, founder and guiding light of Asbury Park for over thirty years, sold the beachfront to the city for $100,000. Before this Bradley had owned the coastal property and thus dictated its development, but now the town was in charge. A local committee considering beachfront improvements issued a report that contained some rather surprising suggestions.

One peculiar idea was to change the boardwalk's planking from crosswise to lengthwise. Although one reason given was that lengthwise planking would make for "smooth and easy walking," another rationale was quite progressive, echoing today's emphasis on equal access for people with disabilities. "In the near future there will be many invalids here who will make use of wheel chairs. With planking lengthwise of the walk these chairs will [roll] smoothly and without jar."

Among the other unorthodox ideas the committee considered were placing all buildings on the east side of the boardwalk, thus

Asbury Park boardwalk as it appeared in 1913. (Collection of Richard Steele)

blocking the ocean view, and constructing an aquarium containing "all manner of salt water fishes."

Most of the committee's unusual ideas, including those mentioned above, did not come to pass. The next significant attempt to change the boardwalk started on September 2, 1916, when a group of local businessmen and city officials proposed the construction of a five thousand-seat structure on the boardwalk that would enable the city to host conventions and similar gatherings. As the *Asbury Park Evening Press* noted that day: "[a] building of this character will be urgently needed next summer when the resort entertains the National Education Association."

Thus began a protracted, decade-long battle over whether to build the Asbury Park boardwalk's most famous structure: Convention Hall. Over the next ten years the pro side argued that such a building was necessary if the resort was to continue attracting large groups, while the con side felt that the financial burdens of such a project would be too great. Finally, in 1926 the city commissioners passed a $2 million financing ordinance for the construction of Convention Hall. By January of 1927 the estimated building costs had jumped to over $3 million.

Unfortunately, by the time Convention Hall finally opened on June 1, 1930, the bloom was off the Asbury Park rose. The country was mired in the Great Depression, tourism was down, and the city itself was close to bankruptcy. Despite its attractive appearance, with its mixed Italian and French architectural designs, Convention Hall never quite lived up to the promise that its backers initially saw when they peered into the future of Asbury Park. Yet, when looking at the hall today, one can still see the ornate handiwork and attention to detail that went into its construction, and can recall those golden years when Asbury Park was the Atlantic City of the North.

◆

Although the Atlantic City Boardwalk came first, the folks at Ocean City weren't far behind their sister city to the north. Possibly mindful of the success that Atlantic City's wooden walkway was enjoying, the founders of Ocean City apparently had no sooner rolled up their sleeves and gotten to work building a town than they started slapping down planks for a boardwalk of their own. In the *First Annual Report of the President of the Ocean City*

Association, the Reverend William B. Wood said: "We have put down 1000 feet of board walk from the wharf on Fourth street to West avenue."

This first thousand feet might well have been the beginning of what, by 1887, was a seven-block boardwalk running from Fourth Street to Seventh Street. A winter storm the following year took its toll on this structure, but you can't keep a good boardwalk down, and soon another pedestrian path sprang up. This was the boardwalk that was to see Ocean City through its heyday in the early twentieth century. Filled with stores, vaudeville theaters, and amusement attractions, the Ocean City boardwalk soon began to threaten the supremacy of its rival in Atlantic City. But whereas the Atlantic City Boardwalk was very much an "anything goes" type of place, the walkway at Ocean City was more genteel, as befitted the town's reputation as a family resort.

Then suddenly it was all gone. A fire that began in a trash pile roared over the boardwalk in a flaming fury on October 11, 1927. In its wake was literally nothing but smoldering embers. The city had lost one of its most prized possessions and visitor attractions.

Characteristically, however, Ocean City bounced back from this disaster. With the summer season hanging in the balance, the new boardwalk was begun at 11:30 A.M. on January 25, 1928. Within a mind-boggling four months and four days it was completed. What makes this feat even more impressive is that it was accomplished during February and March, typically two of the cruelest months at the Jersey Shore. The construction crew often worked six days a week, from six in the morning to ten at night. Owing to the town's Christian character, no work of any type was allowed on Sunday.

"Work was performed under the most trying conditions possible," wrote assistant city engineer N. Harvey Collison in his report on June 7, 1928, citing rain, cold, and storm tides as examples of the foul weather that builders had to face. To help move the job along, a solution of calcium chloride was devised to accelerate the hardening of the concrete used for the pilings, beams, and girders.

The length of the new boardwalk was 3,687 feet, and its width was 60 feet (quite a difference from the 10-foot width of its original rival, the first Atlantic City Boardwalk). It contained 5,800 cubic yards of concrete and 660 tons of steel reinforcing and used

800,000 board feet of spruce from Oregon and Washington. The new boardwalk was built one-half block closer to the ocean (a decision that has taken on critical importance today in light of the subsequent severe beach erosion).

This boardwalk built so quickly and yet so well in 1928 is the one that thousands of Jersey Shore visitors have enjoyed for decades. Despite being battered by several storms and in a perpetual state of erosional warfare with the elements, the Ocean City boardwalk remains one of the Jersey Shore's most pleasing strolls.

◆

Up the coast in Seaside Heights is another of the Shore's most eminent boardwalks. But the road to building this one had more peaks and valleys than a San Francisco street.

It was on January 7, 1916, that the matter of building a boardwalk was discussed during a Seaside Heights council meeting. This might have been considered a bold step for a town that just seven years before had consisted of only three buildings, but clearly the time was right. Within the previous few years the town had grown enormously, helped along by the opening on December 5, 1914, of the first bridge to span Barnegat Bay. (It crossed from the mainland to the barrier peninsula on which Seaside Heights was located.) This bridge made the Heights the closest beach resort to Philadelphia for those traveling by car, and across the bridge they came.

The foundation of the boardwalk had already been laid one year prior to that January 7 council meeting, when Philadelphian Joseph B. Vanderslice constructed a pavilion on the beach, the high point of which was a gasoline-powered merry-go-round. This proved to be a failure. However, in 1916 Frank H. Freeman, later to be mayor of Seaside Heights, took over the pavilion and installed an electrically powered carousel, beginning a long and successful amusement career at the Heights.

So in reality a boardwalk was the next logical step in the development of this resort town, particularly in light of the popularity of similar structures in Atlantic City, Asbury Park, and Seaside's neighbor to the north, Point Pleasant. Although the idea of a boardwalk generally met approval, both the cost and the possibility that it could be washed out to sea raised concerns. It was decided to mount the boardwalk on permanent pilings (town planners were a long way from the removable boardwalk by this time) to give it more durability. As for the cost, the city council determined it was best to find the money for the project as quickly as possible, so that the boardwalk could be built in time for the summer season and used as an additional enticement to visit the growing town.

In late April 1916, the council approved the boardwalk plan, agreeing to issue five-year improvement bonds instead of raising taxes to cover the cost.

But the council's hopes for quick construction were dashed when a battle erupted over obtaining the necessary rights-of-way. For five long years the struggle went on; some parts of the boardwalk were built (by 1919 three blocks had been completed), while other sections were delayed. Finally, in October 1921, all questions concerning rights-of-way were resolved. The boardwalk was completed on December 9, 1921.

Although today the Seaside Heights boardwalk has a cornucopia of amusements, in the beginning it was very different. Up until World War II the wooden walkway had a few amusements and food stands, but it was primarily a quiet place for people, dressed in their Sunday best, to enjoy the brisk ocean breezes. Today's noisy, hectic Casino Pier was a low-key fishing pier in 1930. A big day for families would include a ride on the Freeman carousel and then a visit to Pennyland, where all the latest arcade games cost just one cent apiece.

But the war changed all this; military personnel on leave came to the boardwalk looking for relaxation, and the pathway's popularity grew as new businesses sprang up to meet the demand. Many of those same military personnel returned to Seaside Heights and used their low-interest loans to buy beachfront cottages, fueling the expansion of both town and boardwalk.

In its history, the Seaside Heights boardwalk has been hit with two devastating fires. The first, on June 9, 1955, began at six in the morning, caused by a faulty neon sign. The blaze raged out of control for two hours, fed by cold, fresh air from the ocean. Eighty boardwalk stands, three bars, and a carousel were destroyed, and damage was estimated at $1.25 million.

Almost ten years later to the day, another fire erupted on the boardwalk, on June 10, 1965. Sparks from a welder's torch proved to be the culprit this time; much of Casino Pier was lost in this blaze, which rang up an estimated $2 million in damages.

But these two big blazes didn't stop the Seaside Heights boardwalk from becoming one of the top fun-places on the Jersey Shore. Today it vies for the title of best boardwalk along the central Jersey Shore with its neighbor to the north, Point Pleasant Beach.

♦

Although the Point Pleasant boardwalk is indeed one of the Jersey Shore's most popular pedestrian pathways, what is curious about it is that the entire north end is filled not with amusements but with a colony of homes and bungalows. For an enterprise such as a boardwalk, in which the basic concept seems taken from Atlantic City's "avalanche of attractions" model, to fill an entire section with staid homes instead of rollicking amusements is indeed unusual.

Looking east toward the foot of Arnold Avenue in Point Pleasant Beach in 1890, showing the isolation of what is today a bustling beachfront. On the left is the St. James Hotel Pavilion; to the right is King's Pavilion. Both buildings were destroyed during an 1892 storm. (Photo courtesy Jerry Woolley)

Early boardwalk on Point Pleasant Beach leading to the inlet, circa 1912. (Photo courtesy Jerry Woolley)

Point Pleasant's boardwalk got its start around 1880, when the Point Pleasant Land Company, which was busily transforming the sleepy little stretch of coastline into a resort, laid planks lengthwise along the beach. The pathway, which seems to have been literally just boards lying on the beach, was needed for the growing resort's many guests, who took a horse-drawn trolley (one of the first at the Shore) down Atlantic Avenue to the beachfront. Obviously, this first boardwalk was portable in every sense of the word.

But this crude system proved useful because two years later a pavilion was built on the beach, and the planks were redirected toward it. Finally, in 1885, a more formal boardwalk was erected. Built in sections that were removed each winter, it was quite similar to the early models in Atlantic City. Five years later another boardwalk was constructed in place of the 1885 version. However, although this new one was also meant to be portable, somehow it was still sitting defenselessly on the sand when a mammoth winter storm came along in 1892 and washed the entire thing out to sea.

Another portable boardwalk, measuring six hundred feet in length, was quickly built in time for the upcoming summer season. Throughout the next twenty years this boardwalk would

The same location in Point Pleasant today, showing how development has completely changed the face of the Shore. (Photo by Pat King-Roberts)

be extended (until it was approximately six blocks in length), illuminated by electric light, and even rebuilt, but all during these changes it remained portable. Finally, in a fit of progress, the town built its first four hundred feet of permanent boardwalk in 1912. The temporary boardwalk still extended from either side of this sole stationary section, but the future had been foretold. Over the next decade or so, the permanent boardwalk gradually nudged out its movable cousin. By 1925 the permanent walkway ran from the Manasquan Inlet in the north all the way to the Beacon Hotel in the south, a distance of approximately two miles. However, a bad storm in 1938 destroyed much of the south end of the boardwalk. This section was never rebuilt, which is why today the Point Pleasant boardwalk ends so abruptly at New York Avenue. Several devastating fires have also changed the boardwalk's character, including one in 1975 that destroyed the historic Wuest Pavilion, which dated from 1892.

Now about that group of houses.

The bungalow colony was begun in 1921 at the north end of the Point Pleasant beach, where people previously had been pitching tents. Within a few years this entire area had been built up to the extent that it is now, with houses and small cottages extending along the boardwalk approximately one mile. In 1925, when the boardwalk was extended north to the Manasquan Inlet (replacing the plank walk that had been there previously), it naturally went past this brand new group of small homes. Today, although the Point Pleasant boardwalk has changed greatly over the years, the bungalow colony is a throwback to a bygone era—and an oddity in the annals of boardwalkdom.

♦

The final stop on our journey along Jersey Shore boardwalks takes us all the way to the southern tip of the state—to the tremendous concentration of rides, amusements, food stands, and multifarious other forms of entertainment that has made the Wildwood boardwalk famous.

Like all other wooden walkways along the Jersey Shore, Wildwood's boardwalk went through a slow and steady evolution. The first version was a portable path laid directly on the sand in the vicinity of Atlantic Avenue in 1895. At this time Wildwood, although just beginning to grow, was more like a jungle than a part of the Jersey Shore. Trees of numerous varieties grew in abundance there, thus giving the town its name.

But the town fathers knew that a boardwalk was de rigueur for a developing Shore community, and so even though the trees might well have outnumbered the people, onto the sand went the planks. Prior to this there had been other activities at the beachfront. At Blaker's Pavilion, built in 1892, local Baptists had held meetings over the din of the horses and chariots blaring from a nearby merry-go-round. And in 1894 the now-venerable custom of throwing flowers into the water to honor fallen naval heroes was originated on a pier at Wildwood Avenue. A boardwalk only promised to add to the growing enthusiasm for visiting the town.

In the summer of 1900 a new boardwalk was built at the intersection of Maple and Atlantic avenues. A few years later the Wildwood city council passed a resolution to provide for a "wide, elevated boardwalk nearer the ocean than the present boardwalk along Atlantic Avenue," so the existing footpath was moved 180 feet to the east. (It would be on the move a few times more over the next two decades, always toward the sea.) A squadron of hungry worms were reported as eating the pilings under the boardwalk in 1908, requiring more than 150 pilings to be replaced. In 1910 more repairs to the walkway were needed.

Meanwhile, the neighboring community of Holly Beach had also built a boardwalk. The town council passed a resolution on August 24, 1904, calling for "a [32-foot wide] boardwalk along Atlantic Avenue in Holly Beach." When Holly Beach became a part of Wildwood in 1912, the boardwalks apparently merged as well.

Some of the attractions on the Wildwood boardwalk throughout the years call to mind Atlantic City's raucous atmosphere. In the past the boardwalk has offered such entertainment as alligator wrestling and, in one test of ball-throwing prowess, a pig that ran down from an elevated platform every time a ball struck a particular target. Unfortunately, the outcome of one of these carnival-type amusements proved tragic.

In 1938 a lion named Tuffy was featured in a motorcycle act on the boardwalk. When not performing, Tuffy was kept in a cage at Oak and the boardwalk, and it was from here that he escaped at 5:30 P.M. on October 5, 1938. The lion attacked Thomas Saito as he was entering his parked car on Oak Avenue. The beast dragged the man underneath the boardwalk and killed him. Before it could do any more harm the renegade lion was shot and killed by patrolman John Gares, who was part of a posse formed to track the beast.

Fire has also played a part in the Wildwood boardwalk's history. One of the worst fires occurred on what is normally one of the most joyous nights of the year—Christmas Eve. On December 24, 1943, flames destroyed Ocean Pier, which had opened in 1905 and offered visitors, among other things, hot and cold sea baths.

The fear of fire hangs over boardwalks like a sword of Damocles, yet Wildwood has managed to shrug off the devastation wrought by flames to create a wondrous walkway of delight. Today, with over two miles of attractions, the Wildwood venue is another in the long line of Jersey Shore boardwalks carrying on the tradition started by Atlantic City over a century ago.

♦

As we contend in our Introduction, the Jersey Shore is indeed more than just beaches and boardwalks. Yet this is not meant to slight the contribution of boardwalks to the history of the Shore. From the beginning of the modern boardwalk in Atlantic City right down to today's glittering, excitement-filled walkways that line our coast (as well as those more peaceful pathways that offer strollers a walk in the moonlight and the gentle kiss of a sea breeze), the boardwalk has been an integral part of what makes the Shore so unique. From the modest hopes of a group of businessmen that a walkway of boards would help to keep sand out of their hotels, the boardwalk has grown to be a larger-than-life part of the culture and heritage of the Jersey Shore.

SIX

TRADITIONAL JERSEY SHORE CRAFTS

〜〜〜〜〜〜〜〜〜〜〜〜〜〜〜〜〜〜〜〜〜〜〜〜〜〜〜〜〜〜

S ome people think the Jersey Shore is strictly one-dimensional, composed solely of carnival games, sun-splashed beaches, and innumerable restaurants and motels. In reality, nothing could be further from the truth.

The Shore contains a heritage as rich as any in the United States. It's the home of traditions that reach back to a person's basic desire to do something and do it well, and a philosophy that says give me my tools and my materials and let me do what I do best.

A long time ago we used to call people with this type of outlook craftsmen—a simple word that essentially refers to those who have mastered a particular skill. The Jersey Shore has such people who, like their counterparts nationwide, are being inexorably mass-produced into extinction by an age that demands speed rather than precision and quantity rather than quality. But the masters of any craft are important to us not only for what they do but for who they are. These people are living reminders of the way life used to be at the Shore: uncrowded one-lane highways, unpolluted rivers and bays, and uninhabited stretches of coastline where the air was rich with the tangy odor of ocean salt and the view was unencumbered for miles. Sadly, like those bygone days, these people are disappearing from our midst.

We will not see their like again. They are relics of a dying age.

◆

Harry V. Shourds II's "showroom" for his duck decoys is a rambling old red barn near his Seaville home that also doubles as his work area. Like the man himself, the arrangement is a masterpiece of simplicity and functionality. He works in the shop, molding, shaping, and painting wood into decoys of powerful grace and beauty. When customers come into his showroom he simply puts down his tools, wipes off his hands, and walks through the connecting door to wait on them.

That's all there is to it. No bells, buzzers, beepers, or talking mailboxes. Just Shourds, his tools, and his decoys. It's neat, clean, and perfect.

It's good that things are set up that way, because Shourds gets a lot of customers. His decoys are known and admired far beyond the Jersey Shore. In 1989 he was awarded a five thousand dollar National Heritage Fellowship from the National Endowment for the Arts, which recognizes exemplary master folk artists and artisans. He was the first New Jersey resident to receive this coveted award. His decoys are in homes all over the world, and a news team from Tokyo traveled halfway around the world to sit in the cedar-scented air of his barn and interview him.

Not bad, you might think, for a man who by his own words seems as if he accidentally stumbled into this line of work.

"I started, really, in '62, when I moved over here [to Seaville from Ocean City]," says the white-haired Shourds, his eyes sharp and keen behind his glasses. "I was doing jobbing, like carpentry work, and I put a sign out: Decoys. I've been here ever since."

But probe beneath the surface of that statement, and Shourds's true heritage comes bubbling up. His grandfather was the renowned Harry Vinuckson Shourds, commonly acknowledged as one of the finest decoy carvers who ever lived. Vermont's prestigious Shelburne Museum, which contains an extensive collection of Americana, calls Harry V. Shourds "one of the outstanding craftsmen of his time and the most prolific carver of shore bird decoys on the eastern seaboard."

The man's skill was legendary, even in his own time. He averaged two thousand decoys per year for more than forty years. His primary tool was an ordinary pocketknife, and his proficiency with it was so great that he could whittle a decoy head while waiting for a shave in the barber's chair.

"I guess he carved them in his sleep, the way he knocked them out," says Shourds with a smile.

Harry V.'s son, Harry Mitchell Shourds (the current Harry Shourds's father), also became a noteworthy decoy carver. He was a housepainter who, when the weather was bad, would carve decoys. Shourds would watch his father but seldom help. His father was particular about who handled his tools.

Although Shourds creates a variety of birds out of wood—and even an eclectic collection of Santa Clauses in such guises as clammer and hunter—he is best known for his duck decoys. They are made in the Barnegat Bay tradition: round, smooth, flat-bottomed, and with no feathers painted on. Decoys made in the Delaware River style, on the other hand, have round bottoms with little wing feathers carved and painted on. The differences stem from a fundamental disparity in hunting styles: Barnegat Bay hunters hid close to where their decoys were, while their Delaware River counterparts would wait several hundred yards away. Since the river gunners had farther to go to sneak up on the unwary ducks, their decoys had to hold the ducks' interest much longer: they had to be more realistic, both in appearance and in the way they acted in the water.

Today, however, those ruddy-faced gunners—who knew every inch of the bay as they knew their own living rooms and patronized both Shourds's grandfather and his father—have given way to a new breed of customer who thinks of decoys mainly as ornaments. Decoys have become big business, a fact that probably gives Harry V. many a chuckle in bayman's heaven. (One of his goose decoys recently sold for sixty thousand dollars; when he was making them he got fifteen dollars a dozen.)

Even though he knows full well that most of his decoys will probably wind up on a bookshelf rather than in the water, Shourds still makes them as if some grizzled gunner is anxiously waiting outside to drop them into the water of Barnegat Bay.

All the tools he uses are hand tools, except for a band saw. He has a hatchet from his father, with "H M SHOURDS" carved in the handle. However, either out of respect or because he knows how particular his father was about his tools, he never uses it.

Before carving a piece of Jersey cedar (technically it's Atlantic white cedar, but no one who lives in New Jersey and works with it calls it anything but Jersey cedar), Shourds seasons the wood until he's satisfied that it's ready to be used.

Master decoy carver Harry Shourds in his Seaville workshop. (Photo by Pat King-Roberts)

"You don't want the heartwood," he says, speaking with the quiet authority of one who has cradled thousands of pieces of cedar in his skillful hands. "The outside of the tree is better. Then you've got to let it dry out. A two-inch plank takes about a year to season. You can tell [when it's ready]; it doesn't weigh as much as when you bought it."

He uses the band saw to cut two oval sections that will become the decoy body. Then, with surgical precision, he shapes each piece with an ordinary hatchet until he achieves the proper dimensions.

Next he hollows each section by cradling it between his legs and using a hammer to drive a chisel deep into the wood. The hammer slams into the large, sharp chisel with a loud crack, propelling it into the wood with jackhammer force, sending cedar chips flying in every direction and creating a sense of amazement that Shourds has never impaled himself.

The hollowed-out pieces are next brought to his battered workbench. After jamming the end of one piece against his stomach and securing the other end in a vise, he uses a double-handled tool called a split-shaver to smooth the wood until it has the look and feel of polished stone. He then joins the two pieces using both glue and nails, because he fully trusts neither.

"I always say it's like the guy who wears a belt *and* suspenders," he laughs. "You don't trust the belt and you don't trust the suspenders."

Finally, Shourds uses a simple pocketknife—his favorite is a Schrade Old Timer, although he thinks any good pocketknife will do—to carve the decoy's head and neck. He moves the tiny, razor-sharp blade with lightning-quick thrusts over the soft wood, creating a seemingly endless series of random lines and gashes that, when completed, have somehow magically taken on the appearance of the neck and head of a real duck. The last step is painting.

"I get carried away painting sometimes," Shourds chuckles. "Probably when they [the decoys] are finished, they have about four coats of paint on them."

Sometimes Shourds works early in the morning, listening to sparrows wake the world as sunlight steals over the grass. Other times he toils well into the night, bending over his work as the light melts into darkness, big band music from the radio playing softly in the background and his Labrador retriever, Candy,

*Harry Shourds shapes the wood in the early stages of carving a decoy.
(Photo by Pat King-Roberts)*

stretched out on the floor nearby. Time, which is the master of so
many of us today, might not even exist for Harry Shourds.

But when he looks around outside his workshop, he can't help
but be aware of time, and what its passage has wrought. Like
other longtime Shore dwellers who love the area and what it
means to them, he quietly mourns the loss of what used to be.

"When I first moved here, I had a neighbor who farmed the field
next door, grew cabbage and string beans," he recalls. "Farm

help would be out there singing, and the beans would be piling up over the edge of the baskets; they were getting paid piecework. And so the state comes along [and says] you've got to pay them by the hour, got to do this, got to do that. They worked one year [under the new system] . . . you ought to have seen the difference. They were out there fooling around all day. The next year he sold the land."

Even more distressing to this lifelong bayman is the steady desecration of the bays and rivers due to overdevelopment. As wilderness areas disappear, so do the homes of animals, birds, and fish.

"For a few years, they were building houses like crazy," Shourds says. "You can't keep banging, banging, banging . . . the world's only so big."

But he will not get caught up in regrets. He likes his life, is proud of his work, and can't imagine doing anything else. Although self-effacing, his pride in maintaining this traditional craft, of keeping the circle unbroken that began with his grandfather, is obvious.

"There's factories today that make decoys," he says. "They're not that bad, really. But it's nice to keep the handiwork."

Somewhere, Harry V. and Harry M. are smiling.

♦

It's fitting that John Suralik himself built the cedar-shingle house in Tuckerton where he lives, as well as the garage workshop in which he makes the unique Jersey Shore tool known as clam tongs. Almost no one builds his own home at the Shore anymore; almost no one goes clamming anymore either.

"Clamming is dying out," says the lean, friendly Suralik. "This place used to be bustling and hustling . . . everybody was catching clams, everybody was having a good time. We used to go off Parkertown, and when the tide and the wind were right in the summertime you could walk from boat to boat for a hundred yards and never get your feet wet, and everybody was catching clams. You don't see that anymore."

He says this matter-of-factly, accepting the deterioration of the Jersey Shore clamming industry as a natural consequence of time. Suralik is resigned to the hard truth that change is inevitable, no matter how desirable it would be to turn back the clock.

Clam tongs look and act much like a giant pair of scissors. They're made out of two rounded pieces of wood joined together, called handles. On the ends are the "heads," which are baskets with teeth attached. The clammer lowers the open tongs into the water (most tongs are between twelve and sixteen feet in length and open about sixteen inches wide), so that the teeth bite into the soft bottom where the clams are buried. When the handles close, the heads come together and capture whatever is in the teeth's path, including (hopefully) clams. The clammer then lifts the tongs to the surface and investigates the catch.

Today Suralik is considered a master craftsman. People have come from as far away as Florida to purchase a pair of his clam tongs. Yet, although he's been living at the Jersey Shore for most of his life, Suralik didn't learn his craft until later years. His involvement with clam tongs began by accident—literally.

A construction carpenter by trade, Suralik suffered a near-fatal accident in 1975 on a job site. The mishap landed him in the hospital and left him with several permanent reminders of how close he had come to death, including a right arm that he cannot raise above his head and a permanently shattered elbow. He was out of work for five years.

But life often has a way of evening things out. While he was recuperating, a friend who owned a shop that clammers frequented asked him to make a clam tong handle.

"And from there on I was making tong handles," Suralik says of his excuse-me introduction to the craft.

Every master has a mentor. In Suralik's case it was the late Joe Reid, an almost legendary figure among Jersey Shore artisans. Reid, whose skill as a garvey builder is spoken about with quiet pride when baymen get together to talk about boats, told Suralik that "the only way to make them [clam tongs] is to get involved with it." Then Reid gave him one more taciturn piece of advice: "Get good wood."

Suralik knew the wisdom of Reid's words. On the Shore, wood is the artisan's canvas; with it he creates his masterpiece. For clam tong handles, the only wood to use is mahogany.

"You've got to use a certain kind of mahogany," says Suralik, "what they call ribbon band or ribbon stripe—straight grain mahogany. The grain runs almost the whole length of the board, so you have no cross-grain in the handle when you make it." This last point is crucial; wood with cross-grain might crack clean

John Suralik working on a pair of clam tongs in his Tuckerton garage workshop. (Photo by Pat King-Roberts)

through under the strain of moving the tongs through the mud and muck at the bottom of the water.

Suralik used to be able to get his mahogany from Trenton. But now it comes from overseas, and so he must travel to New York State for the wood. However, even that source is drying up because of import quotas on mahogany. Soon he may not be able to get the wood at all.

To conserve wood, Suralik makes both handles out of one long board (it takes a board fourteen feet long to make one pair of twelve-foot handles). He does this by tracing the design of each so that the curves and angles virtually lock together, making them fit on one board as snugly as shoes fit into a box. He then opens the door of his garage workshop and feeds the long board into his band saw.

One of the most important parts of a clam tong is the outside of the handle. Again, like a shoe, comfort and fit are critical.

"The old-timers [like] Joe Reid used to tell me that the outside of a handle wants to be shaped just like the outside of a clamshell, so it fits the palm of your hand," Suralik says. "That's what I go by."

After shaving and planing the wood, he joins the two handles with stainless steel plates and a pin, then attaches the copper baskets and spring steel teeth. When Suralik buys the teeth, they point straight out; he bends them with an ordinary pipe wrench.

"I bend the teeth so they're at about a ten-degree angle," he explains. "The minute you start working the handles, [the teeth] are sliding clams into the basket already. If [the teeth are] too straight, the clams won't slide, but go sideways into the mud."

A pair of clam tongs. (Photo by Pat King-Roberts)

When clammers purchase tongs from Suralik, they get a very important piece of advice that has been passed down from generations of clammers: Don't use them until they're wet.

"Tong handles are better when they're wet," Suralik says. "Usually I'll tell the guys to throw them overboard and soak the wood; that makes it more pliable."

Not too many years ago, the demand for clam tongs was so great that Suralik would stay out all night cutting handles. No matter how high he stacked the tongs in his garage, he inevitably sold every one. But the rapid decline of clamming as a viable Jersey Shore industry has made those days only memories now.

"The bay is going bad," he says quietly. "I hear different guys talking. There's what they call 'gray water' coming down; they got trouble with septic systems around here. The state says it's OK, but something's happening to our bay."

He says this with the same ingrained sadness that all longtime Shore residents exhibit when they talk about the slow, senseless destruction of the bays and rivers they love. Water is the critical common denominator that nourishes and sustains everything that lives at the Jersey Shore. To watch the water being insidiously destroyed is like helplessly watching a loved one die—especially when, like Suralik, you can remember so easily the way things used to be.

"I was treading for clams before I was even married," he says. "You'd be out there at the crack of dawn treading five or six hours, then go back out again in the evening and tread 'til almost sunset. If we couldn't catch five hundred clams an hour we would move. Now, they're working all day for a thousand clams and then some."

Even though the demand for clam tongs has diminished, Suralik is still out in his workshop, cutting and sanding and shaping the wood, while the music plays and the insects buzz and his black cat Nicholas lazily twitches its tail. He wouldn't have it any other way.

"It's enjoyable. . . . I get out in this garage and it's like I'm in another world."

♦

The initial impression one gets of the David Beaton & Sons boatyard is that it's merely a place where summertime sailors come every weekend to summon forth their boats for a lazy afternoon on the open water. But there's really much more to this place than that. Here, nestled amid the cattails in Mantoloking, is one of the few boatyards left on the Jersey Shore where traditional wooden boat repair is done.

Since the advent of fiberglass boats in the early 1960s, the demand for wooden boats has gone down faster than mercury in a blizzard. Because of this, finding someone to patch a leak or plug a hole in a wooden boat has become next to impossible.

At Beaton's, however, they still do things the old-fashioned way. While the boatyard is thoroughly modern, it's also a place where wooden boats are respected, not scorned.

But this should be expected from a business that has its roots sunk deep in the moist and sandy soil of the Jersey Shore. The boatyard was founded by David Beaton in the 1930s. He was a Scottish emigré whose father had also been a boat builder. After cutting his American boat-building teeth in the shop of Bay Head's famed Morton Johnson, he struck out on his own and set up shop in Mantoloking. Initially he built a variety of skiffs, then switched to small sailing craft as his market veered toward racing boats rather than workboats. He was succeeded by his son Lachlan, who today has given way to *his* son, Tom. Boat building does indeed run deeply in the Beaton veins.

The reason the Beatons prospered, when so many of their contemporaries vanished, is that they recognized the coming of King Fiberglass in the early 1960s and decided to switch rather than fight. They shifted the emphasis of their business to boat storage rather than boat building and thus avoided the fiberglass wave that rolled over most of the other wooden boat builders. But once the smell of freshly cut wood gets into your soul, it never really leaves, and so Beaton's has remained true to its roots by continuing to offer a safe haven and a friendly hammer and saw to those old wooden war-horses that need them.

According to Tom Beaton, the usual problem with a wooden boat is that its owner has let it down.

"Usually what happens is that [the owners] don't keep up with the maintenance," he says. "It's like what happens to your mouth if you don't go to the dentist for ten years." Besides periodic painting, wooden boats need refastening, recaulking, frequent examinations of stress points to detect and repair cracks, and other work to fix the ravages of time and use.

A more serious problem is that wooden boats tend to dry out in the winter, making boards contract and separate. Leaks will develop if the boards aren't allowed to swell and fit snugly again before the boat is put into the water in the spring. Unfortunately, the wood needs time to swell—a few days at least—and in today's instant-gratification world, when a letter can be faxed to Japan in thirty seconds, not many people want to spend three days waiting for their boats to be seaworthy again.

This is unfortunate, because wooden boats do have advantages. Major repairs are often easier on such vessels. This was brought home one cold winter's day at Beaton's, where a gorgeous twenty-five-foot wooden cruiser sat mounted on sawhorses, a two-foot hole in its hull courtesy of a jet ski. The surgeons at Beaton's decreed that with new planking, a little sweat, and some elbow grease, the boat could live to sail another day. A fiberglass boat would almost certainly have been pronounced DOA.

The sturdiness of wooden boats is evidenced by the number of catboats that come to Beaton's for repairs. Many of these single-masted, gaff-rigged sailboats are six or seven decades old and still remarkably seaworthy. When the Shore was still a wild and untamed place, Barnegat Bay and its backwaters were dotted with catboats; the locals used them for both work and pleasure. Later, in the 1920s, a modification to the catboat made it faster for racing (the large gaff was replaced by a "Marconi rig," a tall mast that looks like a telegraph pole). This led to the famous A-cats, with names storied in Barnegat Bay lore such as *Bat*, *Mary Ann*, *Spy*, and *Lotus*. Today, these boats, built by Morton Johnson, are listed on the New Jersey Register of Historic Places. Not only have the Beatons refurbished several of these classic boats, they even built a new A-cat in the early 1980s: the *Wasp*.

Lachlan "Lolly" Beaton, Tom's father, vividly remembers the day the death knell sounded for wooden boats. In the early 1960s he and his dad were doing a brisk business building a small, light boat called a Bluejay. Built out of plywood, the boat had been steadily gaining in popularity, and the Beatons were working on an order for seven Bluejays when word came that the Bluejay Association had approved the use of fiberglass for their boats. Those seven were the last wooden Bluejays the Beatons ever built.

"It's a bygone era," says Tom Beaton. "It's like when everybody had horses and there was a blacksmith in every town. Then cars started to come in, and there wasn't a need for blacksmiths. I think boat building is that way too."

It's a shame; some fabulous Jersey Shore history has been lost with the demise of men like David Beaton. When yards like his were in their prime, the area from Point Pleasant down through Mantoloking was known as one of the top boat-building regions in all of New Jersey. Today there's nothing left but memories—and a few small bastions like Beaton's.

"I believe in history and tradition," says Tom Beaton. "I think they are very important." He points to a sneakbox (another traditional Jersey Shore boat), freshly painted and gleaming in the light, waiting to feel the gentle slap of the bay's blue-brown water on its sleek, white hull.

"You don't want to [be able only to] *tell* your grandchildren about a boat like this," he says, respect and reverence creeping into his voice. "You want to take them out, [point to a boat], and say, 'There's one sailing now.'"

◆

It was an injury that began the transformation of John Petzak into a master Jersey Shore boat builder. After a stroke in the early 1950s left him idle and looking for a way to keep active, he decided to build boats. He built one rowboat, then switched to garveys, a type of boat he had had no prior training at building. But Petzak was confident of success.

"I knew what boats were all about," says the Parkertown resident with a smile.

Indeed he did. Today the good-natured Petzak has few peers when it comes to building garveys, an indigenous Jersey Shore boat that has faithfully served baymen since it was conceived two centuries ago by Garves Pharo, who lived in what is today West Creek.

At first glance a garvey may well qualify as one of the ugliest boats ever built. Squat and square with a long, flat bottom, a garvey is never going to be anyone's choice for zipping over the water on a sunny summer's day. But as a functional Jersey Shore workboat, a garvey has few peers. Its flat bottom enables clammers and oystermen to stand and lift their heavy rakes and tongs from the bay's bottom without risk of toppling either themselves or the boat. Furthermore, a garvey's draw (the amount of water that a

John Petzak of Parkertown puts the finishing touches on a garvey. (Photo by Pat King-Roberts)

boat needs to float) is a mere six inches, which means the boat can be maneuvered through all the shallow, narrow channels and backwaters that baymen often must follow before they reach open water.

At one time, finding a garvey at the Shore was as easy as finding open water; some craggy-faced veteran bayman always seemed to be building one in his garage or basement. Today, however, Petzak is one of the last of his kind, a man who still makes handbuilt garveys out of cedar. He works behind his house on U.S. Route 9, in a converted garage that's barely big enough to hold a finished garvey (which usually averages sixteen feet in length).

His method of "advertising" is refreshingly simple. When a garvey is done, he places it in front of his house with a For Sale sign on it. Inevitably, within a few days someone passing by on the busy highway purchases the boat. He then begins another one, working at his own leisurely pace. He's not a man to be hurried, particularly now, when the years and the decline in clamming and gunning have taken their toll on his clientele.

"There ain't nobody doing it [clamming and gunning] anymore," he says. "All the old guys are dying off."

Petzak used to use Jersey cedar for his garveys. But a precipitous decline in quality has forced him also to use western cedar (which comes from the West Coast of the United States), although the wood's heavy oil content bothers him.

"I'm not using [as much] Jersey cedar anymore. The hell with [the wood cutters]," he says unequivocally. "They give you a lot of bad stuff." Boats built from bad wood, he explains, will start to fall apart within a year, a time frame totally unacceptable to a prideful builder like Petzak, who expects his garveys to last at least twenty years. "I want to build something I know is good."

The shop behind his house is filled with the clutter of wood, scrap, and tools. A fine layer of sawdust covers everything. These days he works slowly, carefully assembling the boat piece by piece, cutting and sanding and shaping the cedar. He has patterns but doesn't use them; after forty years of boat building, his rough, strong carpenter's hands move automatically over the wood.

"If I can't build 'em by now they ought to take me away somewhere," he laughs.

When Petzak got the cedar fresh from the Pine Barrens, it was often green and wet—unsuitable for use. To dry it out he stacked the wood in the shape of a pyramid, so that the air blew through it. Within a few weeks the cedar would be seasoned to perfection.

Although the garveys he makes today are basic, no-frills clamming and gunning boats, in years past he would "jazz them up" by including windshields, cabins, and other small accoutrements.

Much to his surprise, these boats were extremely popular. Petzak says he stopped making them that way because they were "too much work," but one suspects his sense of tradition was offended by something fancy on a boat that's meant to be stained with the dirt and sweat of baymen.

A Philadelphian by birth, Petzak started out building boats during World War II, when he worked at Adam Price's boat shop in Parkertown. It was at Price's that he was introduced to a variety of Shore boat types, including garveys.

Throughout his many years of building boats he has always worked alone, with one notable exception. His wife, Dot, has frequently assisted him in everything from clamping and gluing the heavy boards to painting the boat. "I can't do it without Dot," he says.

In the days when he had orders to fill and deadlines to meet, Petzak (with Dot's help) could build a garvey in three weeks. Now he builds no more than several a year, and he clearly enjoys taking the time to make sure every detail is to his liking.

Petzak has made a few concessions to modern times. Now, rather than run heavy iron rods through the side boards, he uses glue for the same purpose. Instead of caulking to prevent leaks, he uses fiberglass. But these are minor, commonsense compromises to new realities. What riles him is when people say that a wooden boat is not as dependable as a boat made of modern materials.

"You've got to take care of it," he says. "A boat belongs in the water." Too often people take wooden boats out of the water and let them sit on land for months without any cover, exposed to the blistering effects of sun and wind. Then, when the boards dry out and separate, the boat is considered unreliable because it had the audacity to succumb to the relentless attack of the elements. When properly taken care of, a cedar boat is like a giant tortoise, rolling on and on in defiance of the years.

Quite often, someone who has heard of Petzak stops by his neat, two-story house and asks him how to build a garvey. Being an accommodating man, he's willing to show them, but deep inside he feels that the effort needed to make a boat the traditional way is too great for most people today.

"If you're going to do it nice, it's going to take time," he says. "You can't do anything nice fast."

Yet time is the one thing that Petzak does not have to worry about. Even though it might take him several months to build a boat in his sawdust-filled garage, compared with a few hours in a shiny modern factory, there are some things that cannot be measured by time. John Petzak's craft is one of those things.

♦

For nearly fifty years, Charles Hankins of Lavallette has been building the Sea Bright Skiff, a boat recognized throughout the world as having originated at the Jersey Shore. If you've ever seen a white, wooden "lifeguard boat" lying upside down on the beach, you've seen a Sea Bright Skiff.

At one time, these skiffs were the dominant boat along the northern Jersey Shore. There, in tiny beachfront fishing villages with long-forgotten names like Galilee and Nauvoo, men went forth every day to try to wring a living out of the treacherous Atlantic. The lives of these men and their families depended on the reliability of the Sea Bright Skiff, and it almost never let them down—which is why the skiff became a logical choice for a lifesaving boat.

The people who lived in the small shacks and huts that constituted these villages made their living solely by ocean fishing. Too far removed from any inlets or bays that would provide easy access to the sea, they needed a boat that could be launched directly from the beach through the rough surf. When the fishermen returned, the boat, laden with the day's catch, had to be able to glide again through the often-steep seas and land safely on shore.

The Sea Bright Skiff, with its one-foot draw, was ideal for this purpose. The skiff's unique slanting stern helped it to come through the breakers without overturning, while the flat bottom enabled it to sit on the beach without tipping over.

Hankins—a big bear of a man, with white hair and a forthright manner of talking—learned to build these boats as a boy by watching and helping his father, who established the business in 1912. Back then there was no thought of carrying on a Jersey Shore tradition; skiff builders were as plentiful as grains of sand on the beach. But now only Hankins remains.

"You had four [boat builders] right in Bay Head," he says, his eyes traveling up the wall of his shop, searching for a time and a place that exists only in his memory. "You had the Johnson Brothers, Hubert Johnson and Morton Johnson, Barber. . . ." He stops and smiles sadly. "The whole damn bunch of them that were there, they're all gone."

Possibly more than any other Jersey Shore craftworker, Hankins is the living embodiment of a legacy that reaches back more than a century. His skiffs are essentially the same—in size, shape, and materials—as those in which the coastal fishermen battled the sea. His method of building them has remained unchanged, except for the use of a few power tools, since his father began showing him how it was done over six decades ago.

Hankins's barnlike workshop is filled with tools from another era, when people built things by hand and their tools were like extensions of their fingers. He's got special planes to make moldings, a boat builder's slick that removes chunks of wood with a single thrust, and a drawknife that could strip the bark off cedar fresh from the Pinelands swamps. None of these tools are being made any longer.

Since Hankins is so steeped in tradition, it should come as no surprise that the wood he uses to build skiffs is Jersey cedar.

"Cedar is light and swells good," he says in his workshop. "It's almost next in weight to balsa wood. It's a very light wood and durable." The only other type of wood needed is oak, which he uses to frame the boat. "Some oak you want green and some you want dry," he says, running his finger down a thin, pale yellow strip of wood. "If you've got to steam it and bend it [to the shape of] the boat, you want it green; then when it dries out, it dries to the shape you steamed it."

Hankins estimates he's built at least four thousand boats since he came back to Lavallette from World War II in 1946 and took over the family business from his father, who had suffered a heart attack. Since his brother's death in 1953, Hankins has worked on his own. But although he hasn't budged from his Lavallette location, his fame as a master boat builder has spread throughout the world; his boats can be found from South America to Alaska to Turkey. One gets the impression that Hankins is amused by the people who have beaten a path to his door anxious to buy that which he was only too glad to make.

"I built a lot of different kinds of boats for a lot of different people," he says. "I've built for some of the richest people in the United States, and for people who had just enough money to pay. . . . I've met all kinds of people."

At one time Hankins had a crew of several men who assisted him, but finding helpers today is virtually impossible. No one seems interested in investing years to learn the subtle nuances and techniques that raise this trade from a profession to a craft.

Although Hankins professes not to care, you can sense he once harbored hopes that at least one of his former helpers might have taken over the business and kept the tradition alive. But the demise of the fishing villages destroyed a principal market, and the rise of fiberglass boats has destroyed the demand for traditional wooden boats. Anyone taking over the business today would be in the odd position of offering an excellent product for which there are no takers. Even the Shore towns that used to buy skiffs as lifeguard boats have been forced to cut back due to financial pressures. It's sadly ironic that Hankins, known the world over for building Sea Bright Skiffs, has not built one in several years. To hear him talk, it doesn't seem as if he expects to build one again.

"I stopped building skiffs three or four years ago," he says. "I had a couple of good guys that worked with me, but when the last one left I just decided the hell with it. It's just not worth it."

In other respects, it's as if some things haven't changed for Hankins. His workshop has remained virtually the same for over four decades. It's a place that his father would undoubtedly feel at home in today, a place of warmth and light and the tangy odor of cedar. It's easy to imagine it filled with men building Sea Bright Skiffs, talking and laughing as they work, the air ringing with the sounds of hammers and saws.

But these are just phantoms. Today Charles Hankins stands alone in his silent shop. And when he walks out of it for the last time, the curtain will go down forever on a skill that has played a vital part in the history and heritage of the Jersey Shore for over a century. It might be thoughts like these that cause him to muse to himself, almost in disbelief: "I'm one of the last survivors of this industry."

◆

He is an incredible, frenetic, seemingly out-of-control bundle of energy. He scampers around his backyard workshop like an elf hurrying to get the sleigh loaded on Christmas Eve, rarely pausing after finishing one step before starting another, and never staying in one place more than a few seconds. Never. If he was a car, he would have been recalled long ago due to a constantly fast-running idle.

What he is, in fact, is a Jersey Shore boat builder of the highest renown named Sam Hunt, and what he builds is probably the quintessential Shore boat: the sneakbox.

What we've come down to now is the very essence of the Jersey Shore. If the Shore was an onion and you could peel away each of its layers, what you'd find at the core would be the sneakbox. Stripped of all pretense, laid bare of everything except the water and the land from which it sprang, the Jersey Shore is the sneakbox and the sneakbox is the Jersey Shore.

To call the sneakbox a legendary boat is almost trite; it is too pragmatic for that. In the days when the Shore was just another place to live, the sneakbox represented life there. Early each day, in that eerie in-between time when night has ended but morning has yet to begin, a man could slip out onto the water in his sneakbox and move soundlessly through the still-black water until he reached his favorite cattail-covered river bank. There he could nudge the boat alongside the bank until the vessel became almost a part of it. He could do this because a sneakbox is short (typically twelve feet), light (made of Jersey cedar), and has a wide beam for added stability, so it can fit into places where most other boats wouldn't dare go.

But the real beauty of a sneakbox is that it draws as little as four inches of water, so it can move easily through the shallows. This, combined with the fact that a man sits on the floor of the boat, with just his head sticking up (instead of on seats), makes the sneakbox appear to ducks like just another floating piece of wood rather than the boat of a hunter. A man could wedge himself next to a riverbank until he was nearly invisible, spread some weeds or cattails on the top of the boat, put a few decoys out on the water, and wait for the unwary ducks to alight practically alongside him. (They don't call it a sneakbox for nothing.) On a good day he could bring home dinner and maybe something extra to sell to a local restaurant. Families depended on their sneakbox back then to keep their lives going as people today depend on their cars.

While the creation of the sneakbox is often attributed to Hazelton Seaman of West Creek in 1836 (he called it a "devil's coffin"), the man who brought this boat to the attention of the world was Nathaniel Bishop. Adventurous and highly literate, Bishop came to the Barnegat Bay region sometime before 1864 and became interested in the sneakbox. So highly did he think of the boat that he used a sneakbox to journey from Pittsburgh to Florida by means of the Ohio and Mississippi rivers. His 1879 book, *Four Months in a Sneakbox*, popularized the boat for all time.

That, then, is the story of the sneakbox. But what of Sam Hunt?

As best he can recollect after a rather full life of eighty-plus years, Hunt's introduction to boat building came sometime around age ten, when he began working after school and on weekends for J. H. Perrine's boatyard in Barnegat, which was to sneakboxes back then what General Motors is to automobiles today. Now, over seven decades later, there seem to be few kinds of boats that Hunt hasn't built.

Unlike most other Shore boat builders, Hunt works outside, in the pine tree–filled backyard of his Waretown home, with only God's original canopy—the sky—over his head. As might be expected from a man who's been working with wood longer than most of us have been alive, he's developed several tricks of workmanship that make his sneakboxes as unique as a signature. One is that he coats virtually every piece of cedar and oak (the only types of wood he uses in a sneakbox) with pure linseed oil preservative. This gives the wood almost indestructible qualities. "Those timbers will be around long after you and I are [gone]," he says confidently.

He also steams his oak strips to make them supple. He does this in a large, long tube about ten inches in diameter. One end is connected to a small stove, while the other has a flap that can be opened and closed. When the fire is good and hot and the tube is filled with steam, Hunt opens the flap and slides an oak strip into the tube. When he takes the strip out, the wood is, for a brief period of time, as pliable as if it were made of rubber. He can then bend it to fit whatever shape is required.

"I'm the only one building them [sneakboxes] this way," he asserts. He's been steaming wood for his boats all his life, ever since, as a boy, he saw wagon wheel builders steam wood so they could bend it into the circular shape they needed.

But his most startling "secret" is so simple it's almost unbelievable. Hunt does not—and will not—fiberglass the bottom of a

Sneakbox builder Sam Hunt in the yard of his Waretown home. (Photo by Pat King-Roberts)

boat to keep leaks out. Instead, he takes long strands of ordinary cotton and twists them into pencil-thin strips that are so strong an ordinary person cannot pull them apart. He rolls these strips into the thin spaces between the bottom boards, then coats the entire hull with linseed oil. It's a caulking method that has worked flawlessly for years.

"When I sell a boat I guarantee it," he says with fierce pride. "If it leaks one drop when you put it in the water, you get [to keep] the boat and [get] the money back." His chin juts out defiantly. "I ain't lost one yet."

He's always worked alone building sneakboxes, and this is possibly why he dashes about his open-air workshop like a man with a hotfoot, at an age when most people are welded to their easy chairs. There are many things to do when building a boat, sometimes all at the same time, and it becomes especially frantic when you're the only one doing them. After several decades of moving at the speed of light, Hunt knows no other way.

Talking to Sam Hunt is like opening a wild and wonderful Pandora's box; you never know what's going to emerge, but finding out is all the fun. He mixes boat-building chatter with colorful stories without missing a beat, and an interviewer quickly discovers that the best course is to give up all attempts at questions and simply let the words come flooding out. Within the space of five breathless minutes you'll not only discover what the most difficult wind is in which to sail (a west wind, because it's unpredictable), you'll also find out that Hunt's father and Buffalo Bill were buried on the same January day in 1917, that Hunt was putting a windshield on a forty-two-foot boat the day the *Hindenburg* erupted into a ball of fire at Lakehurst in 1937, and that he was putting the windshield on another forty-two-foot boat the day Pearl Harbor was bombed. (Fortunately, he doesn't put windshields on forty-two-foot boats too often.)

Hunt's talents for building, while directed primarily at boats, don't stop there. He has built some of the world's only left-handed banjos (for left-handed banjo pickers, of course) and a rocking chair that former President Ronald Reagan tried unsuccessfully to tip over when Hunt displayed it during the New Jersey exhibit at the Smithsonian Institution in 1983.

But his forte was, and always will be, the sneakbox. Everything that he does—from building them outside, just as it was done hundreds of years ago, to the singular methods he uses—stamp him as the quintessential Jersey Shore boat builder.

◆

Artisans and their traditional skills are like anchors in our lives. The more rootless we become, the more we need the foundation that they represent. It lets us know who we are, what was here before us, and, most important, the reason why things are the way they are. When these masters and their ways are no more, it will mean that something profound has left our lives—and we may not even know that it is gone. Watch for it.

Old-Time Bird and Waterfowl Names

Long before scientists and naturalists came onto the scene and decided that standardization was required, Jersey Shore baymen had their own ways of referring to the birds and waterfowl that lived there. Below are some of the old-time names, along with their modern equivalents.

Old Name	Modern Name
Bullhead	Black-bellied plover
Hell-diver	Horned grebes
Sea pigeon	Eastern dowitcher
Hay-bird	Pectoral sandpiper
Sicle bill	Long-billed curlew
Oystercrackers	Oystercatchers
Blue peter	Coot
Hairy-head	Hooded merganser
Butterball	Bufflehead
Fish duck	Red-breasted merganser
Creaker	Pectoral sandpiper
Niggergeese	Cormorants
Summer duck	Wood duck
Yelpers	Yellowlegs

CHAPTER

SEVEN

I LOVE LUCY
AND HER PALS

Technically, she might be considered an architectural folly—
but don't let her hear you say that, or you might hurt her
feelings.

In fact, if you want to get sticky about it, there are a great
many things you can throw in her face, starting with the rather
disquieting information that "she" might not even be a she. You
can follow that with how some people think she hasn't spent her
whole life on the beaches of Margate, and how she's lost two sib-
lings over the years, and you might well bring her close to tears.

But it wouldn't be nice to make an elephant cry—especially
such a fine old girl as Lucy the Margate Elephant.

For over a century, Lucy has gazed out at the Atlantic Ocean
with her huge, unblinking eyes. During those years she's seen
a lot, including the transformation of the once-deserted area of
marshlands where she began her existence into a bustling community and summer tourist haven. But even though she shines
now like a piece of polished metal in the sun, it hasn't always

been so pleasant for this prodigious pachyderm. There was a time when she was so dilapidated and worn-out that she seemed headed for the elephant graveyard. However, thanks to the efforts of a dedicated group of people who refused to let her die, Lucy is today what she will hopefully always be: an enduring symbol of the Jersey Shore.

◆

The story of Lucy begins with a man and his dream. The man was a mustachioed Irishman named James Vincent de Paul Lafferty, Jr., and his dream was to sell real estate in what was then—in 1881—as unlikely a place for selling land as there ever could be. South Atlantic City, as the area was optimistically known, was nothing more than scrub pine, bayberry bushes, and dune grass, with a few wooden fishing shacks thrown in for good measure. The only way even to reach the place was when the tide was low. Lafferty's dream seemed more like a nightmare.

But Lafferty was an inventive man, not easily put off by the inhospitable look of the barren beachfront. Long before the movie, Lafferty knew the power of the *Field of Dreams* philosophy: If you build it, they will come. What he needed was an "it" so spectacular that people couldn't help but come—and buy some land as well. But what could "it" be?

For reasons known only to himself, Lafferty chose a gigantic elephant. Perhaps he was influenced by the prevailing atmosphere of Victorian America, an uninhibited era that delighted in encouraging oversized, overstated methods of self-expression. Architecture was not immune to these desires; jumbo, outrageous buildings were all the rage. In fact, this entire genre has been labeled "architectural follies" and is considered a legitimate architectural form.

But whatever his motivation, Lafferty knew exactly what he wanted. In his petition to the commissioner of patents on May 19, 1882, he succinctly described his "it":

> My invention consists of a building in the form of an animal (i.e. an Elephant) the body of which is floored and divided into 2 rooms, closets, etc., and the legs contain the stairs which lead to the body, said legs being hollow so as to be of increased strength for properly supporting the body, and the elevation of the body permitting the circulation of air below the same, the entire

device presenting a unique appearance, and producing a building which is well ventilated and lighted.

Just in case the commissioner missed the fact that he was being asked to grant a patent for a six-story elephant, Lafferty added the following line: "It will be seen that the structure is novel and unique."

To help design his novel and unique structure, Lafferty engaged a Philadelphia architect named William Free. Another Philadelphian, a Quaker named J. Mason Kirby, was the builder. Among those who helped construct it were two men who would later become famous in the annals of Atlantic City: John L. Young, who built Young and McShea's Ocean Pier on the Boardwalk, and William Somers, who many say should be given credit for popularizing—even inventing—what we call today the Ferris wheel.

These men obviously knew what they were doing. One of the reasons Lucy is still around to thrill us is that her structure was carefully braced with diagonal members, providing a rigid framework that has withstood all that nature has thrown at her for over a century. Included among the materials used to build the elephant were 12,000 feet of lumber, 200 kegs of nails, 4 tons of nuts and bolts, and almost 5,000 square feet of tin for her hide. Most, if not all, of this was probably brought to the site by boat. Although the cost had been estimated at $25,000—a considerable sum in 1881—Lafferty always claimed the final total was $38,000.

As might be expected with anything that's been around long enough to celebrate over one hundred birthdays, there are many legends associated with Lucy. One of the earliest is that Lafferty used a live elephant chained to the beach as a model. No evidence has been found to support this allegation.

When Lucy finally opened (the exact date seems to be lost to history), Lafferty employed a brass band to play beside his elephant to help lure people to the lonely shoreline. His ads in various newspapers offered building lots in "fast booming South Atlantic City." Sightseers and potential customers came primarily by trolley from Atlantic City; they would hear property being auctioned off as they gathered around the elephant. Incredibly, Lafferty originally had the elephant painted white, as if he were whistling in the dark over the unfortunate connotations of a white elephant.

He should have whistled harder. When you realize that Lucy was the first building in South Atlantic City, you get a better understanding of what Lafferty was up against. Beachfront property didn't have the same magnetism in the nineteenth century that it has today; many people undoubtedly thought the whole idea of buying land in such a desolate spot quite foolish indeed, even though Lafferty's asking price was reportedly only twenty-five dollars per lot. People came down to see the giant elephant that served as a real estate office, but when they left, their money usually left with them.

Within a few years Lafferty had overextended himself through his various real estate ventures at the Jersey Shore and elsewhere. In 1887 he sold the elephant, along with some other property, to Anton Gertzen of Philadelphia. Eleven years later the man who had created Lucy was dead. Sadly, he didn't

Lucy, the Margate Elephant, circa 1895. (A Copyrighted Photograph of Lucy, The Margate Elephant, the representation of which serves as a service mark and registered trademark of The Save Lucy Committee, Inc., P.O. Box 3000, Margate, New Jersey 08402. Photograph reprinted by permission of The Save Lucy Committee, Inc.)

survive to see his dream become a reality; by 1926 lots in Margate (the name was changed in 1909) that had sold for two hundred dollars just three years earlier were selling for up to ten thousand dollars.

But Lucy would witness all this and more. When she joined the Gertzen family, she began an association that would span eighty-three years and take her through a bewildering variety of careers. Although real estate promotion wasn't her line, it was plain that as a curiosity the great elephant had no peers. John Gertzen, one of Anton's sons, took over the elephant and began charging visitors ten cents to tour the furnished interior and climb up to the howdah on her back. From here, approximately sixty-five feet above ground, people could look out for miles over this relatively undeveloped part of the Jersey Shore.

By this time Lucy had a new neighbor. It was the ornate Turkish Pavilion, with its stained glass windows and onion-shaped domes. Built in 1876 for the Centennial Exhibition in Philadelphia's West Fairmount Park, the palatial structure was purchased by Anton Gertzen after the close of the fair. He had it disassembled, moved to Margate, and reconstructed right behind Lucy. Eventually John Gertzen acquired this building also and turned it into a popular night spot. This has given rise to another erroneous legend about Lucy, that she had been built for the Centennial Exhibition and then shipped to the Shore along with the Turkish Pavilion.

Having already embarked on one new career, Lucy took up another in 1902 when an English physician and his family rented her as a summer home. Lucy's interior was converted into four bedrooms, a dining room, a parlor, and a kitchen. In one of the small closets in her front shoulder a bathroom was installed, complete with a miniature bathtub. Her trunk was used as a chute for ashes.

The next few years were bad ones for Lucy. On October 10, 1903, she was battered by a coastal storm, causing her to sink up to her knees in sand. A house mover named Rufus Booye raised Lucy and set her fifty feet farther back from the ocean. On top of that indignity came another, when the peaceful pachyderm was turned into a tavern. The combination of drinking, oil lamps, and a wooden elephant was a sure recipe for fire, and disaster almost struck on several occasions when the lamps were knocked over.

Finally, after one particularly harrowing incident in 1904 that very nearly turned Lucy into a pile of charred timbers, her days as a tavern ended. Possibly to prevent the elephant from going up in smoke, a local bartender named Phil Rohr Sr. is credited with installing electric lights in 1905.

In 1916 John Gertzen died, leaving Lucy in the care of his widow, Sophia. In conjunction with her elephant attraction, she began a tourist camp where people lived in tents along the beach. The success of this venture caused others to follow her lead, until the beachfront looked like a sea of tents. When concerned city fathers banned all "Habitation in Tents" on the beach, the resourceful Sophia converted the former Turkish Pavilion into a rooming house (in 1920 Prohibition had ended its days as a tavern anyway). This, and the ten cents per person she received from visitors to Lucy, became the only source of income for her and her two children, Caroline and Joseph.

Sophia Gertzen plays an important part in Lucy's history. Not only did she keep the elephant going for nearly fifty years, but she also is widely believed to have been the person who gave Lucy her name and changed her sex!

In the early days, the elephant was popularly considered to be a he. This would be in keeping with the tenor of the male-dominated times. Even as late as 1936, an article in the May 24 edition of the *Sunday Press*, a local newspaper, refers to the elephant as "taking his cup of tea." (At this point Lucy seems to have still been in use as a rooming house of some type; the article noted that the "entrance leads to the recreation room . . . the dining room, kitchen and four bedrooms.")

It was right around this time that the change from nondescript male to the personable female we know as Lucy might well have taken place. In a 1938 interview Sophia Gertzen said, "We've had Lucy so long that she's one of the family. I call her my oldest daughter." A story in the *Atlantic City Press* on Sunday, August 28, 1938, gave additional impetus to the sex change, also calling the elephant Lucy.

As an added bit of historical proof, Beverly K. Gertzen, Sophia's granddaughter, wrote in the early 1980s: "The elephant is, indeed, an architectural phenomenon, but a large chapter of Lucy's 'life' was indelibly carved in time by Sophia, who added a touch of love and named her 'Lucy.'"

Reflecting on the remarkable achievements of a single woman in a male-dominated world, Beverly Gertzen went on to say: "Sophia Gertzen, who brought the elephant through World War I, Prohibition, Woman's Rights, the Great Depression and World War II, must be the very heart of Lucy's historic personality."

She might also have added the hurricane of 1944 to the list of crises that Lucy has survived. This storm, one of the most vicious of the twentieth century, tore up the Jersey Shore from Cape May to Sandy Hook. It destroyed the Margate boardwalk (which has never been rebuilt), but Lucy escaped relatively unscathed.

Of course, along with the major disasters there were numerous minor incidents over the years that Lucy tolerated with her stoic good humor. In 1929 a storm ripped off her attractive howdah, which was subsequently replaced by a less ornate version. Four years later a dancer named Drucilla Taggart whirled about on Lucy's head while newsreel cameras clicked away. During the elections of 1938, someone stuck a Republican campaign sign on her that read "Let's Go Places With Walter Jeffries In Congress," despite any known evidence of Lucy's political affiliations. (Rumor has it that she's not even registered to vote.) She's also gone through several different colors over the years, including black and brown.

Through it all, Sophia Gertzen maintained Lucy with the same good grace and gentle humor that characterized her long stewardship of the great beast. However, Sophia's death in 1963 marked the end of an era for Lucy. For some time the elephant's physical condition had been declining. The terrible March storm of 1962 that devastated much of the New Jersey coast took a further toll on the aging elephant. Sophia's children, Caroline and Joseph, continued to run the business, but clearly Lucy had reached a crossroads. For eighty years she had triumphed over every hardship, but she couldn't beat Father Time.

Lucy had become an eyesore. Margate Mayor Martin Bloom said in July 1963: "The elephant downgrades the entire area. I would like to see a high-rise apartment or hotel built in its place." The final blow came in June 1964, when Margate building inspector R. Bayne Williams toured Lucy and ordered her closed. His inspection had revealed that the once-proud pachyderm was in "a state of utter disrepair through age, rot, weather, and a total lack of proper attention over a period of many years." The ultimate indignity was that Lucy, after surviving numerous fires, was now labeled by Williams as a fire hazard.

But even as public officials were marshalling forces against Lucy, concerned citizens were coming to her defense. Bloom's unflattering remarks were picked up by the wire services and sent around the nation. Almost overnight something called the Society for Prevention of Cruelty to Margate's Elephant sprang up and bombarded the mayor with protest letters and phone calls. On July 20, 1963, more than one hundred pickets demonstrated around Lucy, chanting "We want the elephant!"

With Lucy's popularity now demonstrated, Margate officials began searching for a way to save her. But for six long years the situation remained at a standstill. Unable to buy Lucy and unable to finance a restoration of such magnitude, the town fruitlessly sought a solution as the proud creature continued to die a little bit each day. A headline in the July 25, 1969, edition of the *Catholic Star Herald* said it best: "Lucy the Elephant Just Wasting Away." The description of the once-elegant elephant was heartbreaking: "Sections of her rusting tin sides flap with the passing breezes. Pitiful holes pock the once-impressive body . . . a gaping, almost symbolically tear-shaped hole under the elephant's right eye has become a home for pigeons who nest and raise their young there. She is being allowed to fall apart."

But then, just at the darkest hour of Lucy's long existence, a little light began to shine. The Margate Civic Association was formed and began searching for a way to save the famous landmark. Before restoration could even begin, it was decided to move Lucy to a vacant piece of municipal beachfront property two blocks south of where she had stood for so many years. To clear the way for the move, the Gertzen family gave the elephant to the city, ending an association with Lucy that had spanned more than three-quarters of a century. The Save Lucy Committee was formed and began frantically doing everything it could to raise the approximately twenty-five thousand dollars needed to move the elephant. Even schoolchildren pitched in to help the grand old lady of the Jersey Shore, donating proceeds from cake and crafts sales. Somehow, all the obstacles were overcome (including a last-minute injunction to stop Lucy's relocation, filed by a corporation claiming that in her new home she would deflate the value of adjacent property it owned), and July 20,

1970, was designated as the day for Lucy to pack up her trunk and move.

On that sunny summer's day, Jersey Shore history was made. While hundreds watched and the news media sent the story out to the rest of the country, the creaking, deteriorating elephant captured the heart of a nation. Slowly, almost regally, Lucy moved down Atlantic Avenue in Margate, pulled by a small yellow pickup truck. There was something poignant and poetic about her as she inched down the street on her special platform, raised by house jacks and stabilized by wooden cribbing placed underneath her crumbling body; something about her will to live touched a chord in everyone who witnessed her short but remarkable journey that day. Donations for her restoration began flooding into the Save Lucy Committee from people around the world.

For Lucy, as well, it must have been a strange journey. For almost ninety years she had stared silently out to sea, while all

Lucy, the Margate Elephant, showed the ravages of age and neglect in 1973 just after she was moved to her present location. (A Copyrighted Photograph of Lucy, The Margate Elephant, the representation of which serves as a service mark and registered trademark of The Save Lucy Committee, Inc., P.O. Box 3000, Margate, New Jersey 08402. Photograph reprinted by permission of The Save Lucy Committee, Inc.)

Lucy, the Margate Elephant, as she appeared in 1976 after being restored. (A Copyrighted Photograph of Lucy, The Margate Elephant, the representation of which serves as a service mark and registered trademark of The Save Lucy Committee, Inc., P.O. Box 3000, Margate, New Jersey 08402. Photograph reprinted by permission of The Save Lucy Committee, Inc.)

around her a new world had grown up. But even though the deserted sand dunes and weather-beaten fishing shacks that had once been her neighbors had long since given way to paved streets and concrete and steel buildings, and although she was badly in need of a total make-over, she was still the same majestic creature she had been when the likes of Woodrow Wilson, Henry Ford, the Astors, and the Rockefellers had passed through her decades before. This was not lost on anyone who watched or read about her journey that fateful July day, when she made the transition from elephant joke to courageous heroine.

Today, thanks to the herculean efforts of the Save Lucy Committee, the shore's unofficial mascot has been restored to her former glory and can be toured again. Money is a perpetual worry for the committee; it takes more than just peanuts to continue the restoration and also keep Lucy in fresh gray paint. And she needs to look her best, now that she keeps such exclusive company. In

1977 the United States Department of the Interior designated Lucy a National Historic Landmark, putting her in the same select group as the Alamo, Independence Hall, and other famous structures that are considered important in the heritage of this country. At ceremonies honoring Lucy's selection to this elite group, one speaker proclaimed, "Viva la Lucy!"

That's a sentiment well worth repeating: Viva la Lucy!

◆

While Lucy was, and is, the First Elephant of the Jersey Shore, she wasn't always the only elephant of the Jersey Shore. In fact, Lucy used to have two cousins. One was a distant relative living among the bright lights and carnival sounds of Coney Island, New York; the other parked his trunk just down the road a bit, on a lonely stretch of beach in Cape May.

On May 9, 1884, the weekly newspaper *Star of the Cape* carried the following story:

> Ground was broken on the beach at Cape May for the erection of a white Elephant Bazaar from plans drawn by N. H. Culver, Architect. The builder, J. W. Bradley, has contracted with T. M. Reger, of Philadelphia to have it finished by July 1st. The dimensions [are] 87 feet long [and] 65 ft. high, surmounted by a howdah or observatory from which a grand view of the ocean, bay, and surrounding country for 50 miles can be had. Entrance and exit through the rear limbs.

This was the birth announcement of Lucy's first cousin, officially called the Light of Asia but more popularly known as Jumbo. Although the original dimensions, as carried in the newspaper story, would have made Jumbo larger than Lucy, the actual elephant was just forty feet tall (fifty-eight feet tall when the howdah was counted), and its tusks were eighteen feet long, four feet shorter than Lucy's.

One of the mysteries of the Light of Asia is whether or not James V. Lafferty, Lucy's creator, had anything to do with it. Sometimes he is referred to as the builder of Jumbo and sometimes not. The most likely scenario is that while Lafferty wasn't directly responsible for Jumbo, as he was for Lucy and her Coney Island cousin, he did give approval for his elephant design to be used. Surviving photographs of Jumbo show a similarity between it and Lucy, even down to the trunk being deposited in a feeding container. However, the meticulous attention to detail and realism that marked both Lucy and the Coney Island elephant were missing from the Light of Asia, which was more squared off and not as realistically shaped as its two cousins. It can only be assumed that this was because Lafferty was not intimately involved.

While Lucy seems to have been built with a minimum of fuss and bother, it was quite a different story for Jumbo. Located in a meadow close to the ocean between Cape May City and Cape May Lighthouse, the elephant took much longer to construct than anticipated. This was despite great public interest and curiosity in the giant beast. Under "West Cape May Jottings" in the May 16, 1884, *Star of the Cape*, the paper stated: "One of the first building improvements in the new borough is the much-talked of Jumbo, the elephant being erected on the West Cape May beach front." Just a few weeks later, the paper again spoke of Jumbo: "Our new white elephant structure is already a point of considerable attraction. It is not only a novelty in the way of buildings, but as a spot for a pleasant, quiet, enjoyable hour, it will doubtless receive much patronage."

But the elephant wasn't finished by July, as initially stipulated. The July 4, 1884, issue of the *Star of the Cape* announced that "work on the mammoth elephant . . . is being pushed forward. It will probably be completed in time for use this season." However, this again turned out not to be the case. And even though it has sometimes been reported that the elephant was finished in January of 1885, in June of that same year the *Star of the Cape* said the elephant "remains uncompleted." Possibly trying to speed things along, the paper added that the "owners should get it ready if possible, for the coming season's business."

When the Light of Asia finally opened, it had shops, concessions, and amusements inside it. Souvenirs and refreshments could also be purchased at stands located in the elephant's front legs. Robert C. Alexander, who has chronicled much Cape May history, wrote that a friend recalled taking a trolley to see the elephant, where his mother bought him a glass of lemonade. There were tables located underneath Jumbo, where one could sit and have the dubious distinction of gazing up at the belly of the beast while enjoying a cool drink and the salty sea breezes. The giant creature could also be seen from the train that ran between Cape May and the pier where the excursion steamship *Republic* docked.

Unlike the mysterious origin of Lucy's name, the reasons behind both Light of Asia and Jumbo seem clear. Light of Asia probably came from the supposedly sacred white elephant of the same name that showman Adam Forepaugh brought to the United States in the spring of 1884. Jumbo was most likely due to the incredible popularity at that time of Phineas T. Barnum's eleven-foot-tall, 6-ton elephant, known affectionately to Americans as Jumbo.

In 1887 some members of the Mount Vernon Land Company acquired Jumbo. Emulating their elephant neighbor a few miles to the north, they sought to use Jumbo as a sales gimmick and painted "New Mt. Vernon" across the elephant's side.

But like Lucy, the Light of Asia wasn't good at pushing real estate. And although many people visited, Jumbo was not a profitable venture for the principals involved, who reportedly never made a penny on their eighteen thousand dollar investment. Eventually neglected and ignored, the great wooden creature drifted into decline. Its legs fell through the wooden platform it was mounted on, and it became a ramshackle, rundown wreck.

Finally, as the new century dawned, Captain Samuel E. Ewing was contracted to dismantle Jumbo. The May 19, 1900, issue of *Star of the Cape* carried the news about the Light of Asia's sad demise: "Capt. Samuel E. Ewing has a force of men tearing the elephant to pieces. . . . The structure was built with the intention of using it as a pleasure resort, but it has met with an inglorious end." The *Star* added that Ewing accomplished Jumbo's destruction "without much trouble."

But the story of Jumbo has a strange codicil. According to tales that began to circulate while the ill-fated elephant was still intact, the Light of Asia was beset by "strange sights and unearthly voices." Rumors spread that the beast was haunted.

One possible explanation for these "mysterious occurrences" could be that vagrants were attracted to Jumbo after it began falling apart. Indeed, Alexander wrote about a West Cape May resident who, as a boy, knew of a secret entrance through a loose board in the trunk by which he and his friends could sneak into the elephant without paying the ten cents admission fee. If

Jumbo had people hiding inside it, they might well have been responsible for the sights and voices reported.

Unfortunately, we'll never know. Unlike Lucy, the Light of Asia has passed into history.

♦

One thing is for certain about Lucy's other cousin: he could never have been happy in the serenity of a deserted beachfront. The Elephantine Colossus was a born party animal.

Of course, living in Coney Island he'd have to be, for this was during the time when the Brooklyn amusement park was synonymous with zany, unpredictable fun. In the outrageous world of bearded women and midgets that was Coney Island, a 122-foot-tall, tin-skinned wooden elephant fit right in.

The Elephantine Colossus was built by James V. Lafferty, Lucy's creator, in the spring of 1884, at a reported cost of sixty-five thousand dollars. It took 263 men 129 days to complete the job. Lafferty's influence can clearly be seen in surviving pictures of the giant creature. The Elephantine Colossus bore a much closer resemblance to Lucy than did the Light of Asia.

When completed, the Coney Island elephant, also known as the Colossus of Architecture, was something of a sensation due to its immense size. Long before skyscrapers were common, the gigantic elephant—which was nearly twice the height of Lucy—afforded a view from its telescope-equipped howdah of more than fifty miles. It faced the ocean across Surf Avenue in Coney Island, near the famous Sea Beach Palace. Its legs were sixty feet in circumference. The front legs held a cigar store and a diorama, while the back ones provided the entrance and exit. Huge lights inside the four-foot-tall glass eyes burned at night like angry beacons from heaven.

Inside the enormous creature were seven stories of exhibits. However, unlike Lucy, who began life as a real estate office, the Elephantine Colossus was meant from the beginning to be a working hotel. Rooms for the night were available in the thigh, shoulder, hip, or cheek. Those who wanted to know what it felt like to live inside a giant hypodermic needle could squeeze into the eleven-foot-around trunk for a one-night stay.

Unfortunately, Lafferty had picked a bad place to build his colossal creation. The somewhat seedy area around the Elephantine

National Historic Landmarks Along the Jersey Shore

Lucy is not the only National Historic Landmark along the Jersey Shore. Here's a list of the history you can find:

ATLANTIC CITY CONVENTION HALL. On the Boardwalk between Pacific, Mississippi, and Florida avenues. The glory of Atlantic City is embodied in this famed structure, site of the Miss America Pageant and numerous other events.

ALL SAINTS MEMORIAL CHURCH COMPLEX. Navesink Avenue and Locust Road, Middletown. Designed by famed architect Richard Upjohn and built in a Gothic Revival style.

CAPE MAY HISTORIC DISTRICT. Gingerbread and Victorian architecture gone wild in one of the most beautiful and historic cities in the world.

COVENHOVEN HOUSE. 150 West Main Street, Freehold. Headquarters of Sir Henry Clinton, British army general during the American Revolution.

FORT HANCOCK AND SANDY HOOK PROVING GROUND HISTORIC DISTRICT. Fort Hancock, Sandy Hook. One of the hubs of American military preparedness during several wars, and a site for testing new weapons.

GEORGIAN COURT COLLEGE. Lakewood Avenue, Lakewood. Former estate of Jay Gould, railroad executive and financier.

HANGER NUMBER ONE, LAKEHURST NAVAL AIR STATION. Route 547, Manchester Township. Where the *Hindenburg* went down in 1937, taking dirigible travel with it.

HORN ANTENNA. AT&T Bell Laboratories, Crawford Hill Facility, Holmdel. Where two scientists accidentally discovered the remnants of the big bang explosion that created the universe.

LUCY, THE MARGATE ELEPHANT. Decatur and Atlantic avenues, Margate City. Gee, this sounds familiar. . . .

MONMOUTH BATTLEFIELD. Route 522, Manalapan Township. Site of the Battle of Freehold during the American Revolution, and the place where Molly Pitcher fought her way into history.

SANDY HOOK LIGHTHOUSE. Sandy Hook. The oldest continually operating lighthouse in the United States.

SHADOW LAWN. Cedar and Norwood avenues, West Long Branch. Built for the president of the F. W. Woolworth Company, this mansion served as Woodrow Wilson's "Summer WhiteHouse."

T. THOMAS FORTUNE HOUSE. 94 Bergen Place, Red Bank. Home of one of this country's pioneering black journalists.

Colossus was popularly known as the place where a man looking for a good time could find a woman more than willing to accommodate him. This led to the phrase "seeing the elephant" (probably accompanied by a few sly winks), which became part of the sexual vernacular of the times.

Eventually, Lafferty sold out to the Philadelphia syndicate of Hall & Garretson. But they could do nothing to turn the great beast's fortunes around. Then, on the night of Sunday, September 27, 1896, observers spied smoke and flames coming out of the elephant's second-story windows. As the next day's *New York Times* reported: "An alarm was raised at 10:30 p.m., but as the structure was of wood and the water was scarce, the fire could not be put out. The elephant fell within half an hour." According to the paper, the structure "had been unoccupied for several years."

But it would be a mistake to think that, because of the Elephantine Colossus's unsavory reputation, its demise was not mourned. The September 28, 1896, edition of the *Brooklyn Daily Eagle*, under the heading "Loss of An Old Friend," paid a fitting tribute to the mighty beast:

"News of the death of the Coney Island elephant, which occurred last night at 10:30 o'clock will be received in Brooklyn, as elsewhere, with feelings of profound regret. He died as a hero, not exactly like the boy on the burning deck, but faithful to those who had admired and loved him and anxious even in his last moments to contribute to their happiness. It was a singularly pathetic career that was thus brought to an untimely end, a career full of promise at the start, but marred by the intervention of events over which there could be no control. Crowds came from far and near to witness his expiring gasps. The youth and beauty of Coney Island were there and its chivalry too, and as the flames mounted fifty feet to the sky and lighted up the Atlantic, to say nothing of the palatial residences in the immediate vicinity, there was a general feeling of sadness. Every person in the throng felt as though he or she had lost a friend, and it was a loss the magnitude of which could not easily be exaggerated."

However, some good did come from the fiery death of the enormous creature. A few years later, when Frederic W. Thompson was building his fabulous Luna Park amusement complex directly behind Coney Island, the remains of one of the Elephantine Colossus's legs were found while workmen were clearing the land. Thompson regarded it as a good luck charm, and thereafter he was always partial to elephant acts. This seems an apropos final chapter to the career of the Elephantine Colossus—Lucy's biggest cousin and brainchild of James V. Lafferty, who always hoped that his "novel and unique" creations would bring him luck but instead found only immortality.

EIGHT

Spirits of the Jersey Shore

The man and woman were walking slowly along the deserted beach, hand in hand, engrossed in the delightful solitude of sand and surf. Except for the squawking of sea gulls overhead and the whisper of waves on the beach, an eerie, almost unnatural quiet filled the air. It was the sound of utter isolation.

A desolate beach is a curious thing. Is an abandoned beach ever truly abandoned, or is it filled with the energy and memories of what has occurred there in the past, from yesterday's volleyball game to last century's shipwreck? Is the quiet real, or is it an illusion, blurring the tenuous boundary between fantasy and reality?

The couple were about to find out.

Suddenly, they realized they were not alone. Just a few yards behind them was a woman, dressed in a curious, old-fashioned style. She seemed to be searching for someone, or something. Her eyes swept the beach and the ocean like lighthouse beacons, but whatever she sought remained hidden.

For a time she followed the couple, never getting too close but never paying them any attention either. All she did was wander about the beach, staring this way and that, her actions becoming more and more puzzling. Her presence began to unnerve the couple. Her dated clothing and eccentric manner were very odd indeed. Suddenly the isolation of the beach, so appealing moments before, was ominous and frightening. Help—if they would need any—was far away.

Somewhere over the water, a solitary sea gull cried out.

Then the mysterious woman did a very strange thing. As the couple watched, she turned and walked straight into the ocean. Seemingly unaffected by the waves, she continued walking as the water swirled and eddied around her. Within seconds her head slipped beneath the black water.

She never emerged.

◆

Stories such as this are far more common at the Jersey Shore than might be expected. Tales of seashore spirits abound from Sandy Hook to Cape May.

Maybe it's the way the moonlight sparkles off the glassy ocean at night that stirs people to concoct bizarre and fanciful stories. Maybe all the violent and untimely deaths from shipwrecks and other catastrophes are too much for fertile imaginations to resist on nights when the moon is full and the hissing of the waves sounds like the whispered laughter of phantoms.

Or maybe it's because the shore is still essentially a wild, untamed place. Despite many efforts to bend it to our will, the shore remains beyond mortal control, as anyone who has ever witnessed a raging coastal storm knows all too well. The sea, sand, and wind are wily, capricious, and unrelenting—possibly just the right combination of natural powers to attract restless, unearthly spirits.

Some tales of ghosts and spirits have been handed down through generations, their origins long obscured. Such is the case with the supposedly haunted building on the south end of the Fort Hancock military complex on Sandy Hook. Descriptions of the specter vary. Some say it's a floating head covered with blood; others claim to have seen ghostly shoes walking up stairs; still others report seeing a ghostly guard soldier, holding a rifle, standing on the front porch of Building 20.

Reports of spirits at the Jersey Shore have also come from the most respected of sources. Before finding fame as the author of *The Red Badge of Courage*, Stephen Crane in 1895 related a spooky Shore tale to readers of the *New York Press*. It concerned a ghostly white lady who walked beaches in the Metedeconk area—"a moaning, mourning thing of the mist," said Crane. "Her hair fell in disheveled masses over her shoulders, her hands were clasped appealingly, and her large eyes gleamed with the one eternal and dread interrogation."

The awful question that this frightful specter supposedly put to every mortal she met on the beach concerned the whereabouts of her lover's body. Those that didn't immediately reply in a direct and lucid manner were doomed to die within a day's time.

It seems that in life this tortured spirit had been the companion of a ship's captain. One day, as he was saying his farewells before embarking on a long voyage to Buenos Aires, she pouted at being abandoned for such a lengthy time, causing him much despair. But no sooner had the brokenhearted man's ship passed Absecon Inlet than the lady regretted her actions and began mourning for his return.

The woman grew thin and pale as she spent each day staring out to sea in silent vigil, awaiting the moment when his sails would be seen again on the horizon. Finally, during a howling winter storm, she spied something rolling in the surf outside her home. But when she went out to investigate, she made a horrifying discovery: it was the drowned corpse of her lover. In true "Monkey's Paw" fashion her secret wish had come true; he would never go to sea again. But her eternal soul paid the price for her pettiness.

Crane also reported on other specters that haunted the Barnegat Bay region, including an Indian who was stalking the young bride he had buried for putting too much salt in his muskrat stew and a young man and woman whose ghosts, "impalpable as sea mist," still keep their lovers' rendezvous on the beach.

Crane's most nightmarish story of the Jersey Shore concerns the ghost of a black dog that maintains an eternal vigil on the beach over the body of its master, who was killed in a shipwreck: "The phantom of this black hound is what the fishermen see as they return home from their boats and nets late at night. There is a dreadful hatchet wound in the animal's head, and from it the phantom blood bubbles. His jaw drips angry foam and his eyes are lit with a crimson fire. He gallops continually with his nose to the ground as if he were trailing some one. If you are ever down upon the New Jersey coast at midnight and meet this specter, you had better run."

Usually, however, it is men and women who are condemned to walk the beaches until Judgment Day, often in retribution for misdeeds in life. Such tales are widespread along the Shore. There's the story of a ghostly sea captain cloaked in black who appears on the Brigantine shoreline just before a storm hits. Some say he was the captain of a ship that wrecked off Brigantine in a savage storm years ago, who possibly did not do all he could to prevent the tragedy. Now, eyes wide with terror, hair whipping around his head in the growing wind, he rushes up to any mortals he meets on the beach, trying to get them to seek shelter before the storm arrives. But in the perverse logic that governs the world of the damned, his warnings are never heard. Inevitably the swirling wind muffles his words, leaving his mouth moving without a sound.

Long Beach Island, with its storm-swept history, seems to be a favorite haunt for ghostly beachwalkers. According to legend, a white female figure can sometimes be seen wandering over the island's beaches, then falling to her knees and bending over with clasped hands, as if grieving over a corpse. Supposedly this is the spirit of a young woman who in life was a member of a band of "wreckers"—land pirates who lured ships to their doom on the shoals just offshore and then pillaged both the cargo and corpses that washed up on the beach. One night, as the gang was hard at work on the remains of a ship they had caused to crash, the woman screamed in horror and threw herself atop one of the water-swollen corpses. It was the body of her seafaring lover, who had escaped from a wreck near England and was returning to meet the woman he loved—on the ship that she had just helped to destroy.

Even grimmer is the modern tale of a little girl who appeared without warning one summer night in the Beach Haven bedroom of a vacationing family.

The man, an amateur artist, and his wife were asleep when he suddenly awoke to find the strange child standing beside his bed.

Dress torn, hair disheveled, her entire body soaking wet, the girl whimpered and gurgled pitifully. But when he tried to help her, she glided backward through a sliding glass door and vanished. Moments later, after waking his wife, the man and woman spotted the young girl walking along the beach. As they watched, she simply strolled into the surging sea and disappeared.

An even greater shock came the very next day, when the man checked the painting of a beach scene he had been working on. During the night, something new had been added to the canvas: the mysterious little girl who had visited him in the bedroom.

Was the apparent violence of the girl's tragic death the catalyst that made her reappear in the world of the living, re-creating her last desperate moments of life when the sea closed around her? Certainly, violent death has been the prime reason for the strange sounds and sights that have been reported on the beach in Barnegat Light, at the northern tip of Long Beach Island.

It was here, along a stretch of beach just south of where Barnegat Lighthouse now stands, that more than twenty American privateers were murdered in 1782 by a band of marauders led by John Bacon. This grisly episode is described in the next chapter on war at the Shore; its ghostly aftermath is perfectly suited for this chapter. There have been persistent reports of strange shapes and sounds coming at night from this stretch of sand. Some say the shapes resemble people, and the sounds are those of human laughter and moaning. Could these unearthly occurrences be the spirits of those men whose lives were so tragically snuffed out over two centuries ago?

◆

Scoffing, of course, is easy to do and part of human nature. No one wants to admit there may be more to the sometimes mysterious sights and sounds on the beach at night than just the wind or the sea. But no amount of scoffing can change what happened to the Mansion of Health. It's possibly Long Beach Island's most famous ghost story.

Opened for business as a resort in 1822, the Mansion of Health (so named because its founders thought it the most "healthful" place on the island) was a rambling, three-story structure located near the beach in what is today Surf City. Measuring 120 feet long, its immense size made it the largest hotel on the Jersey

Shore at the time. One of its distinguishing features was a balcony that ran along the entire top floor, providing a stunning view of the glistening ocean that lay just a few hundred feet from the front door. Although not luxurious, the Mansion of Health attracted many people eager to enjoy the quiet and serenity of the Jersey Shore, and for years the great building prospered.

The downfall began on Sunday, April 18, 1854. On that day, one of the worst storms in New Jersey's history raged along the coast, claiming among its victims the packet ship *Powhattan*. The ship was filled with German immigrants—many of them wealthy—who were seeking a new life in America. But all they found was death.

The savage storm drove the *Powhattan* onto the shoals. There, as the ship lay helpless, the howling winds and pounding waves systematically destroyed it. Every one of the 365 people on board died in the churning sea. For hours the bodies of men, women, and children washed up on shore like pieces of driftwood. Mothers still clutched their babies to their bosoms in a macabre embrace of death.

But the next day, when the living arrived to take charge of the dead, they were surprised to discover that the bodies contained no money whatsoever. The wreckmaster (the person responsible for filing reports of any shipwrecks in the area) was a man named Edward Jennings, who was also the manager of the Mansion of Health. He declared that when he had arrived on the scene he hadn't been able to find a single coin on any of the victims.

A few months later, a pile of empty money belts was discovered buried not far from where the bodies had washed up. Every belt had been cut open. It was widely suspected that Jennings had robbed the bodies of the unfortunate immigrants, but proof was lacking and Jennings was never brought to justice.

However, justice of a different type was meted out at the Mansion of Health. Word quickly spread that the ghosts of the *Powhattan* victims were haunting the large hotel. Reports flew about ghostly figures being seen in the mansion, including that of a woman holding a baby in her arms and staring sadly out to sea. Needless to say, business quickly dried up. Within a few years after the *Powhattan* tragedy the Mansion of Health was an abandoned ruin, haunted by the memories of better days—and, quite possibly, by something else as well.

Storms and their terrible aftermath are an indelible part of the Jersey Shore. Years ago, sailing ships were more at the mercy of the elements. As a result, they would routinely be flung onto the rocks and shoals that lie scattered along the New Jersey coastline, sending both bodies and cargo washing onto the beach. Because of the frequency of shipwrecks, it should come as no surprise that the Jersey Shore has its share of ghost ship stories. Some are of the typical Flying Dutchman variety: a ruined, rotting hulk of a ship, tattered sails flapping in the breeze, is sighted on the water, gliding silently along in defiance of its dilapidated condition until it disappears into a fog bank.

Other tales take a more unusual tack. Baymen from the Barnegat region used to tell of seeing a ship lying broken in the surf on the morning after a bad storm. Strewn along the beach and bobbing in the shallow water like corks were barrels, planks, pieces of cargo, and numerous other objects that could only have come from a wreck.

The men would go off to organize a salvage party and then head back to the ruined ship. But when they arrived on the beach, the ship would be gone. The ocean that had been teeming with evidence of the tragedy was clear and quiet. It was only then that the baymen knew they had seen a ghost ship fated to continually reenact the scene of its destruction until the end of time.

♦

Located on the Delaware Bay side of Cape May Point, Higbee Beach has long been considered haunted. No doubt the terrain has aided this impression. Although it is a popular spot for sunbathers, fishermen, and bird-watchers, Higbee Beach is a rugged, desolate place. The wind moans across the sand dunes, rustling twisted underbrush that is more reminiscent of the Transylvania of vampire lore than New Jersey. Often the air is filled with the uncanny cries of unseen animals and birds. It seems the perfect place for spirits to call home.

Apparently, some already have. Stories endure of strange sights and sounds at Higbee Beach—of phantom figures gliding across the sand and then disappearing into the water, accompanied by disembodied voices and strange laughter. Some trace the source of these disturbances back to claims that old man Higbee was buried facedown so that he could meet Satan face to face, and

How Sailors Prevented Ghosts from Haunting Their Ships

The sea is a wild and mysterious place, full of unseen relics of ages past. Alone on a misty, moonless night, staring out at the never-ending ocean, sailors have often sworn that they've heard and seen things that are not of this earth. To keep the spirits of the dead from haunting their ships, sailors would resort to several different methods.

Drowned sailors were more likely to haunt their former shipmates if they were not given a burial at sea. To do this the body would be washed and then dressed in clean clothes. The sailmaker would sew a canvas shroud around the deceased, and, after the crew had mustered on deck, the captain or mate would read the burial service. The weighted body would then be cast overboard—hopefully for good.

It was thought that merely to mention the names of dead sailors would bring back their ghosts. Those who did find it necessary to speak of their departed shipmates would never refer to them as dead, but rather would always precede their names with "poor."

Sailors would carry a variety of amulets, rings, lucky stones, and other objects thought to possess magical properties and ensure smooth sailing. (The number of these charms would depend on the degree of a sailor's superstitions.) To keep away evil spirits, sailors often kept foul-smelling charms on their persons. (Charms with a pleasant aroma were thought to attract friendly ghosts.)

It was believed that drowned sailors either remained at or returned to the place where they had died. This was particularly true of sites up and down the Atlantic coastline where greedy "wreckers" had used false signals to lure unsuspecting ships to a watery tomb. Since the Jersey Shore had more than its share of such wrecks (it wasn't called the Graveyard of the Sea for nothing), local sailors undoubtedly took great caution when heading out to sea or returning to port.

Seabirds—particularly the petrel and the albatross—were thought to be the spirits of drowned sailors. Sailors believed that killing one of these birds would bring extremely bad luck, yet they also felt that the birds themselves were good omens. (However, since sailors also thought it was good luck to have a seabird defecate on them, it might be prudent to take their bird beliefs with a grain of salt.)

that it's his feisty spirit that roams the beach. Others say the area is inhabited by the ghost of one of the Higbees' personal slaves, who was assigned in life to watch over his master's grave and has continued his long vigil to this very day. There's also the timeworn story about ghostly pirates still guarding treasure that they supposedly buried there centuries ago.

Not far from Higbee Beach is the site of another supposedly supernatural occurrence in the Cape May region. It's known as the haunted bunker, and the name fits it well. Sitting in the surf just off the beach at Cape May Point, the old, battered relic from World War II looks like the military equivalent of a haunted house. Decay hangs over the squat structure like a shroud; erosion and years of exposure to the corrosive effects of salt air and water have battered the concrete hulk worse than any enemy shells ever could. Built in 1942, when hysteria about German submarines attacking the East Coast was at its zenith, the bunker has been abandoned for more than thirty years.

Or has it?

Many people report hearing a phantom gun crew still performing their duties on the bunker—cursing, yelling, laughing, and crying out to watch the seas for signs of an enemy that has long since been defeated. Some who've approached the bunker claim to have seen crew members scurrying around on top of the structure, only to find it deserted when they draw closer.

If there are indeed ghosts still on duty at the bunker, they couldn't have picked a more suitable place to be eternally marooned. The entire Cape May area is crawling with stories about ghosts, spirits, and strange phenomena. Perhaps ghosts are attracted to Cape May because the region's strong Victorian heritage has locked it into the past. Possibly spirits feel they belong in this living relic of an era long gone.

Whatever the reason, several of the grand old structures in and about the graceful town have ghost stories connected to them. Some are bed-and-breakfast establishments that seem to be haunted by the spirits of those who stayed there when alive. Guests who have encountered these supernatural visitors report seeing strange, wavering shapes moving in halls or throughout rooms, or hearing voices when no one else is present. At other times the ghostly occurrence takes a more traditional form: a feeling of extreme cold that lasts only a few seconds.

There are also those who report the most unnerving feeling of all: that of not being alone, even when they know they are. People who've slept in rooms and shopped in stores rumored to be inhabited by ghosts claim to have had just such a feeling—a quiet, tingling, instinctive awareness that someone or something was very near them, despite the apparent absence of another living thing. Such is the case at the Hildreth House, one of the most well-known haunting sites in the Cape May area.

Built in 1722 and later moved to its current site on U.S. Route 9 in Rio Grande, Hildreth House is today part of Winterwood, a Christmas and gift shop. There have been so many reports and sightings of ghostly activity in and about the house that a sign outside tells visitors all about the apparition: ". . . Do not be disturbed by the resident ghost, Hester."

It's good to be warned of such things, for Winterwood seems to be a bona fide case of supernatural phenomena. There have been many reports of footsteps, voices, and loud thumps and rumblings coming from empty rooms. Other creepy occurrences include objects moving, music boxes playing by themselves, and malfunctioning electrical equipment such as lights and burglar alarms. Workers have had tools scattered about, and wall-mounted displays have slipped from their hooks without apparent cause.

The Hildreth House ghost has a physical—or metaphysical—presence as well. A white-robed figure has been seen gliding across the lawn, then vanishing when it reached the old Hildreth family burial ground that lies in back of the house. Others claim to have seen a mist-cloaked figure crossing in front of a doorway in the house.

Events such as these prompted a team of psychic researchers to investigate Hildreth House in 1979. Their conclusion, presented the following year at an international parapsychological conference, was that the house is the site of poltergeist activity by a "deceased agent."

The investigators also added a new wrinkle to the theories about the identity of the spirit. Before the research, it had been widely assumed that the Winterwood ghost was one of two spinster Hildreth sisters, Hester or Lucille, who lived in the house during the first part of the twentieth century. Hester died in 1949, and Lucille followed her to the grave six years later. But one of the sensitives who investigated the house reported a male presence, saying it was a cousin of Hester and Lucille's.

Others believe the presence is a former male slave whom the Hildreths were supposed to have educated during the Civil War. A popular legend holds that the spirit is a British soldier from the American Revolution who was given refuge in the house. In gratitude, he carved the beautiful wooden mantlepiece that is located in the shop today.

Another bit of evidence that points to a male rather than a female ghost is the words of a six-year-old boy who came to Winterwood one day with his mother and asked for "Hector's box." This request baffled those who worked in the store until the child's mother explained that, on a previous visit to the store three years before, the boy said he had met a man named Hector who lived there in a box. The boy had been agitating since that time to go back to Winterwood and see his friend Hector again.

Was this just the product of a child's overactive imagination at work? Maybe. Maybe not. If the conclusions of the research team are to be believed—they ruled out the possibility of a hoax—then something out of the ordinary is indeed present at the old Hildreth House.

What raises a ghost story to a level above the typical tale we've all heard countless times—a luminescent spirit floating along the ground, then abruptly vanishing into thin air—is the assertion by psychic experts that there might well be something more to it than just whimsy. At the Spy House, psychics have been pointedly saying just this for quite some time.

The Spy House is probably the most haunted building on the Jersey Shore. So many spirits seem to inhabit this museum of Bayshore history located along Shoal Harbor in Port Monmouth (near Sandy Hook) that its curator and guiding light, Gertrude Neidlinger, says they stopped counting when the number reached thirty!

Built around 1663, the Whitlock-Seabrook House (the Spy House) is considered the first house built on the New Jersey shoreline. During the American Revolution it was converted into an inn to protect its neutrality and save it from being plundered by the British. Its unusual nickname dates from the Revolution. Colonial spies would watch the British leave their ships and come to the inn for supper, then attack the undermanned ships anchored in the harbor. This so-called whaleboat warfare (because the Americans would steal up to the unsuspecting ships in whaleboats) hampered the British war effort considerably.

The Spy House as it appeared in 1894. (Photo courtesy Special Collections and Archives, Rutgers University Libraries)

Like the Hildreth House, what makes the Spy House exceptional is that its reputation as a ghostly haven comes not from hoary stories told after a night of too much rum but from the experiences of both psychics and ordinary people. Indeed, there seems to be such a plethora of phantoms at the Spy House that it's more surprising when an encounter doesn't occur.

Among the spirits is an evil sea captain who, during the 1600s, supposedly killed children and American Indians and engaged in devil worship. Once the captain's spirit, dressed in a long black robe with a hood, was spotted by several children. But when he turned around, there was only smoke where his face should have been.

A later owner of the house, Reverend William Wilson, has been seen by psychics leading a funeral service in front of a bedroom fireplace. (Wilson's wife and mother-in-law died within ten days of each other.) In another bedroom a woman named Abigail, with a baby in her arms, gazes sadly out the window, searching for her husband, who was lost at sea. Loud sobbing has been heard from this room. Abigail's evening appearances at the window are so regular that people sometimes sit in their cars in the Spy House parking lot, waiting for a glimpse of the mournful spirit. Occasionally a small boy, most likely her son Peter, is seen with Abigail. Neidlinger feels that he is the mischievous soul who occasionally switches on the tape recorders placed throughout the house that explain its history.

One of the strangest Spy House experiences involves a blonde-haired mannequin with broken hands and no legs that sits in an old rocking chair in one of the bedrooms. A female psychic claimed that the spirit of Lydia Wilson (Reverend Wilson's wife) was "coming right through the mannequin." Men have become dizzy when walking past the door. Another man felt a burst of static electricity—strong enough to make his arm hair stand on end—shoot through his body when passing that room.

Sometimes the appearances of Spy House spirits can be quite deceiving. Late one evening, a member of the museum's board of directors was walking to his car when he saw children playing in the parking lot. He was about to tell them to go home when he noticed the many different styles of dress they wore—a mixture of pioneer, colonial, and eighteenth-century garb. The children were spirits.

Once, according to the unflappable Neidlinger (who tends to casually describe paranormal activity at the old house as "hair-raising"), a psychic visiting the Spy House witnessed a ghostly reenactment of the massacre of a mother and her small children by American Indians. Rapes and other acts of brutality have also been re-created by spirits who performed those deeds in life.

Why is the Spy House such a magnet for the supernatural? Is it because the age of the house enables it to act as a doorway between the thin veil that some say separates the spirit world from our own? According to Jane Doherty, psychic and president of the New Jersey Society of Parapsychology, one of the main reasons is the proximity of the water.

"Water is an energy source," she says. "Spirits are energy, and they seem to be able to gather energy to materialize for us because of water. Also, there's been a lot of killings and a lot of violent history there. Spirits can be confused by a violent death."

Doherty knew the Spy House was unique the first time she visited it. "I went through the house picking up impressions," she says. "[Downstairs] I felt the impression of a woman standing by the fireplace. [Upstairs] I saw a murder taking place—a man stabbing another one at the top of the steps. I also felt the presence of a man walking with a limp who I felt was a pirate." In another room Doherty saw a sea captain looking out the window. In the room where Abigail is supposed to be, she had the impression of a woman standing by the window and also heard a baby crying.

Doherty has been back to the house several times. On one visit both she and her son saw the phantom children that others have reported seeing at play in the backyard of the house.

It was during a séance Doherty conducted at the Spy House that the spirit of a pirate named Robert spoke through her. "He said that he had done a lot of wrong deeds and that he was afraid [to move to the next spiritual plane]," she says. "He [said] he was sorry for all the killings he had done."

Robert also revealed the existence of heretofore secret underground tunnels leading from the house to the harbor.

Doherty explains that there seem to be rooms along the sides of the tunnels—little hiding places in which are hidden treasures, books, and other objects. She also feels that bodies are buried there.

These startling revelations have led to a project to excavate the tunnels. Doherty feels that Robert revealed the secret tunnels to her—an act that apparently drew the wrath of another pirate spirit, a bad-tempered captain named Morgan—to make up for all the killing he did when alive. According to Doherty, the remorseful pirate hopes he is "righting his wrongs"—Robert's own words—through his current actions.

There's just one spot in the entire house that bothers Doherty. It's a cellar that, when she enters it, has a negative feeling that "just shouts" out at her. She feels that murders were committed there.

Another psychic who has had similar experiences at the Spy House is Fran Doran. Sometimes she has seen a woman with long hair peering out from a window in the room where Abigail has been spotted, as well as candles floating in that same window. Occasionally she detects the peppermint scent of baby powder, or a cold draft. Once, while sitting in a car in the driveway, noises like those of a blacksmith's shop began coming from a nearby shed. At one point the door even opened slightly, then closed again. Later, curator Neidlinger explained that the shed door was always firmly locked.

Doran has also had a close encounter with Captain Morgan. After hearing an awful pounding coming from upstairs—"like someone pounding the walls off"—she went up to the attic to investigate. Finding nothing, Doran started back down the steps. However, at the second-floor landing the sound of pounding suddenly began coming down the steps after her, as if someone were chasing her down the stairs. Apparently, Captain Morgan had resented her invasion of the upstairs regions where he reportedly dwells.

Doran predicts that the tunnels revealed by Robert contain "coins . . . uniforms, dresses, and jewelry" packed into the soft mud of the earthen walls. About the tunnels themselves, Doran says that, during the Revolution, George Washington lived in a nearby church and would come to the Port Monmouth shore in a rowboat. He would enter one of the underground tunnels and come up into the Spy House through a trapdoor under a stairwell that has since been removed. An investigation revealed that the trapdoor was right where Doran said it was and that Washington had indeed stayed in a church in South Amboy.

Will we ever know the truth about the Spy House? Sadly, the answer might well be no. The years may be numbered for this venerable old witness to over three centuries of Jersey Shore history. A gathering of spirits has reportedly revealed to a psychic that the house will burn to the ground at some undetermined date in the future. If fiery destruction is indeed the fate of the Whitlock-Seabrook House, then it will be unfortunate indeed that future generations will not have the opportunity to further explore the many mysteries of the Spy House.

◆

Is the Jersey Shore haunted? The answer to that question is easy: yes.

It's haunted by the memories of what was, for there is a sense of immortality about the Shore. Each year, like some supernatural creature, the Shore comes to life, and everything that happened the year before—children laughing on the beach under a bright summer sun, people screaming in mock terror as they whiz around on a rollercoaster, boardwalk barkers urging passersby to try their luck—occurs again with an eerie, almost identical sameness.

But then, after Labor Day, when the chill of winter hangs heavy in the air, the Shore returns to its sleep, and the haunting begins. Can anyone who has ever walked along a deserted boardwalk in the cold, with everything boarded up tight and the wind moaning across the empty beach, deny that the ghostly echoes of days past still linger? And what is a haunting if it's not the past colliding with the present?

But as for the more traditional haunting, with its ghosts, spirits, and things that go bump in the night, it's up to the individual to make that decision—a decision helped along by stories such as the following:

The night was bright but cold as the old man drove his wagon along the Mantoloking beach, just off the point where, during a terrible storm some years before, a ship had gone down, killing hundreds. For days afterward bodies had been disgorged by the ocean, covering the shoreline like some horrible blanket.

The old man's wagon was heavy with provisions, making it hard for the horse, but she was a game mare and gave it her best. Suddenly, however, the mare stopped and began to tremble. He gave her a bit of the whip, but she refused to go on. That's when the old man looked ahead and saw a man lying across his path.

Even as one part of his mind was telling him how curious it was to see a man stretched out across the road on such a bitter night, another part was formulating a plan for dealing with what was obviously someone passed out cold, most likely from too much drink. He decided to drive around him and nudge the prone figure with his whip as he passed.

But despite his urging, the mare would not move. Finally frustration set in, and the old man laid the whip heavily onto the mare. With that the horse took off straight ahead and made a tremendous leap over the body, dragging the heavy wagon behind her—right over the figure lying in the road.

The old man felt the front wheels strike the body, lift, and go over, followed moments later by the back wheels. Looking back, he could see the man's clothes, see his hair straggling out over the ground. He didn't see any flesh, but he supposed that was because the man's face was turned away from him. As soon as he got the mare quiet, the old man jumped down off the wagon and rushed back to see what assistance he could provide.

There was no one there.

CHAPTER

NINE

WAR AT THE SHORE

ᘒᘒᘒᘒᘒᘒᘒᘒᘒᘒᘒᘒᘒᘒᘒᘒᘒᘒᘒᘒᘒᘒᘒᘒᘒ

Like every other corner of the world, the Jersey Shore has been touched by war. From the time of the American Revolution all the way up to the present day, the Shore has been involved in each of the wars in our nation's history. This fact sometimes surprises people, because the Jersey Shore seems so removed from blood and battles; how could war's dark shadow possibly have fallen on the quiet beaches, the peaceful towns, the gently lapping waters of the ocean?

But fall it has—sometimes with more impact than expected.

◆

Today a stone marker near the entrance to Barnegat Lighthouse State Park commemorates the Long Beach Island Massacre, one of the most savage incidents of the American Revolution. Time has washed away the blood, and local legend has obscured many of the facts, but the infamy of the deed will live forever.

It was October 25, 1782, and the American privateer ship *Alligator* was about to make a spectacular find. Cruising off the northern shore of Long Beach Island, the privateer, captained by Andrew Steel (or Steelman, depending on the source), spotted a British cutter stranded on the shoals. As a privateer, the *Alligator*'s mission was to harass enemy ships; if the enemy happened to be stuck on a shoal and unable to maneuver, so much the better. Cautiously Steel brought the *Alligator* and its twelve-man crew in for a closer look at the cutter. The ship was deserted. In the hold, however, was a trove of supplies intended for the British army in New York. Steel and his men had hit the jackpot. Realizing that he would need more men to unload so fat a prize, Steel sent word across Barnegat Bay for assistance. His request was answered by about a dozen men, who rowed over to Long Beach Island to help him. Unfortunately, Steel's plea was also heard by another man, who had something very different in mind.

John Bacon was a notorious Jersey Shore Tory (an American loyal to England during the Revolution). He led a marauding band of thieves and murderers—called Refugees by the populace—who used the war as an excuse to prey on innocent citizens. In late December 1781, Bacon's band had plundered throughout Ocean County and, to add insult to injury, escaped a trap set by the local militia. In his base on Island Beach on that fateful October 25, Bacon somehow found out about the rich cargo being unloaded on the shore of Long Beach Island from the stranded British ship.

That night, Bacon and his band of killers slipped silently across Barnegat Inlet in the sloop *Heroes Revenge* and arrived on the island undetected. There they found the men who had unloaded the British cutter asleep on the beach, the remnants of a small fire smoldering nearby. Steel and his men had worked all day, unloading cargo and splashing through the surf to bring it to the beach, and by nightfall they had grown wet, tired, and cold. Apparently finding the beach an inviting place to spend the night, they had built a fire and gone to sleep.

Bacon and his band fell upon the sleeping men like wolves on a herd of sheep. Twenty of the men—maybe more—were ruthlessly slain. Only a few escaped. Almost six months later, John Bacon's murderous career ended when he was shot and killed in a house between West Creek and Little Egg Harbor.

The Jersey Shore was also the scene of several conflicts between colonists and British soldiers. The most famous is the Battle of Monmouth at Freehold. General Charles Lee's ill-timed retreat caused a near disaster for the American Continental army that was rectified only at the last minute, when George Washington hinself rode into the thick of the battle and rallied the troops. Another massacre, this time of forty American soldiers by British soldiers on Osborn's Island near Chestnut Neck (now Egg Harbor), occurred on October 15, 1778. In March 1782 the village of Toms River, which had been a hotbed of American privateer activity, was attacked by English troops. Virtually every house in the town, along with a gristmill and sawmill, was burned. In command of the twenty-five-man American militia contingent defending the town was Captain Joshua Huddy, whose name is enshrined in Jersey Shore lore for all time.

Huddy was a well-known patriot whose exploits during the Revolution were already becoming legendary. Gustav Kobbe, in *The Jersey Coast and Pines*, described Huddy's raids as "a series of daring deeds in the guerrilla warfare waged all along the New Jersey coast between the Tory refugees and their former neighbors." He was such a thorn in the side of the enemy that sixty British soldiers set out for his house in Colt's Neck in September 1780. After holding off the soldiers with the aid of only his wife and a servant girl, he was captured and placed in a small boat on the shore of Black Point (between the Shrewsbury and Navesink rivers) that took him to a nearby English ship. However, a band of patriotic militiamen appeared and began firing at the boat before it got too far offshore. In the confusion Huddy jumped overboard and swam to shore, thus giving the name Jumping Point to this area near Rumson.

So it seems likely that the British were eager to get rid of Huddy. After capturing him in the battle at Toms River, they saw their chance and were determined not to let it slip away again. On April 12, 1782, Huddy was taken to Gravelly Point, near the Navesink Highlands, and hanged on a trumped-up charge of murdering Philip White. White was a Tory who had been captured and then killed while trying to escape, with no involvement by Huddy whatsoever, but the facts were of little consequence. As Huddy was hanged, a Tory supposedly said, "Up goes Huddy for Phil White." These words became a famous rallying cry for the patriots, much as Remember the Alamo! would become a half-century later. Although Huddy's cold-blooded execution provoked outrage among the Americans, who made plans to retaliate by hanging a captured English officer, Huddy's death was never avenged.

◆

The little-known war with the Barbary pirates (called the Tripolitan War) brought fame to another Jersey Shore soldier, but it also cost him his life. Richard Somers, a member of the family who gave their name to the modern Cape May County town of Somers Point, was a naval commander in 1804 when the United States was fighting the Barbary pirates. In early September 1804, the American frigate *Philadelphia* was captured in Tripoli harbor. Somers proposed sailing a small ship packed with explosives into the harbor and igniting it, thereby creating confusion so the *Philadelphia*'s crew could escape and perhaps destroying some enemy ships as well. It was a suicide mission from the word go, not helped at all by the fact that the crew of Somers's ship numbered (unluckily) thirteen. But on the night of September 4, Somers loaded a ketch with fifteen hundred pounds of powder and a variety of cannonballs and other explosives, and he and his men slipped into Tripoli harbor. About ten o'clock there was a tremendous explosion. When the smoke cleared, the ketch was gone and the *Philadelphia* crew were still prisoners. Although some badly mangled bodies were later recovered, no identifiable trace of Somers was ever found. In recognition of Somers's supreme sacrifice, Congress erected a monument to him at the Washington Navy Yard, and the navy has continually maintained a commissioned ship named after him.

The two subsequent wars—the War of 1812 and the Mexican War—didn't have much impact on the Jersey Shore, although the English blockade of the East Coast and renewed privateer action during the War of 1812 caused some spirited sea battles. This second conflict with the British also resulted in one of the more humorous Jersey Shore war stories. On July 4, 1813, the fishing boat *Yankee* leisurely set sail in Sandy Hook Bay, as if deliberately baiting the British sloop *Eagle*, which was patrolling the waters off the Hook to enforce the blockade. Upon sighting the *Yankee*, which was under the command of "Mad Jack" Percival,

Early War Heroes of the Shore

When the call to arms came during the American Revolution, many Jersey Shore residents selflessly responded. Below are some of those whose actions, while unheralded, were nevertheless heroic.

CAPTAIN ADAM HYLER. Hyler gained fame along the Shore as a daring privateer. He plagued British ships from Sandy Hook to Egg Harbor, leaving more than one flaming vessel in his wake. One of his most renowned exploits occurred in October 1781, when with only one gunboat and two whaleboats under his command he captured five British ships off Sandy Hook—without losing a single one of his own men!

CAPTAIN REUBEN RANDOLPH. The captain of the militia in Manahawkin, Randolph had many harrowing moments. He was once surprised in bed by a local band of Refugees (Americans loyal to England), who took him to a swamp and bound him to a tree. (He somehow managed to escape, though history provides no details.) Later the Refugees again tried to take Randolph prisoner. As they invaded his house and scoured the rooms, Randolph lay hidden in a cask of feathers, and the Refugees went away empty-handed.

REBECCA STILLWELL. While living at Beesley's Point, Stillwell one day spotted a British gunboat anchored offshore. When she saw a longboat full of soldiers rowing toward the beach, she knew that the English were almost certainly after a large shipment of salt and supplies stashed at a nearby store. Although most of the local men had been called away by the war, the patriotic Stillwell proved that the Shore defenses were in good hands. Rushing to a nearby cannon that had been primed and loaded in anticipation of just such an attack, Stillwell aimed the piece and lit the fuse with a burning brand from the fireplace. The shot passed close enough to the longboat to cause the rowers to stop. Then a young boy on shore began blowing a call to arms from an old hunting horn. Suddenly faced with the daunting prospect of a pitched battle, the soldiers in the longboat returned to the ship, which sailed away.

THOMAS LEAMING. A respected lawyer in Cape May County prior to the war, Leaming ultimately became one of the Revolution's most famous privateers. During the years of fighting, he and his men captured about one thousand British sailors.

(continued)

Early War Heroes of the Shore (*continued*)

JOHN GRACE. A Cape May County native, Grace served in the Third New Jersey Battalion and participated in the battles of Brandywine, Monmouth, and Yorktown. One of General Washington's most trusted scouts, he kept for many years a note written by Washington that described him as a man "British gold can not buy."

the *Eagle* came alongside and threatened to open fire if the ship didn't drop anchor. Percival (who, according to Kobbe, was acting like "a half-witted boor") responded brightly: "Dad's big molasses jug is on deck, and if you broke that he'd make you sorry for it!" While the British were still wondering what to make of this non sequitur, Percival nosed the *Yankee* practically up against the bigger ship. Moments later a group of thirty armed men rushed from their hiding places on the *Yankee* and overpowered the *Eagle*'s crew. The triumphant Percival and his men then sailed the captured ship to the Battery in New York, where, according to a newspaper account, it was greeted by "the plaudits and shouts of thousands of spectators, assembled on the Battery to celebrate the anniversary of our independence."

◆

Since no Civil War battles were fought on or near the Jersey Shore, the impact of that bloody conflict was primarily in the terrible toll of human suffering and death that it extracted from families throughout New Jersey, including the coast. The most striking example of this was the macabre lottery of death inflicted on a Cape May captain in the Union army.

Henry Washington Sawyer was a thirty-two-year-old Cape May carpenter when he answered Abraham Lincoln's first call for volunteers in April 1861. By June 9, 1863, he had risen to the rank of captain in Company K, First Calvary Regiment. That day, during a fierce battle at Brandy Station, Virginia, Sawyer was wounded in the thigh and in the right cheek, the bullet passing out of his neck near the spinal column. As Sawyer was reeling from his wounds, his horse was shot out from under him. The captain fell to the ground, sustaining a concussion. When he awoke he was a prisoner. When Sawyer was sufficiently recovered, the Confederates sent him to the infamous Libby Prison in Richmond, Virginia, a former tobacco warehouse where men were packed into rooms like cattle herded into slaughter pens.

On the morning of July 6, 1863, Sawyer and seventy-four other prisoners with the rank of captain were called outside. Whatever the men were expecting—news of parole, or of a prisoner exchange, perhaps—they were stunned to hear that two of them were to be executed in retaliation for the execution of two Confederate officers by Union General Ambrose Burnside, who had caught the Rebels recruiting for the southern cause within federal lines.

With their hearts in their throats, the men watched as each of their names was written on a piece of paper and put into a box, from which the two unfortunates were to be chosen. The first name picked was Sawyer's; the second was that of John M. Flynn (or Flinn) of the Fifty-first Indiana Regiment. A reporter from the *Richmond Dispatch* recorded the scene: "Sawyer heard it with no apparent emotion, remarking that some one had to be drawn, and he could stand it as well as any one else."

There is some indication that the executions were to be carried out immediately but were delayed for ten days due to an unknown reason. However, William Nelson, in his 1902 *The New Jersey Coast in Three Centuries*, reports that the sentence was always intended to be eight days hence (July 14). Either way, it gave both men time to inform their families of their impending fate. Sawyer's letter to his wife is heartrending yet lucid for a man facing imminent death. After remarking that his "prospects look dark" and explaining what was in store for him, Sawyer asked her to come to him, saying: "let me see you once more, and I will die becoming a man and an officer; but, for God's sake, do not disappoint me. Oh! It is hard to leave you thus. Farewell! farewell!! and I hope it is all for the best."

Sawyer and Flynn were then confined to a damp, dark, underground dungeon where the air stank of mildew, and here they waited for death. But they had not reckoned with Sawyer's resourceful wife. Immediately upon receiving her husband's letter she had sped to Washington, D.C., where she procured an audience with President Abraham Lincoln. The compassionate president promised to aid her, and he quickly found the perfect device: two Confederate prisoners were ordered into close confinement, and word was sent to the Confederates that if Sawyer and Flynn were killed, the two Rebels would also be executed. One of the Confederates was the son of Robert E. Lee.

Lincoln's tactic worked. Eight months after they were condemned to die, Sawyer and Flynn were exchanged for the two Confederates whose fate was intertwined with their own. Sawyer went on to a successful career after the war, including serving as a member of the Cape May city council, before dying in 1893. Flynn, however, wasn't so fortunate. Whether it was from the physical hardships suffered while in captivity or the mental anguish of having his life dangling by a thread, Flynn died six months after being released from prison.

During this bloodiest war in the nation's history, work continued on a granite fort begun in 1857 at Sandy Hook. During the Civil War, federal troops were stationed at the partly completed fort, although they were usually outnumbered by the construction crews. But with the close of the war, one thing became shockingly clear: advances in weaponry had made stone forts like that being built at Sandy Hook obsolete. Construction halted in 1868 while the government tried to figure out what to do with its three-quarters-completed, now-useless fort.

Sandy Hook Proving Ground soldiers, circa 1910, pose on a sixteen-caliber gun, reportedly the largest gun ever built up to that time, weighing 284,500 pounds (Photo courtesy Moss Archives, Sea Bright, N.J.)

I'd like to load a gun like this
 With a message and perhaps a kiss
To let you know how proud I am
 That you have backed up Uncle Sam

Patriotic postcard picturing a close-up view of a gun being loaded at Fort Hancock. (Photo courtesy Moss Archives, Sea Bright, N.J.)

Then in 1874 someone had the inspired notion to establish the U.S. Army's first official proving ground at Sandy Hook. A proving ground is a place to test weapons and ordnance ("prove" them), and the Hook's relative isolation made it a perfect choice for the task. The sound of weapons testing began echoing over the peninsula, and it would continue for many years. The weapons would be set up at the north end of the beach and shot into large dunes down the length of the sand, a distance of about four miles. All types of weapons, from Gatling-type machine guns to gigantic cannons, were developed and tested at Sandy Hook.

Then in 1886 came the pivotal event that was to transform the still-lonely stretch of sand into a bustling military complex. A federal panel investigating America's coastal defenses decided that the country was poorly prepared to protect its most important harbors and ports, and it called for an immediate beefing up of these defenses. With the most important port in the world—New York City—just a few miles to the north, Sandy Hook received top priority. Among the components of these new fortifications were high-powered gun and mortar batteries mounted in concrete emplacements, submarine mine fields, rapid-fire guns, floating batteries, and torpedo boats.

Almost all the partly completed fort on Sandy Hook was demolished by 1890 to make way for the new equipment. This advanced
weaponry included the first and only battery in the United States
with disappearing guns. Battery Potter, named after Civil War
General Joseph Potter, had guns that were raised and lowered by
elevators through the roof of the bunker. The Hook also had the
country's first mortar battery. On October 30, 1895, the "installation at Sandy Hook," as it was known, was officially christened
Fort Hancock, after another Civil War General, Winfield Scott
Hancock. (According to Sandy Hook historian Tom Hoffman,
there is no truth to the persistent old story that the installation
was originally named Fort Lincoln.)

Of course, all the soldiers that were now manning these batteries and weapons systems needed places to live, and so construction began on barracks, officers' homes, and support structures
(many of which were built with tin ceilings instead of plaster, so
that the occupants wouldn't get beaned by pieces of plaster
shaken loose by vibrations from the weapons testing). To the
booming roar of big guns being tested on the peninsula were now

*A turret with twin-mounted 14-inch guns that was tested at Sandy Hook
Proving Grounds in 1915, later shipped to a fortification at Manila Harbor. (Photo courtesy Moss Archives, Sea Bright, N.J.)*

added the sounds of hammers pounding and saws hissing, creating a near constant din that blanketed Sandy Hook like a fog.

By the dawn of the new century, Sandy Hook had become the nation's premier military installation. The proving ground (a totally separate entity from the gun batteries; same army, two distinct military operations) was banging away full tilt, the defensive weapons and gun batteries were in place, and the grounds of Fort Hancock were swarming with soldiers, workers, and support personnel. The once-quiet Hook resembled a miniature city.

Despite stories to the contrary, Sandy Hook/Fort Hancock never saw any wartime action. A supposed attack on Fort Hancock by a German U-boat during World War I never occurred. Interestingly enough, however, another persistent legend about a secret tunnel does have some basis in fact. During the 1890s there was an underground room that contained a control panel connected by electrical cables to underwater mines located in New York Harbor. At the touch of a button these mines could be detonated. The so-called secret tunnel, however, was just for the cables and was not a last-ditch escape route for soldiers.

Activity at Sandy Hook increased even more during the two world wars. World War I saw an average of 7,000 soldiers stationed at Sandy Hook, while the average for World War II was 12,000 (peaking at a staggering 18,000 men and women in 1945; it's a wonder Sandy Hook didn't sink from the weight).

Soldiers in formation at Fort Hancock, circa 1902–1906. (Photo courtesy Moss Archives, Sea Bright, N.J.)

But even as more and more military personnel poured onto the Hook, changes were in the offing that would eventually spell the end of its army days. Advances in weaponry soon made Battery Potter, the Dynamite Gun Battery, and other defenses obsolete. As weapons became bigger and more powerful, they quickly outgrew Sandy Hook's limited four-mile firing range, and the proving ground moved to Aberdeen, Maryland, in 1919.

The range and power of the weapons introduced during World War II—including long-range aerial bombers and the atomic bomb—made the idea of protecting harbors with artillery emplacements rather pointless. Although the army maintained its presence on Sandy Hook through the 1950s and 1960s, the installation was a veritable ghost town compared with the boom times during the two world wars. Finally, on August 15, 1974, Sandy Hook's era of protecting the nation's most important harbor formally ended when the army deactivated missile units of the Sixteenth Air Defense Artillery Group at Fort Hancock. The fort officially closed on December 31, 1974.

But we've jumped ahead of ourselves. Let's go back to World War I and one of the greatest controversies in the annals of warfare—one in which the Jersey Shore may well have played a part.

◆

The sinking of the British passenger liner *Lusitania* on May 7, 1915, by a German U-boat off the Irish coast killed nearly twelve hundred people and was one of the reasons for the United States's eventual entry into World War I. But did the message to attack the ship come from a mammoth, 820-foot radio tower in Tuckerton? Today, over thirty-five years since the tower was destroyed, three colossal concrete blocks and a blockhouse—the remains of the Tuckerton Tower—stand in mute testimony to suspicions that will not die.

The Tuckerton Tower was the brainchild of Dr. Rudolph Goldschmidt, a brilliant German scientist who advanced the principles of wireless communication past those established even by Marconi. Goldschmidt conceived the idea of a transoceanic wireless and built one station at Eilvese, Germany. The other station he situated on Hickory (now Mystic) Island on the Jersey Shore, three miles south of the small community of Tuckerton.

The Tuckerton Tower, from which it was rumored a message was sent to a German submarine with orders to sink the Lusitania. *(Photo courtesy Tuckerton Historical Society's Giffordtown School Museum)*

Hickory Island was an ideal spot for the gigantic radio tower. The firm, level ground offered an unobstructed view of the broad Atlantic. The tower's location was extremely desolate; only a crude two-lane dirt road led to the site.

According to an interview over a decade ago with Tuckerton resident Charles Beulow, who helped build the tower as a seventeen-year-old boy, Hickory Island was chosen because the weather conditions were too severe in the north and there was too much static in the south. Beulow also revealed the fascinating bit of information that the tower almost *wasn't* built on the island. He claimed that a site in Manahawkin had already been chosen, but then Goldschmidt changed his mind and picked Hickory Island because of its isolation.

On May 21, 1912, work crews began building the Tuckerton Tower. Everything was built, assembled, and tested in Germany, then dismantled and shipped to the United States. Each section of the tower was as long as the flatcar that carried it by rail from New York to the Tuckerton railroad station, from where it was trucked to the construction site. Although many local residents worked at the site, the construction bosses and engineers were Germans.

When completed on March 31, 1914, the tower was truly one of the wonders of the world. It was 20 feet wide and rose to an incredible height of 820 feet, making it at the time the second-tallest structure ever built. Cable junctions were spaced every 250 feet; four cables on each of the tower's three sides were connected to three 1,100-ton concrete blocks set on the ground approximately 600 feet from the base of the structure. At the very top was a 60-foot-high wooden pole to which the antenna was attached. The tower maintained a staggering 500,000 volts—the highest voltage of any radio tower in the world.

Incredible as it may seem, the U.S. government was totally unaware that this massive communications device was being constructed on American soil by a country whose increasing belligerency was causing grave international concern. The first official blink of recognition came in May 1913—over one year after construction had begun—when the U.S. Navy was asked to inspect the operation. Government bureaucracy being what it is, it took another year for the navy to inspect the tower, which was then cleared for broadcast and given the station call letters WGG.

Blissfully unaware of the awesome new power of German communications, the world received a rude awakening on July 28, 1914, when World War I began. Suddenly an age that still used the letter as the primary form of communication realized that Germany, which was now engaged in a naked grab for power and territory, could send messages hurtling across the vast Atlantic Ocean at astounding speed. It was a sobering thought.

Almost immediately the Tuckerton Tower came under sharp scrutiny. Both England and France protested to the United States that the tower was communicating with German ships at sea, which would be a violation of international neutrality agreements. President Woodrow Wilson, having declared the United States neutral in the conflict, was facing a dilemma; he wanted to shut Tuckerton down because of the alleged violations, but the station was the only American radio link to Germany, and Wilson felt that communication with the various warring powers was a key ingredient in stopping the war. So the president let the tower remain operational. Shortly thereafter, the Germans who ran the tower made things easier for him by communicating with their cruisers *Dresden* and *Karlsruhe* in the North Atlantic. In response, Wilson sent a U.S. naval censorship team to oversee operations at the Tuckerton Tower.

But the censorship procedures were apparently lax. Naval censors first approved messages to be sent, then listened to their transmission; German personnel were reportedly still allowed to receive messages. While it's true that with naval authorities listening, an outwardly nonneutral message could not be sent or received, it's probable that messages with disguised, seemingly harmless meanings could have gone to and from Tuckerton. Britain and France seemed to think something was funny as well; they continued to protest that the Germans were using the Tuckerton Tower for military purposes.

There is further evidence that American censorship was not as firm as it may have seemed. The October 3, 1914, edition of *The Pathfinder* newspaper talked about problems the government was having with radio stations linked to foreign governments: "the Washington authorities let the stations operate, but under government censors, who were to see that strict neutrality was preserved. A botch was made of this plan. The censor at Siasconset [a Massachusetts station with ties to England] loafed on the job and allowed the British to transmit some messages to their ships, thus violating the neutrality rule."

With American censorship seemingly as tough as wet tissue paper, the stage was set for the events of May 7, 1915. The British passenger liner *Lusitania* was just off the Old Head of Kinsale on the southwest coast of Ireland when a long, cylindrical shape sped through the water toward it. A few moments later the torpedo, fired by the German submarine U-20, struck the ship. In just eighteen minutes the mighty liner went down, sending 1,198 people to their death.

It is one of the tenacious legends of history that U-20 commander Walther Schwieger received the terse message "Get Lucy"— an order to attack the *Lusitania*—and that this order came from the Tuckerton Tower. There is no documented evidence that Schwieger ever received such a command; no such message is listed in his meticulously kept war diary. However, since the tower was under censorship at the time, it is unlikely that so obvious a message could ever have been sent. But another message, seemingly harmless, is well within the realm of possibility. Government records prove that although censors at Tuckerton attempted to weed out nonneutral messages, some slipped through. And the attack on the liner was certainly no accident. Germany had marked the *Lusitania* for destruction and took out newspaper advertisements warning against sailing on the ship. If such a message was sent to a U-boat far out at sea, the Tuckerton Tower was one of the few places that could have done it.

The U.S. government ordered an investigation into just that possibility shortly after the *Lusitania* went down. The results were inconclusive; the government has never confirmed or denied the "Get Lucy" report.

The Tuckerton Tower continued to be a trouble spot until the United States entered World War I on April 6, 1917. The U.S. military immediately took over the tower and ran it for the duration of the war. Thereafter it was operated by RCA and then the military again during World War II.

On December 28, 1955, having outlived its usefulness and with Mystic Island set for residential development, the Tuckerton Tower was demolished. Cut up for scrap, the giant structure yielded eight hundred tons of steel.

Today once-deserted Mystic Island is teeming with houses, and it's hard to imagine that the world's second-tallest structure was ever there. But still remaining (probably until the end of time, for they are over twenty feet tall and are sunk at least twenty feet into the ground) are the massive concrete blocks that were the tower's anchors. Like the questions that just won't go away, these giant blocks are perpetual reminders of the curious case of the Tuckerton Tower.

The word *curious* might also be used for another World War I artifact at the Jersey Shore—the concrete ship *Atlantus*, now slowly sinking into the sandy seabed a few hundred yards off the Cape May Point shoreline, at the foot of Sunset Boulevard.

Of course, it's not too surprising that a ship made of concrete would sink in the first place; after all, when was the last time anyone saw a piece of concrete floating lightly along the surface of the water? But during World War I, concrete ships were considered to be the ideal solution to a growing steel shortage. Ships built with a steel frame overlaid with concrete needed only one-third as much metal as regular ships. The U.S. government eagerly endorsed the project and commissioned forty-three concrete ships to be built at five different shipyards throughout the country.

But by the time the 250-foot *Atlantus* slid into the water, on April 20, 1918, the war was winding down, and the idea of concrete ships was fast losing its appeal. Only a dozen ships were launched before the project was canceled in 1921. The *Atlantus* was towed to Norfolk, Virginia, where it was left to die in a graveyard for ships aptly named Pig Point.

But then along came Colonel Jesse Rosenfeld of Baltimore, a friend of Theodore Roosevelt and a man with big dreams. He announced a plan to establish ferry service between Cape May Point and Lewes, Delaware. To help build the ferry dock on the New Jersey side, Rosenfeld's group—The National Navigation Company—bought the *Atlantus* and brought it to Cape May Point in June 1926. The idea was to sink three concrete ships in the shape of a Y to form the base of the dock.

What happened next is still a matter of dispute in Cape May. Some longtime residents claim the *Atlantus* broke loose from its moorings in a storm and sank; others say the ship was deliberately sunk as the first step in the ferry project. Either way, the *Atlantus* hit bottom sometime in late June or in July of 1926, and there it remained—for good. No amount of equipment, human labor, or divine inspiration, could move it.

National Navigation soon went broke, its scheme for ferry service between Cape May Point and Lewes destined not to be realized for another thirty-eight years. Today the *Atlantus* has been designated a historic site by the state of New Jersey. With each successive year the now-decrepit ship sinks a little deeper into the sand.

◆

Far removed from the amusing incongruity of a concrete ship was the deadly seriousness of the Second World War. These years were nervous times at the Jersey Shore; German submarines prowled the East Coast, attacking ships with impunity, making every skipper feel that the next voyage could well be the last. Often the morning's light would reveal a beach covered not with clamshells and seaweed but with burnt wood, pools of fuel, and twisted metal—the grim debris of a ship that had been attacked and sunk during the evening. Shore residents wondered if the next footsteps they heard would be those of invading German soldiers.

To counteract the threat of invasion from the sea, the U.S. Coast Guard established patrols along the beach. At first the effectiveness of these patrols was questionable, since they consisted of one man armed merely with a flare. As the official Coast Guard publication *The Beach Patrol and Corsair Fleet* puts it, "There is no doubt . . . that the work of the beach patrol was not taken seriously."

Then, in June 1942, a lone Coast Guardsman surprised a group of Nazi agents who had just landed from a U-boat on the beach near Armagansett, Long Island. Needless to say, the beach patrols suddenly received a much higher priority. Besides giving the patrollers weapons, the Coast Guard also gave them dogs. The first dog patrols began at Brigantine in August 1942. They were soon instituted up and down the East Coast.

One month later, in September 1942, horses were authorized for use by the beach patrollers. As a young sixth-grader vacationing in Seaside Park in 1942, Watchung resident Jean Thompson Weiler vividly remembers the sight of these friendly night riders galloping over the sand.

"You'd walk up to the beach and everything would be pitch black [because of wartime blackout regulations]. All of a sudden, in the distance, you'd hear hoofbeats. It was really a very creepy thing the first time [you heard it]." She added that the most frightening thing about the experience was hearing the hoofbeats before seeing the riders. "Suddenly, [the riders would] be there," she said. "It was scary. You had no idea what was going on."

For young Weiler, war and its unpleasant necessities changed what had always been a warm, comforting place to vacation into one of mystery and danger. Even a formerly harmless pastime such as swimming was changed by the war; Weiler remembers having to use a strong solvent (possibly kerosene) to remove tar and oil from her feet before going into her house after swimming.

World War II also changed the physical appearance of the Jersey Shore. From the ocean the usually bright, cheery boardwalks looked like ghost towns as blackout curtains cut off (or at least reduced) as much light as possible from the concession stands. The normally gay Atlantic City Boardwalk became a virtual military institution. An estimated 250,000 soldiers trained on the beach, marched on the Boardwalk, and lived in dozens of the city's hotels. The Chalfonte-Haddon Hall, which is today Merv Griffin's Resorts Casinos Hotel, was a 4,000-bed hospital.

To meet the menace from the ocean, lookout towers began springing up along the Shore. These towers may have been fine for scanning the sea for enemy submarines, but they were none too pleasant as places to pass the time. In a 1990 interview in the *Hudson Lantern Dispatch*, a former Coast Guardsman recalled his time in the Avalon tower: "We had no power and to keep warm you had to pull coal up from below in a bucket on a string to feed the coal furnace. The most modern thing at Avalon was a big batch of kitchen matches and a candle. Once you lit the candle and made your log entry, you had to put the candle out because of the blackout on during the war."

♦

Quite recently, a new chapter began to unfold in the saga of war at the Jersey Shore. This one is a mysterious tale whose ending might not be resolved for some time to come. But as any good fiction writer will tell you, the best mysteries are those that keep you guessing until the final page.

On Labor Day, 1991, professional diver John Chatterton of Millburn was diving off the boat *The Seeker* about sixty miles off

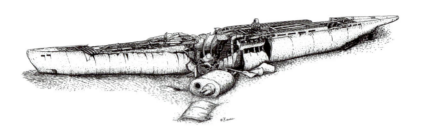

Artist's rendering of the unknown U-boat discovered recently off the coast of Point Pleasant Beach. (Illustration © Captain Dan Crowell)

Point Pleasant Beach. At a depth of 230 feet, he saw something lying on the bottom: "I saw the air cylinders on top, and my [initial] assumption was that it was some type of fuel barge or pipe barge," said Chatterton, a veteran diver who has explored numerous sunken ships, including the *Andrea Doria*. "Then I saw a hatch, looked inside, and saw a torpedo. As soon as I saw a torpedo I knew it was a sub."

Because of poor visibility at that depth, Chatterton at first had no idea whose sub it had been. Later, when the group on board *The Seeker* researched the find, they theorized that it could be a German submarine identified as the U-550. But they soon realized that the 550 had been documented as sinking one hundred miles farther out to sea. American records, which are quite specific, did not indicate a sunken sub of any type near the site of the wreck. So the mystery grew.

Three weeks later, on September 29, Chatterton went back to the wreck. This time he brought to the surface some china—which was, remarkably, unbroken—with the Nazi insignia clearly imprinted on the back. There was no longer any doubt about the nationality of the submarine. A little further research revealed that the 230-foot sub was probably a Type 9, which was the German long-distance boat. Chatterton and his fellow divers had found the first Nazi submarine ever to be discovered off the coast of New Jersey.

But the solving of one mystery only deepened another. What in the world was this submarine doing so close to the New Jersey coast, in defiance of all naval records? And which submarine was it?

"This sub," said Chatterton simply, "is not supposed to be there."

The questions nagged Chatterton like a toothache. Feeling that he just had to find out, he began a personal odyssey that took him to Chicago, to the U.S. Navy in Washington, D.C., and even to Germany, where he met with the curator of the U-Boat Archives. But no matter where he went, no matter how voluminous or detailed the data he studied, the answer was always the same: there is no record of a Nazi submarine going down sixty miles off Point Pleasant Beach, New Jersey. It was as if the mystery sub had never existed.

The boat shows a massive amount of damage. The crew's quarters are crushed as if they were made of cardboard. The top is peeled away like a banana skin. Debris from the sub litters the seafloor around the wreck.

But the great amount of damage may be a clue to the sub's fate. From his research and his experience with other sunken submarines, Chatterton doesn't think a depth charge sank it, because the damage is so severe. The more likely candidate, he feels, is a torpedo. What may well have happened is that the mystery sub either launched a torpedo that circled around and came back to hit it, or it might have been struck by another submarine's torpedo.

During his search for the sub's identity, Chatterton began corresponding with Karl-Friedrich Merten, a former German submarine captain. Now in his eighties and wracked with cancer, Merten feels strongly that Chatterton has found the wreck of a Nazi sub known as the U-851, which has been listed as missing all these years after having gone down—in the Indian Ocean!

It's a long way from the Indian Ocean to New Jersey, but the scenario, as developed by Chatterton and Merten, is credible. The commander of the U-851, a friend of Merten's named Weingartner, was a gung ho captain who wanted to see action during the war. His dreams were apparently dashed when he was given command of the U-851, which had the distinctly noncombat mission of taking supplies from Norway to the Japanese in the Indian Ocean.

But Weingartner might have seen a way to turn his routine delivery run into glory. The U-851 had a range of thirty-one thousand miles. Both Merten and Chatterton believe that the anxious captain, instead of just following the European coast on his way to the Indian Ocean, took advantage of his submarine's great range to make a very, very wide sweep into the Atlantic—a sweep that took him into the New York City shipping lanes. Here the sub could taste combat by quickly attacking a ship or two, then head back for deeper water and resume course for the Indian Ocean. Something, however, went terribly wrong, and the U-851 was never heard from again.

There is one strong piece of evidence to back up this hypothesis. The last time the U-851 was in contact with its home base, the sub was one hundred miles west of where it was supposed to be— a course that placed it heading straight for New York City. The Indian Ocean is listed as the place where the 851 sank only because that's where the sub was supposed to go. There apparently is no physical evidence that it did.

Is this mysterious submarine for which no records exist the long-lost U-851? Has Karl-Friedrich Merten at last found the final resting place of his friend and fellow commander? John Chatterton wants desperately to find out, to put Merten's mind at rest and also to correct a gross inaccuracy that has existed for nearly a half-century.

"The page of history that has [the U-851] on it has got to be rewritten," Chatterton said. "It's incorrect."

Rewriting history is a difficult task; often the past is like a mule: stubborn, unreasonable, and refusing to yield to logic and human effort. But if Chatterton can accomplish his goal, he will have added yet another chapter to the continuing saga of war at the Jersey Shore.

CHAPTER

TEN

SCIENCE AND
INVENTION

〰〰〰〰〰〰〰〰〰〰〰〰〰〰〰〰〰〰〰

Ever since a man named Edison opened shop at Menlo Park
and began creating things that both astounded and changed
the world, New Jersey has been fertile ground for those inquisi-
tive men and women who have a vision and won't rest until
it is brought out of the mind's shadows and into the sunlight of
reality.

Not surprisingly, the Jersey Shore has had its share of intrepid
inventors and scientists. However, because their accomplishments
have been largely obscured by the Shore's overpowering reputation as a place of sun and fun, these pioneers have remained essentially unknown to all but a few scientists and historians.

Just why people don't consider the Shore as a place where inventive minds flourish is puzzling. Up to the early part of the
twentieth century, the isolated, almost primitive nature of the
Shore meant that people there had to live by their wits and hard
work, the two ingredients supposedly necessary for invention. Indeed, it can be argued that the builders who invented some of the

Shore boats—the sneakbox, garvey, Sea Bright Skiff, and A-Cat come to mind—changed not only the Shore but also the world, since many of these boats seem to be plying faraway waters.

Like those long-ago boatbuilders, others have found the Jersey Shore to be the ideal place to test a theory, turn amorphous visions into hard reality, or even revolutionize the world. The names of some of these people are familiar today, while others have unfortunately slipped between the pages of history. What links them together forever is the Jersey Shore.

◆

Slipping between the pages of history is exactly what has happened to Simon Lake. He may well be the Shore's greatest yet most obscure inventor.

Lake was born on September 4, 1866, in Pleasantville, New Jersey, to one of the Shore's most prominent families (his grandfather and uncles founded Ocean City). It would be hard to find another clan as relentlessly creative as the Lakes; invention was in their genes, something to be passed down from generation to generation as other families pass down red hair or blue eyes.

Simon's great-uncle Jesse was credited with a number of inventions, including a whistling buoy, the first calculating weighing scale, and a mowing machine in which the blade could be raised or lowered. Altogether Jesse held close to sixty-five patents, and at the time of his death he was working on yet another new idea: a method of obtaining aluminum from the mud in local meadows.

Ezra Lake, Simon's uncle, invented an improved roller for window shades and subsequently manufactured window shade rollers with Simon's father, John Christopher Lake. As with Jesse, death interrupted Ezra in the midst of a new invention: a ball bearing that needed no oil.

Ezra also invented something called a "sea wagon" that could roll out into the surf and rescue people who were trapped on a stranded ship. An intriguing description of this unique device can be found in the January 2, 1885, issue of *Star of the Cape*, a Cape May County newspaper:

> We were much interested a few days since in learning from Mr. E. B. Lake, Superintendent of Ocean City Association, and inventor and patentee of Lake's Sea Wagon, some additional par-

ticulars of its construction, its possibilities, and results of and impressions from the recent trial trip through the surf. To the inventor himself this trial was perfectly satisfactory, demonstrating the fact that the machine will do all that is expected and desired of it. By this test all weaknesses and defects were made manifest, which are being promptly remedied. The wagon wheels will not bury in the sand, as some feared. It can be run out to a wreck when a boat cannot be launched, and the higher the sea the more quickly it will work its way out. It can be controlled by steering gear, and can be run backwards or forwards by simply changing the gearing by the man in the top. At a wreck, ladders may be run down, not up, to the vessel's deck, long enough to allow for the heavy roll of the ship by the heavy seas, the sea wagon remaining perfectly at rest as the sea sweeps through its skeleton form. The box will be made to seat fifteen or twenty persons, and Mr. Lake says he intends to make it a pleasuring craft, at which the most timid will be able to spend hours of recreation at sea in perfect security.

With all this enterprising spirit raging through his blood, it's little wonder that young Simon Lake displayed his inventive talents early. An antisocial child, he found his true friends in tools and books. When he was ten, he built himself a watch using spare parts he found on his father's workbench. (Unfortunately, because of a wrong-size balance wheel, the watch ran only when laid on its back.) He was better served by his passion for a Jules Verne novel, *Twenty Thousand Leagues under the Sea*. Its theme of submarine travel was to influence the course of Simon's life.

At the tender age of twenty, when most of his contemporaries were engaged in the usual frivolous pursuits of youth, Simon invented a single-screw steering gear for bicycles. He quickly followed this with a means of transmitting motion from one shaft to another. He applied this to a steering gear, then made several modifications so that the part could be made very cheaply. He then moved with his father to Baltimore, where in short order he invented (with assistance from his father) an improved winder for oyster dredging vessels on Chesapeake Bay and a machine that soldered the lids on tin cans of fruit, thus greatly improving the efficiency of canning. (The latter invention worked too well. Because the machine could solder fifty thousand cans per day, the local cappers' union threatened to strike if any company began using it.)

In 1893 a series of events began that would both define and haunt the remainder of Simon Lake's life. The U.S. Navy wanted to develop a submarine that would launch torpedoes, and it put out a general call for designs. Lake, his imagination fired by Captain Nemo's *Nautilus*, began work on a craft similar to that of Verne's troubled captain.

On June 3, 1893, Lake submitted his design for a submarine torpedo boat. It had a double hull, a folding periscope, folding wheels for traveling along the ocean floor, and, in true *Nautilus* fashion, an air lock in the bow. Divers would enter the air lock through a heavy door that closed on rubber packing to ensure that the main quarters of the vessel would remain airtight. The divers would then open a valve to admit compressed air into the diving compartment. When the air pressure in the compartment equaled the water pressure outside, the door in the bottom of the sub could be opened and water would not flood the vessel. From this vantage point Lake could observe the underwater world, watching fish swim silently by as he ruminated on the peace and serenity he found below the surface.

Possibly the most ingenious aspect of the craft was how it kept on an even keel. Lake accomplished this via horizontal rudders at both the bow and the stern, as well as through controlled, movable weights that compensated for the crew's movement fore or aft. Large side fins also contributed to the stability of the vessel.

All this was innovative for the 1890s, and for a man like Lake, who had little if any practical boat-building experience, it was quite remarkable. The navy formed a board to judge the various designs that had been submitted, and four out of the five members thought Lake's plan feasible. Unfortunately, because it was just a design, the submarine contract went to the Holland Torpedo Boat Company of Paterson, New Jersey, which had offered actually to build a vessel. (Building it and making it work turned out to be two very different things. Holland's vessel, a steam-driven craft called *Plunger*, was spectacularly unsuccessful and was finally abandoned in 1900. Reportedly the only time it had submerged was when it accidentally sank at the dock.)

Undaunted by the navy's rejection, Lake journeyed to New York City in 1894 and tried to raise the capital necessary to build a small submarine. According to the *Genealogy of the Lake Family* by Arthur Adams and Sarah A. Risley, a privately printed vol-

Simon Lake (in sub) and his cousin Bart with Lake's first submarine, the Argonaut Jr. *(Photo courtesy Submarine Force Library and Museum, Groton, Conn.)*

ume published in 1915, Lake's encounters with prospective investors would usually go something like this: "Often in describing his vessel, when Mr. Lake told how a door could be opened and no water enter the vessel, a look of terror came into the eyes of the financier, who would reach out and press a button, whereupon his clerk would call his attention to an important engagement, thus terminating the interview."

Investors, of course, are notoriously conservative, and the visionary aspects of Lake's idea probably struck them as the sheerest form of lunacy. Finally, after six months, Lake grew weary of the terrified stares and withdrew to Atlantic Highlands, where he found a much more receptive audience at the home of Anna M. Champion, his aunt. She and her husband supplied the funds necessary for the young inventor to build the *Argonaut Jr.*, a wedge-shaped craft of yellow pine that was fourteen feet long and five feet deep. The little sub had three hand-cranked wheels, a soda fountain tank for storing compressed air, and a plumber's hand pump for discharging water ballast. Power was provided by a hand-turned propeller crank. By the summer of 1895 *Argonaut Jr.* was ready to take the big plunge. Assisted by his cousin Bart Champion, Lake took the tiny submarine into the nearby Shrewsbury River.

The results were spectacular. *Argonaut Jr.* passed its maiden voyage with flying colors. The only mishap occurred when the vessel first submerged, a bolt hole that Simon had forgotten to plug began spewing water. Coolly Lake plugged the hole with a stray piece of wood.

Throughout the remainder of that summer, Lake and Champion put the *Argonaut Jr.* through its paces. It must have been a curious sight for the local populace to see the small craft cutting through the bustling Shrewsbury River, which was filled with steamboats, cargo ships, and numerous other vessels, then suddenly disappearing beneath the surface.

One of the most wondrous aspects of Lake's submarine was that, through the open door of the air lock, it was possible to reach out and spear a fish or pluck an oyster off the river bottom.

Simon Lake's Argonaut Jr. *years after its historic voyages. (Photo courtesy Submarine Force Library and Museum, Groton, Conn.)*

Once, when viewing a demonstration of Lake's invention, local officials wrote their names on a wooden shingle and threw it into the water. Down went the *Argonaut Jr.*; soon it returned, along with the shingle. Lake even built a diving helmet so that, with the help of weights on his arms and legs, he could roam through the water himself, getting a firsthand look at a world of boundless mystery and delight.

The tiny sub's success caused investors to stop being terrified and start regarding the young New Jerseyan much more seriously. Lake soon raised enough money to form the Lake Submarine Company. From it emerged, in 1897, the *Argonaut*. This cigar-shaped submarine, propelled by a thirty-horsepower gasoline engine, was thirty-six feet long, had tubes that projected above the surface to take in fresh air and release exhaust, and could roll about on folding wheels.

The *Argonaut* was successfully run hundreds of miles on the bottom of both the Chesapeake Bay and the Atlantic Ocean, and in all types of weather. Word of its amazing abilities traveled all over the world. In what must have been a singular thrill for Lake, he received a congratulatory telegram from Jules Verne, whose tale of submarine travel had stirred his soul so many years ago. The *Argonaut*'s "conspicuous success," Verne said, would "push on underwater navigation all over the world." Proving himself a prophet, Verne also said that "the next great war may be largely a contest between submarine boats."

Lake continued to modify his invention. To improve its handling he added a free-flooding superstructure of light plating over the conning tower and decks, creating an enlarged bridge that extended the length of the hull. This helped the vessel cut through the water easier when surface cruising and set a precedent for submarines to come.

Surprisingly, the U.S. Navy did not beat a path to Simon Lake's door on hearing of the *Argonaut*'s success. This was probably because rival submarinemaker John Holland had also been busy producing the USS *Holland*. Although it had no periscope—forcing it to rise to the surface when sighting a target—Holland's vessel did have a fifty-horsepower engine and was the first to employ the dual-propulsion system characteristic of submarines built during the next fifty years, in which a gasoline engine powered the sub on the surface and a steam engine propelled it during submersion.

The Submarine Firsts of Simon Lake

Given Simon Lake's prodigious genius, it is not surprising that the inventor recorded many firsts in his drive to perfect the submarine. Several are mentioned in the chapter; others are listed below.

The *Argonaut*'s thirty-horsepower engine was the first gasoline engine ever installed on a submarine.

In 1898, on returning from a trial run in the Chesapeake Bay, the *Argonaut* became the first submarine to operate successfully in an ocean (the Atlantic).

During an *Argonaut* voyage in 1899, Lake became the first American to take underwater photographs, which were later published in *McClure's Magazine*. (Lake almost became the first ever to take underwater photos; that first was recorded only two years earlier by a French diving scientist named Louis Boutan.)

Lake's *Protector* was the first submarine to have a practical periscope (which Lake called an "omniscope") and to have a small gun mounted on its foredeck.

In 1904 Russia ordered several of Lake's *Protector*-style submarines. One, the *Gray Mullet* (renamed the *Kefal* by the Russian navy) became the first submarine to navigate under ice when it remained submerged for one hour and thirty-two minutes in ice-choked Ussuriy Bay, near Vladivostok.

Yet the naval powers-that-be had not forgotten Simon Lake. Around the turn of the century he was asked by the navy to submit plans again for a submarine torpedo boat. This he did on June 20, 1901. But even though Lake was congratulated on the superiority of his plans, the congressional appropriation for submarines called for the navy to use "Holland boats exclusively." The Naval Board of Construction told Lake that because Congress had specified Holland boats, Holland boats it would have to be. The inventor was again turned down.

But this time there was a glimmer of hope. The board suggested to Lake that if he could build a submarine that worked as well as the plans seemed to indicate it would, they would recommend its purchase. Acting on this advice, Lake in 1901 built the

Protector. This craft was seventy feet long and had a dual-propulsion system, three torpedo tubes, and a cannon. The boat worked splendidly, and a recommendation was sent to Congress to buy five of these vessels. The purchase authorization passed the Senate but was defeated in the House of Representatives. Although there are indications that politics triumphed over common sense in the defeat of the bill, the bottom line for Lake was the same: rejection.

Eventually, the *Protector* was bought by Russia. Lake moved to St. Petersburg and built more submarines for the Russians. His fame spread; soon Austria became a client, and both Germany and Italy sought Lake for consultation. However, eager for recognition from his own country, he returned to the United States in 1910. He built a shipyard in Bridgeport, Connecticut, where he eventually realized his dream of building submarines for the U.S. Navy.

But by then history had passed Simon Lake by. John Holland had become widely recognized as the father of the modern submarine, and Lake's numerous contributions to submarine development were largely ignored.

Lake lived until June 23, 1945, long enough to see the terrible destruction wrought by submarines during both world wars. Ironically, Lake always felt that the submarine, with its powerful capacity to destroy, would ensure peace among nations simply through its intimidating presence. He would much rather have put his submarines to use salvaging sunken cargo and offering breathtaking views of the ocean floor. But fate denied him his proper place in history, and humanity perverted his dream for the submarine, leaving Simon Lake as merely one of the Jersey Shore's greatest forgotten inventors.

◆

Unlike Simon Lake, Joseph Francis never had to search for recognition in his native country. He received accolades from around the globe, including the Congressional Medal of Honor in 1890, when Francis was living in Toms River. But, like Simon Lake, Francis is largely forgotten today.

Born in Boston on March 12, 1801, Joseph Francis showed the promise of his future career when, at the age of eleven, he built a rowboat with cork in either end, making the vessel unsinkable. A few years later, an uncle who was in the boat-building business gave Francis some space in his factory where the young inventor could pursue his ideas and visions. It was here that Francis built a fast rowboat that incorporated the unsinkable design he had produced earlier. This boat was exhibited at the 1819 Fair of the Mechanics' Institute, earning Francis an "honorable recognition." The young man was on his way.

Throughout the course of his long life (he died at age ninety-two) Francis continued to improve boats and lifesaving vessels. Included among these inventions were a boat, built in sections, that could be taken apart and transported; a reversed-bottom lifeboat (on each side the bilge was laid below the keel line, providing greater stability); and a boat planked with thick strips of one-inch-square cedar that required no caulking.

Although there is uncertainty about the exact year (either 1825 or 1837), Francis realized early on that to be truly successful he would have to become more visible, and the most visible place in the country was New York City. Setting up shop there, he built a wooden lifeboat with cork in its bow and stern, air chambers along the sides and under the thwarts, and a perforated bottom. Proving that his desire to attract more attention to his work wasn't just idle talk, he took his new boat to the foot of Wall Street and cast it, bottom up, into the river. The vessel quickly righted itself as water drained through the sieve-like bottom. A few more public demonstrations of this sort ensued, including one in which the boat was filled with men who tried mightily to capsize it. They failed; the boat remained upright and incredibly buoyant. By 1841 most of the vessels sailing out of New York Harbor were equipped with Francis's "unsinkable" lifeboats.

Given Francis's keen interest in lifeboats, it's not surprising that the enterprising Bostonian soon turned his attention to the problem of rescuing shipwreck victims. Today it can scarcely be comprehended how serious a problem this was in the early nineteenth century, but in an age without any type of floatable device or organized system for aiding ships in distress, a shipwreck was often a death sentence for those on board. Countless men, women, and children were swept away by the churning sea, sometimes with land so tantalizingly close they could see their would-be rescuers standing helplessly on the shore.

Then in 1848, thanks to the efforts of Dr. William Newell, a congressional representative from New Jersey, eight lifesaving stations were built along the Jersey coast. Volunteers would run to the station at the first sight of a shipwreck and haul out the rescue equipment. The main piece of lifesaving apparatus was a surf boat (nearly identical to a Sea Bright Skiff, which is similar to a lifeguard boat). But if the ocean was too rough to launch the boat from the beach, the people on board the stranded ship were still no closer to being saved.

Francis set out to rectify this situation. He first attempted to build a covered wooden boat that could run between ship and shore on a hawser line. But wood proved too fragile against Nature's wrath; during a test in the type of heavy seas that would cause a shipwreck, the boat broke apart. Finally, after many experiments, Francis hit on the idea of a corrugated metal boat as a relatively light yet sturdy vessel that would be able to survive storm-swept seas.

This success led to Francis's most important invention, and the one that ranks him among the top Jersey Shore inventors of all time: the life-car. When seen today, the walnut-shaped life-car is commonly thought to be a submarine because of its tight construction and lack of any openings save the top hatch. But the car, built of corrugated metal, was designed to travel along the surface of the water via a rope and pulley system, much as a flag is raised up and down a flagpole. The lifesaving crew would send the car out to the ship in distress. Once there, five or six people would squeeze inside the small vessel and the hatch would be secured, forming an airtight, watertight seal. Then the rescuers would pull the craft back to the safety of the shore.

Francis's test results with the life-car were so impressive that it was included as part of the equipment at each of the eight original lifesaving stations, even though it had never been tested by an actual shipwreck. But when it saved two hundred people from the British emigrant ship *Ayrshire* on January 12–13, 1850, no one could doubt the life-car any longer. (This episode is described in chapter 11.)

An article from an 1851 edition of *Harper's Magazine* gives some insight into the claustrophobic conditions inside a life-car: "The Life-*Car* is a sort of boat, formed of copper or iron, and closed over, above, by a convex deck with a sort of door or hatchway through it. . . . To be shut up in this manner in so dark and gloomy a receptacle, for the purpose of being drawn, perhaps at midnight, through a surf of such terrific violence that no boat can live in it, can not be a very agreeable alternative; but the emergencies in which the use of the life-car is called for, are such as do not admit of hesitation or delay. There is no light within the car, and there are no openings for the admission of air. [When the hatch was closed, the air inside lasted fifteen minutes.] It is subject, too, in its passage to the shore, to the most frightful shocks and concussions from the force of the breakers."

While riding in a life-car may not have been a Sunday drive in the country, the alternative—drowning—was much more disagreeable. The success of the life-car with the *Ayrshire* and subsequent wrecks cemented Francis's reputation. His fame now secured, Francis went on to a long and glorious career as one of America's most ingenious men. His clientele included the rich and powerful throughout the world. Rulers from across the globe ordered iron barges from his New York factory, and Russia ordered a fleet of corrugated iron steamers and floating docks for use in the Aral Sea.

In 1868 Francis was drawn back to the area that his life-car had done so much for; he built a Victorian mansion in Toms River. The elegant building, which stood on a cliff overlooking the Toms River, later became the Riverview Hotel. (On Christmas night 1964, the structure burned to the ground.)

It was while he was living in Toms River that he built, in 1878, a circular yacht, the only one of its kind in the world. Measuring twelve feet long, twelve feet in the beam, and sixteen inches deep, the boat was sloop-rigged and could accommodate ten people. Francis, who used a tea saucer as his model, believed that the new form advanced the theory that a vessel would move faster if it was broad and flat, thereby floating on the surface rather than cutting through it.

Among the many honors that Francis received during his long career were gold medals from King Ferdinand III of Sicily and entrance into the Royal Order of Knighthood of St. Stanislaus, granted by the tsar of Russia. Going the Russians one better, not only did Napoleon III of France also make Francis a knight, he presented the American inventor with a gold snuffbox studded with eighty-six diamonds, each set in blue enamel. One year before he died, in April 1892, the ninety-one-year-old inventor received a singular tribute when he was introduced to the U.S. Senate by unanimous consent of that body.

But possibly the honor that meant the most to Francis occurred on April 12, 1890, when he was awarded the Congressional Medal of Honor in the Blue Room at the White House in Washington, D.C. Francis wrote about the ceremony in a letter to Captain Thomas Bond on April 21, 1890, his delight clearly evident: "Then he [President Benjamin Harrison] made an elegant address. . . . It was an honor never before done by the President of the United States to himself carry out such an ovation equal to any given to the nobles and Royalty of Europe."

The inscription on the six thousand dollar medal (the most expensive ever bestowed by Congress at that time) was an apt tribute to a remarkable man: "To Joseph Francis, the inventor and father of the means for life saving service to the country."

To that, a simple thank-you would undoubtedly have been added by the countless thousands whose lives were saved because of Joseph Francis and his little walnut-shaped life-car.

◆

Before leaving the realm of submarines and boats, we would be remiss if we did not mention the Swain family of Cape May County. In 1811 Jacocks Swain, along with his sons Henry and Joshua, invented the centerboard for boats. Nothing quite so useful has been invented for a boat since water. The centerboard is a movable plate of metal or wood that can be extended from the keel to help control a boat's leeway (the drift of a boat, as caused by wind and current). Its use revolutionized the handling of boats. When not in use, the centerboard folds upward into a watertight compartment.

Unfortunately, despite its universal application, the Swains reportedly made very little money from their invention. Their patent was evaded by those who placed centerboards between the main keel and the apron instead of through the middle of the keel, as the Swains' patent specified. Thus the Swains have little to show for their pioneering work except entry into the Hall of Forgotten Shore Inventors.

◆

Unlike Simon Lake, Joseph Francis, or the Swain family, the name Guglielmo Marconi is not shrouded in obscurity. People today readily recognize Marconi as the man who first proved to the world that words could be sent through nothing more than empty air, thus setting the stage for the invention of radio.

However, what is not widely known is the role that the Jersey Shore played in helping the brilliant Italian inventor prove the feasibility of the "wireless telegraph." While it's an exaggeration to say that without the Jersey Shore there would be no radio, it's quite correct to say that the Shore was as important to the development of radio as Kitty Hawk was to the development of the airplane.

If anyone is a perfect example of the phrase *boy wonder* it is Marconi. In 1899, at the age of twenty-five, the soft-spoken inventor had accomplished more than most people do in a lifetime. Just three years earlier in England he had given the first formal demonstration of "wireless telegraphy," an event that caused him to be granted the world's first radio patent. Throughout Europe he was known as a genius. But people in the United States considered Thomas Edison the greatest inventor in the world; Marconi was just some upstart.

So it might have been with more than a little trepidation that Marconi boarded the Cunard steamer *Aurania* in Liverpool, England, on September 12, 1899, bound for the United States. He had accepted an invitation from James Gordon Bennett, publisher of the *New York Herald*, to broadcast the results of the America's Cup Races that were to be held off Sandy Hook in a few weeks. The idea was for Marconi to be stationed on a ship in the ocean just beyond the racecourse and transmit details of the contest back to the *Herald*. For Bennett it was a tidy public relations coup, as well as a way for his paper to be the first in the city to carry news of the race. For Marconi it was the chance to demonstrate to a somewhat skeptical American people the practicality of his invention.

In typically breathless fashion, the September 12, 1899, edition of the *Herald* reported Marconi's departure: "Signor Marconi, with four trained assistants, sails from Liverpool today on the Cunard steamer *Aurania*, with all the necessary instruments for use in reporting the races. . . . Every detail of the international struggle between the Columbia [the American yacht, owned by financier J. P. Morgan] and the Shamrock [the British entry, owned by Sir Thomas Lipton] will, by means of this system, submarine cables and land wires, be flashed to the Herald office."

The newspaper went on to explain how it was all going to work: "The transmitting instrument will be placed upon the large ocean going Plant line steamer the *Grand Duchesse*, upon the upper deck of which a tall pole, extending 60 feet in the air above the water line, will be placed. Signor Marconi and two of his assistants will be on this vessel. On board the cable ship anchored near Scotland Light, a similar pole will be erected, and here the other two expert operators will be stationed to receive the message. . . . From the cable ship the message will be flashed by means of submarine and land wires direct to the Herald office."

If Marconi was nervous when he arrived in the United States, he didn't show it. Rather, he was brimming with confidence during an interview in the September 22 edition of the *Herald*: "We will be able to send the details of the racing to New York as accurately and as quickly almost as if you could telephone them. The distance involved is nothing, nor will hills or buildings interfere with the communication." The paper described the young inventor as looking like a "student all over" and possessing "the peculiar semi-abstracted air that characterizes men who devote their days to study and scientific experiment." Marconi was so relaxed that he even found time for humor. After making a half-dozen tiring trips to the Custom House to clear his instruments for entry into this country, he joked, "When does the next steamer start for Liverpool? This is too much of a rush for me."

The joking quickly stopped, however, as the work began in earnest. The races were just days away, and Marconi had to scramble feverishly to make his preparations. Critical to the success of his venture was selecting a site on land high enough to receive the signals he was to send from aboard ship. The choice was obvious: the towering Navesink Highlands bluffs on which stood the Twin Lights Lighthouse. For decades the light shining out across the water from these imposing cliffs had warned mariners that they were drifting perilously close to land. Now the heights would play a much different, yet just as important, role in history.

Marconi dispatched his assistant, William Bradfield, to Twin Lights to set up the 150-foot-high receiving mast. As he worked, Bradfield patiently explained what he was doing to the lighthouse keepers and signal servicemen from nearby Fort Hancock. The men, according to a later account of the incident by Marconi's

daughter Gioia Marconi Braga, "listened silently, spat medita-
tively and looked at him as if he had lost his mind."

"Signor Marconi had a busy day yesterday preparing for the reporting of the yacht races by his system of wireless telegraphy,"
gushed the *Herald*, which was happily milking the most out of its
coup by spotlighting Marconi's actions as much as the upcoming
yacht races. The paper also noted that the military was keenly
interested in the success of the experiments. "Admiral Bradford
[Rear Admiral William Bradford] is taking particular interest in
the matter of wireless telegraphy because of the importance of
the system to the naval establishment," the *Herald* reported.

At last all was in readiness. At sea two stations had been established, one on the steamship *Ponce* and the other on the
Grand Duchesse. Land-based stations had been established at
Twin Lights and on top of a tall building on Thirty-fourth Street
in New York City. Everyone waited for the beginning of the
races. On the Navesink Highlands, the giant receiving mast looked
like an avenging finger pointing to heaven.

But at that moment fate intervened. Commodore George
Dewey had returned from his victory in the Battle of Manila Bay
during the Spanish-American War, and all of New York was in a
tizzy over the arrival of the nation's latest military hero. Because
the water was about to be filled with battleships and cruisers, the
yacht races were postponed. History would just have to wait.

By the end of September everything was again in readiness.
On September 29, Marconi made a trial run on the *Ponce* to test
the equipment, sending and receiving messages. The next day's
Herald blared the news that a new era in communication had
begun: "Message From Parade To Navesink Without Wire." The
paper added: "First Test In America A Complete Success."

On October 2, 1899, another huge *Herald* headline continued
the story: "Wireless Messages Sent From Course," trumpeted the
paper in type so large it could have announced a declaration of
war. "Signor Marconi Sends Despatches [*sic*] from the Steamship
Ponce Aggregating One Thousand Words Without Any Interrup-
tion, Some Over Distance of More Than Twenty Miles." Even the
scoffers had to doff their hats to the Italian inventor. He had
been as good as his word. From Twin Lights, Bradfield sent his
own understated message to Marconi: "Congratulations on today's successful work."

By the time the yacht races were held, they were almost an anticlimax. Bad weather hampered the event, so it wasn't until October 16 that the races finally began. The paper described the frenzied scene outside its New York offices, where people had gathered to eagerly await the updated racing bulletins that the paper was receiving from Marconi and then pasting onto its windows: "the public realized that its only accurate news of the race would come from Signor Marconi. The crowds in Herald square [*sic*], watching the HERALD Bulletins . . . were larger than at any of the preceding trials."

For the record, the *Columbia* won the America's Cup, but Marconi won the public's heart. At one point a rumor swept the city that one of the ships following the race had sunk. Panic reigned until Marconi, in response to the *Herald's* anxious wire, sent back word that the ship was fine. The skeptics were silenced. Marconi had ushered in a new era of instant communication that continues to this day.

Marconi was now an international hero, and the Navesink Highlands had helped him in his quest to prove the feasibility of "wireless telegraphy." But the quiet genius was not yet done with the Jersey Shore. A few years later he came back, bought some land in Wall Township, and built the first commercial transatlantic radio receiving station there. (Now it's part of the U.S. Army's Camp Evans site.) Today, if you go to Twin Lights, you can still see the heavy eyebolts used for the guy wires that were attached to the giant receiving mast—a perpetual reminder of the time when Marconi came to the Jersey Shore and changed the world forever.

◆

Now we stretch the Shore a bit, heading inland a few miles until we reach Holmdel. Known primarily as the site of the Garden State Arts Center, Holmdel has another and even more important distinction: it is the home of the Horn Antenna, which discovered radiant echoes of the long-ago explosion that gave birth to the universe.

This big bang theory, as its called, postulates that the universe we see today is the debris of a huge fireball that created everything in a massive explosion about 16 billion years ago. The theory has its roots in the startling discovery made by U.S.

astronomer Edwin P. Hubble in 1929 that the more distant a galaxy is, the faster it seems to be receding from the earth. This led to the concept that the universe is still expanding as a result of the mammoth explosion that began it. Because of the awesome power generated by the blast, scientists speculated, its radiation should still be detectable today, despite the billions of years that have passed since it occurred.

But discovering the origins of the universe was probably the last thing on the minds of Arno Penzias and Robert Wilson in 1964. The two scientists, working for the Bell Telephone Laboratories in Holmdel, were thinking only of communicating with the first Telstar satellite about to be launched. The original plans had called for a new antenna in France to relay telephone conversations and television signals from Telstar across the Atlantic Ocean to a Bell systems antenna in Maine. But construction of the French antenna fell behind schedule, and as the launch date grew nearer, anxious Bell executives ordered the Horn Antenna

In 1964 the Horn Antenna discovered cosmic background radiation that helped scientists prove the big bang theory. (Photo courtesy AT&T Archives)

modified so it could communicate with Telstar. Penzias and Wilson were assigned the task.

Built in 1959, the fifty-foot-long Horn Antenna is so named because it resembles an alpenhorn (the instrument always used by sheepherders and mountaineers in movies, with a long, mournful, fox hunt–type of sound). By the time Telstar was launched, the French antenna was in operation, and the satellite communicated with all three ground antennas successfully. But before Wilson and Penzias could move on to other projects, they were asked to measure precisely the Horn Antenna's sensitivity, so as to ensure that Telstar's performance had been up to standards.

This turned out to be impossible, because the scientists could not eliminate a low, persistent hiss in the antenna's receiver. The noise was one hundred times more intense than they had expected and occurred day and night, no matter in which direction the antenna was pointed. What followed was almost comical, as the two men tried everything they could think of to eliminate the noise. They cleaned the antenna, put aluminum tape over the rivets, and replaced parts. They even removed two homing pigeons they found nesting inside the horn (they sent them to Bell's offices in Whippany; two days later the resourceful birds were back). But nothing helped. Wilson and Penzias felt they had failed.

Then, in December 1964, Penzias told a friend sitting next to him on an airplane about the unstoppable noise inside the Horn Antenna. A short time later the friend directed him to a research paper about the possibility of detecting the microwave radiation left over from the big bang. Could the noise that seemed to be inside the antenna actually be arriving from all over the universe? Ironically, the paper was written by a member of a group of Princeton University scientists who were preparing to search the skies for exactly the type of "noise" being detected in the Horn Antenna. As soon as both sides got together and evaluated the mysterious noise, they knew they had stumbled onto something momentous. Just thirty miles apart, yet working in total ignorance of each other's efforts, these two groups had made what might well be the most important scientific discovery of the twentieth century.

For their joint discovery, Penzias and Wilson in 1978 were awarded the Nobel Prize for Physics. The Horn Antenna has been designated a National Historic Landmark, thus preserving forever its place in scientific history—and in the heritage of the Jersey Shore.

◆

It's fitting that the last entry in this chronicle of little-known Jersey Shore inventors and discoveries is a man who has possibly been cheated the most by fate. Except for circumstances, what is today known throughout the world as the Ferris wheel might well be called the Somers wheel.

In 1891 William Somers, a member of one of the Jersey Shore's most prominent families, formed a company to erect an "Observation Roundabout" on the Atlantic City Boardwalk. What Somers built is now called a Ferris wheel; the only difference between then and now was that Somers's invention was made of wood, not metal. It turned out to be a critical distinction.

Somers's ride was a huge hit. However, despite reports to the contrary, it does not seem as if Somers can be given credit for inventing the popular amusement ride. Similar devices had been used in the United States since at least 1848, when one was built at Walton Spring, Georgia. But the difference was that the others were not located in a popular pleasure dome on the magnitude of Atlantic City. Word of the Roundabout began to spread.

On June 22, 1892, fire destroyed the Roundabout. Undaunted, Somers quickly built a second, which was actually two wheels, each running side by side in opposite directions. People again lined up in droves to ride Somers's creation.

The next act in the drama is somewhat murky. Somers either contacted or was contacted by officials of the upcoming Columbian Exposition in Chicago. They were interested in having one of Somers's Roundabouts at their fair.

But an agreement between the two sides never occurred. Then, according to William McMahon in his book *So Young . . . So Gay*, fair officials sent a bridge builder from Pittsburgh to study the Roundabout's design. His name was George Washington Gale Ferris. When Ferris returned, he built a wheel out of steel rather than wood for the exposition. Towering to a height of 265 feet, illuminated by three thousand light bulbs, and able to carry 1,440 passengers, the ride was the sensation of the fair. Over a million customers queued up to pay fifty cents—an enormous sum in an era when a merry-go-round ride cost only a nickel—to take the twenty-minute ride. Quite naturally, everyone began calling it the Ferris wheel. "Do whatever you have to do—even sell the kitchen stove—come to Chicago and ride the Ferris Wheel!" wrote one excited North Dakota farm boy to his family.

Somers took exception to what he probably felt was another man stealing his thunder, and a lawsuit between Ferris and Somers ensued. However, Ferris died before it was settled. Ironically, the court found for Somers, but it was too late. The ride was forever to be known as the Ferris wheel. Somers continued to build interesting and unusual amusements; in 1894 he opened a triple-deck carousel on the Atlantic City Boardwalk complete with a dance floor on the top that could hold fifteen hundred people. But his one chance at immortality was gone. Like others before and after him, William Somers had discovered the vagaries of fame.

History can be a cruel taskmaster. Sometimes it ignores you completely. Other times it fetes you for a while then gradually forgets you. Of all the people mentioned in this chapter, just one—Marconi—has had lasting fame, and that is because his achievements were so monumental that even capricious history cannot forget him. Each of these men, however, both astounded and changed the world in some way, and they will forever be enshrined in the heritage of the Jersey Shore.

ELEVEN

THE LIFE-SAVING SERVICE

~~~~~~

It was August 3, 1848. Washington, D.C., sweltered in the equatorial heat that typically marks summer in the nation's capital. Men mopped their brows with handkerchiefs, ladies fanned themselves, and children raced around the streets, seemingly impervious to the sticky, humid air.

On the floor of the House of Representatives, in these days before air conditioning or electric fans, the atmosphere was oppressive. Flies, bees, and the multitude of other winged pests that summer always calls forth were darting about in the stagnant air.

But the heat, the insects, the general stupor caused by the weather—none of this mattered to a thirty-year-old representative from New Jersey named William A. Newell. He was making a speech—the most important not only of his own life but also for the lives of countless others, many of whom were not even born yet.

Newell was arguing for the creation of some organized system of helping shipwreck victims along the New Jersey coast. It was his pet project, and it had long been met by rejection among law-makers. But this time, to make his case, the physician-congress-man was bringing all his guns to bear.

"The coast of New Jersey is more famous for shipwrecks, at-tended with loss of life, than any other part of our country, not even excepting the Florida reefs," he told the House members in attendance. He pointed out that there was a sand bar along the length of virtually the entire New Jersey coast. It varied in dis-tance from three hundred to eight hundred yards out to sea, and in some spots it was covered with just two feet of water at low tide. A vessel that gets stranded on this bar, he said, is cut off from the safety of the beach.

If Newell's voice was tinged with passion as he spoke, it had good reason to be. Nearly nine years before, on the night of Au-gust 13, 1839, he had watched helplessly from shore as the crew of the Austrian brig *Terasto* battled the raging sea. The ship had struck a shoal just off the Mansion of Health, a prominent hotel on Long Beach Island, during a hurricane. Fourteen people, in-cluding the ship's captain, drowned as they tried desperately to swim ashore. In the days that followed, Newell had ample oppor-tunity to brood on their fate; the victims were buried in the Bap-tist Church cemetery in Manahawkin, which was adjacent to his residence. The more he looked at each fresh mound of earth, the more determined he grew to help shipwreck victims.

It is likely that this dreadful night was utmost in his mind when Newell chided his fellow representatives during his speech. "The appropriation asked for [$10,000] is small indeed when com-pared with the great interests of property and life which it is de-signed to protect." Rolling out his heavy artillery, he cited grim statistics that showed the horrible toll of the sea: from April 12, 1839, to July 31, 1848, a total of 338 vessels had been wrecked on the Long Island and New Jersey coasts (122 vessels alone in just a two-year stretch from February 1846 to July 1848). "Our sea-men," said the doctor pointedly, "are entitled to far more care from the Government than they receive."

Although he had been advocating government action for years, Newell had laid the groundwork for this particular moment months before. On January 3, 1848, he had offered a resolution that asked the Commerce Committee to find out whether "any plan can be devised whereby the dangerous navigation along the coast of New Jersey, between Sandy Hook and Little Egg Harbor, may be furnished with additional safeguards to life and property." The resolution had passed without opposition. (Among those who supported it was a young congressman named Abraham Lincoln, who read the resolution and said, "Newell, that is a good measure. I will help you. I am something of a life saver myself, for I have invented a scow that righted itself on the Mississippi sand bars.") Now Newell was attempting to collect on the promise of support implied by the passage of the previous resolution. Alternately cajoling, reasoning with, and imploring the House members, the young doctor pleaded his case on that hot August day.

Apparently he felt that his words had not fallen on deaf ears. Six days after his August 3 speech, Newell attached an amendment to a lighthouse bill that provided for "surf boats, life boats, rockets, carronades and other necessary apparatus for the better protection of life and property from shipwrecks on the coast of New Jersey, between Sandy Hook and Little Egg Harbor."

The bill—amendment and all—passed without opposition. On August 22, Stephen Pleasonton, the fifth auditor of the treasury in charge of lighthouse administration, penned a memo to Robert J. Walker, secretary of the treasury: "In the lighthouse law passed on the last day of the late session of Congress, is an appropriation of a very unusual kind, and I now have the honor to bring it to your attention." Thus was the Life-Saving Service born.

Dr. Newell went on to amass a record of unparalleled public service. He was a two-term New Jersey governor, president of the New Jersey State Board of Agriculture, and governor of Washington Territory, yet his single-minded determination to establish the Life-Saving Service ranks as his finest hour. Ironically, the great success of the service apparently led to many people taking credit for an idea that no one had wanted to support in the beginning. William Nelson, in his *The New Jersey Coast in Three Centuries*, said: "For many years the immediate origin of the present Life Saving Service was a subject of controversy, owing to conflicting claims set up by the friends of various persons who had been connected more or less prominently with it at different times." To set the record straight, Dr. Newell presented a paper to the Monmouth County Historical Association in 1900 (just one year before his death), in which he laid out the facts of how the Life-Saving Service began and his role in the event.

Pleasonton's memo got the ball rolling. Eight sites for Surf Boat stations (as they were initially called) were chosen along the Jersey Shore. With a speed that seems incredible in these days of molasses-slow government bureaucracy, all eight stations were built and equipped by the following May (1849). Even at that, the man in charge of the job, Captain Douglas Ottinger of the United States Revenue Marine, was "apprehensive that it may appear . . . that much time has been occupied in bringing this duty to a close."

The first eight stations, along with those in charge of them (actual locations are in parentheses), were as follows:

Sandy Hook (Spermacetti Cove)—Nathan Wooley
Long Branch (Monmouth Beach)—Edward Wardell
Deal Beach (Deal)—Abner Allen
Shark River (Spring Lake)—Stephen Newman
Squan Beach (Chadwick [or Chadwicks]—a fishing village on the Barnegat Peninsula)—John Maxen
Six Mile Beach (Island Beach)—F. Rogers
Barnegat (Harvey Cedars)—Samuel Perrine
Long Beach (Beach Haven)—Thomas Bond

The following year more stations were built to cover South Jersey and the Long Island coast. Additional Jersey Shore stations were located at Absecomb [*sic*] (Atlantic City), Brigantine Beach (Brigantine), Cape May (Cape May Point), Five Mile Beach (Hereford Inlet, Wildwood), Great Egg Harbor (Ocean City), and Ludlam's Beach (Townsend's Inlet). In a little over one year, the Jersey Shore had gone from no system of shipwreck assistance at all to an organized network of fourteen stations approximately ten miles apart. This number would later swell to twenty-eight stations spaced five miles apart under the provisions of an 1854 law.

◆

The first surf boat stations were anything but glamorous. Essentially they were just garage-size storage areas for the surf boats and other lifesaving equipment, measuring twenty-nine feet long by sixteen feet wide. (The Spermacetti Cove Station can

be seen today at Twin Lights.) The stations were not permanently staffed but run by volunteers, much as some fire stations
are today. When a shipwreck occurred, the volunteers rushed to
the station, got out the equipment, and brought it (either on foot
or by wagon) to the site of the disaster.

Unfortunately, it seems that since the stations were unat-
tended most of the time, frequent theft and vandalism occurred.
(Nelson, in *The New Jersey Coast in Three Centuries*, euphemisti-
cally described the thefts: "all removable property [in the sta-
tions] was converted to private uses.") After building the first
eight stations, what Ottinger had essentially done was leave each
one under the care of a local fisherman or surfman. These keepers, as they were called, could not keep the stations under constant observation; even if no one stole the equipment, it was not
always in the best condition when the time came to use it. Nelson
writes that "dreadful shipwrecks occurred in view of stations
which existed only in name, and which were powerless to render
assistance." In 1854, to remedy this tenuous situation, keepers
were formally appointed and paid two hundred dollars per year to
maintain the equipment and train the volunteer crews.

In the beginning, the lifesavers usually had two options for rescuing people from a stranded ship: the surf boat and the life-car.
Of the two, the surf boat was the first choice, since it could be
launched fairly quickly out toward the ship, which might well be
breaking up in front of the rescuers' eyes as they worked feverishly on shore. The first surf boats were made by Joseph Francis,
inventor of the life-car (see chapter 10). Measuring twenty-six
and one-half feet long with a beam of six and one-half feet, these
boats were modeled on the Sea Bright Skiffs that fishermen in
Nauvoo, Galilee, and other local fishing villages had been launching for years from the beach into the ocean, despite the pounding
surf. Newell, during his August 3 speech in the House of Representatives, had noted how such boats could negotiate shallow and
sandbar-filled waters, unlike a ship's traditional longboat.

Almost without exception these fishing boats were made of
wood (usually Jersey cedar). Since the boats were never out of
the water for long, the wood didn't have a chance to dry out, separate, and crack. But the sporadic use of the lifesaving boats
meant that a more durable material would have to be used, and
Francis settled on corrugated galvanized iron. As Captain Ottinger said in his report of May 21, 1849: "The galvanized iron

surf boats were adopted on account of their durability and not being likely to need repairs for a long time." The only part of the boat not made of metal was the bottom, which was made of wood to withstand the continual scraping along the rough beach sand.

After using these boats, however, rescuers complained that they were too heavy and that the wooden bottoms tended to crack and leak. Subsequent modifications by Francis, including a bottom made of galvanized iron, solved these problems.

The life-car, another invention of Francis's, was designed to be used in seas too steep for launching a surf boat. Built of corrugated metal and totally sealed, the life-car was designed to skim over the waves on a rope and pulley running from shore to ship. The life-car weighed 225 pounds, was eleven feet long, nearly five feet wide, and three feet deep, and it could accommodate from four to six people. Once the hatch was closed, the air inside lasted only fifteen minutes. When first introduced shortly before 1850, the life-car was supplied to all eight of the first lifesaving stations, even though it was untested in actual use. That test came much quicker than anyone would have liked.

On the evening of January 12, 1850, a fearsome winter storm drove the British emigrant ship *Ayrshire* onto the shoals off Squan Beach. (The location of Squan Beach varies with every account of the *Ayrshire* wreck. Some place it at present-day Manasquan, some at Absecon Beach, and some at Chadwick Beach, north of Island Beach on the Barnegat Peninsula. Since most accounts seem to agree that the ship grounded abreast of the Squan Beach lifesaving station, and since John Maxen [often erroneously spelled Maxon], who plays an important role in this drama, was in charge of operations at Squan Beach, we shall assume the location to be around Chadwick Beach.) The surf was so high and the sea so violent that an open boat could not reach the nearly two hundred passengers trapped on the stranded ship. The sea pounded the stricken vessel, sending masts and rigging crashing to the deck below. The passengers and crew huddled together, helplessly awaiting what seemed to be inevitable destruction.

On the storm-swept beach, however, there was hope. Maxen and his crew had brought the life-car to the scene and were frantically readying the mortar that was to launch the hawser line to the stricken ship. It is no easy feat firing a mortar toward a ship three hundred yards away during a violent storm, and Maxen's first shot was wide. The second, however, landed in the mate's stateroom—not the best location, but at least on the ship. As an unidentified eyewitness later wrote: "Mr. Maxon [*sic*] put too much powder in the first shot and too little in the last."

Fortunately, sending a rescue line by mortar to a distressed ship had been common practice in the British navy for some time, and so the *Ayrshire*'s sailors knew what Maxen was trying to accomplish. Working quickly, the lifesavers and the sailors rigged the rope and pulley system on which the life-car rode. Maxen's crew fastened the life-car to the hawser line by rings and chains. Then two lighter lines, called "whip lines," were run out to the ship. Hanging from the stationary hawser line, the life-car was moved back and forth from ship to shore by means of the whip lines and pulley. On shore, the hawser was kept elevated by the "crotch": two long poles in the shape of an X mounted in the sand. The end of the hawser was connected to a sand anchor, which was two pieces of wood fastened together in the shape of a cross and embedded in the beach. By manipulating the hawser, one or two of the lifesavers could keep the line taut and the life-car riding above the waves.

Although the life-car had never been tried during an actual shipwreck, it clearly was better than waiting for the angry ocean to rip the *Ayrshire* to pieces. Maxen and his men completed their preparations and sent the odd-looking vessel skimming out to the wreck. As soon as it arrived, several passengers clambered into it, the hatch was secured, and the car sent back toward shore.

We can only imagine how terrifying it must have been for those inside the sealed, unfamiliar craft as it bobbed over the waves toward shore. Spread out on the floor of the life-car in total darkness, hearing the sea angrily striking the metal walls, some of those inside surely must have thought they would never see their homes or loved ones again. But approximately ten minutes later, the life-car arrived on the beach. The people inside were helped out of the tiny craft, scarcely able to believe that they had cheated death in such a fashion.

"From two to four came off from the ship at a time in the car," wrote the unidentified observer. "They were thus landed and the car sent back. About four or five trips were made in an hour."

This scene was repeated over and over that day and the next, as almost every one of the *Ayrshire*'s passengers was rescued.

The only casualty was a Mr. Bell, who tried to ride on the outside of the life-car when barred from entering the vessel with his sister and her three daughters. He was quickly swept away by the mammoth waves and drowned.

Maxen later wrote about the landmark operation: "I superintended the rescue of the passengers on board the wrecked *Ayrshire*, sending the line on board by the mortar, and, by the means of the metallic Life-car, landed safely all the passengers and crew except one,—two hundred in all,—which, in my opinion, could not otherwise have been done, as the sea was so bad no open boat could live."

The life-car had proved its worth. When this particular one was retired in 1878, it had saved 1,493 lives. Other life-cars went on to record similar spectacular successes. Two hundred and ninety-six people were rescued via life-car on December 3, 1852, from the *Georgia*, which was trapped on the shoals off of Long Beach Island, and five hundred more were saved late in 1854 when the *Underwriter* went aground off present-day Mantoloking. On October 22, 1853, a staggering seven hundred people were rescued with Francis's invention from the *Western World*, which was stranded outside Spring Lake.

But while the *Ayrshire* rescue was important in proving the feasibility of the life-car, it may have actually hurt lifesaving efforts in the long run by illustrating how effective the volunteer system could be, rather than a full-time staff patrolling the coast. In truth, if the *Ayrshire* had gone aground a few miles to the north or south instead of virtually on the front doorstep of the Squan Beach lifesaving station, it might not have been discovered for many hours—more than enough time for the ocean to batter the ship to bits and send passengers and crew to a watery grave. But as it actually happened, the volunteers responded quickly, and that seemed proof enough that the current method worked.

The volunteer system also meant that equipment maintenance was sorely lacking. This point was illustrated in sadly dramatic fashion on November 13, 1854, when the *New Era*, filled with five hundred German immigrants, struck a sandbar off Deal Beach (which is now the northern part of Asbury Park). The captain and several crewmen quickly abandoned the ship, leaving the terrified passengers to fend for themselves. When the lifesaving crew tried to shoot a mortar line out to the ship, their equipment continually malfunctioned due to neglect. The crew was never able to get a line out to the *New Era*; 163 people were rescued, most by the crew and other volunteers on shore who waded into the water and pulled half-dead passengers from the surf. The rest of those on the *New Era* drowned.

Still, as long as this rather slipshod system of volunteers relied primarily on local fishermen, captains, and others intimately familiar with the sea and its mercurial nature, things worked about as well as could be expected and probably better than some feared, with the tragic exception of cases like the *New Era*. The fault certainly was not solely with the crew members, who frequently performed superhuman feats in saving lives and property under conditions that can best be described as horrendous. Frequent recommendations were made to upgrade the system and improve equipment maintenance, but government officials— probably muttering the old saw, If it ain't broke, why fix it?— turned a blind eye to these requests.

During the decade of the 1860s, however, the Revenue Marine Bureau of the Treasury Department—under whose jurisdiction the lifesavers fell—began worrying about the growing number of political appointees given jobs as station keepers. It was bad enough appointing a keeper who didn't live near the station, but when that person didn't know the bow from the stern in a boat, he had no business trying to orchestrate a life-and-death rescue operation.

But with the nation preoccupied in the 1860s by the Civil War and its aftermath, the volunteer lifesaving service had to limp along as best as it could. Things continued this way until 1871, when Sumner Kimball arrived on the scene.

♦

When Kimball became general superintendent of the Revenue Marine Bureau of the Treasury Department, he launched an immediate reorganization. Within a year, the loose confederation of lifesaving stations became one centralized system: the Life-Saving Service. Thanks to Kimball's efforts, the new service was well on its way to being the envy of the world.

Kimball's reforms were legion. He instituted beach patrols during nights and bad weather, so that wrecks could be quickly spotted. He expanded the number of stations: the Jersey Shore soon boasted a staggering forty-two stations, or approximately one every three miles. He initiated a system of visual signals (with flags during the day, torches at night) so that rescuers on shore could communicate with crews on board ship. And he began a modernization program to refurbish old stations and build new ones.

Most important, Kimball scrapped the volunteer system and replaced it with a regular paid staff headed by a keeper. Crew members received forty dollars per month, and keepers sixty. These men were on duty during the "active season" (when most storms occurred), which lasted from September 1 to May 1. The lifesavers lived at the station, like lighthouse keepers. Their families, however, did not live at the stations with them. During the busy winter months in particular, a crew member could go for weeks at a time without seeing his loved ones.

Each station's crew complement was determined by the number of oars required to pull its largest boat. Normally this meant a six-man crew. A seventh man was usually added beginning on December 1 to deal with the increased threat brought by winter storms.

To aid the lifesavers, a new piece of rescue equipment was introduced called the breeches buoy. The name could not have been more apt; the breeches buoy was literally a short pair of canvas pants sewn into a large life preserver. It worked on the same

The Lyle gun, a mortar that shot rope out to distressed ships, is tested during an early Life-Saving Service drill. (Collection of Richard Steele)

An early Life-Saving Service crew testing their boat. (Collection of Richard Steele)

principle as the life-car, moving between ship and shore via a rope and pulley system and a hawser line, but with one significant difference: only one person at a time could use it. Obviously, a ship packed with passengers and in imminent danger of breaking up was not a good candidate for the breeches buoy. Also, women complained that dangling in the device made their bare legs show, but when the choice was dignity or drowning, dignity was quickly abandoned.

During the active season, the lifesavers didn't just sit around waiting for a shipwreck. Along with the previously mentioned beach patrols—which were lonely and often frigid walks in soft sand over long stretches of dark, deserted beaches—and regular housekeeping duties, there were drills, drills, and more drills. Both the crew and the equipment were meant to be constantly in tip-top shape. As Nelson wrote in *The New Jersey Coast in Three Centuries*: "If in one month after the opening of the active season a crew can not accomplish the rescue within five minutes, it is considered that they have been remiss in drilling, or that there are some stupid men among them. They are cautioned that if upon the next visit of the inspector a marked improvement is not shown, some decisive action will be taken to secure it."

All these changes infused the Life-Saving Service with an esprit de corps that would hardly have seemed possible a few years before. A spirited rivalry often existed between crews of nearby stations to see who could perform their drills faster and better. Crew members were issued regulation uniforms, just like members of the armed forces. The uniform and badge were worn proudly.

In time, as trains and highways served more of the shore, families began to move closer to the stations to be near their husbands and sons. The stations became the focal points of small communities, everyone connected by the common bonds of dangerous work and selfless devotion to duty.

That the work was indeed dangerous was something no one wanted to talk about, but each lifesaver knew that the very same harsh conditions that spelled disaster for a ship could prove his undoing as well. One such sad event occurred on February 12, 1886, at Life-Saving Station No. 17 at Barnegat Shoals. The *Karl Jevica* had gone aground about one and one-half miles off shore, too far for a mortar line to be used. The lifesaving crew launched the surf boat, which struggled through the high seas out to the ship only to find it deserted. The crew turned their boat around and headed back for shore. What happened next is chronicled in an unidentified newspaper clipping contained in Leland Downey's compilation of Jersey Shore shipwrecks entitled *Broken Spars*: "When close in to shore and the danger was about over, a wave, higher and stronger than the others, suddenly gave the rudder a wrench and before she could be brought under control the life boat capsized. The men struggled in the surf and most of them kept themselves afloat until they were washed to the beach. When those who had escaped death picked themselves up from the sand they saw that three of their companions, Solomon Soper, John Soper and John Perrine were missing. When night was falling, the bodies of the men were washed up on the beach and taken to the station house."

Ironically, the *Karl Jevica*'s thirteen-man crew had cast off in two boats almost the moment the ship hit the shoal, making the surf boat trip unnecessary and the rescuers' deaths even more tragic. Six *Karl Jevica* crewmen made it safely to shore; the others drowned.

These were the type of unpredictable, dangerous situations that the lifesavers faced each time they ventured forth from the comfort of the station house into a storm's fury. Because of these men's repeated bravery, their deeds became the stuff of legend. The later part of the nineteenth century was a time when the United States was maturing and making its presence felt on the world stage, and the lifesavers were the living embodiment of the new national confidence. The crews were ordinary people performing extraordinary feats, perfect illustrations of the credo that there was nothing Americans couldn't do if they put their minds to it.

Ordinary citizens understood this larger-than-life role. The following letter, from *The Asbury Park Journal* of April 28, 1877, is typical of the public admiration enjoyed by the lifesavers: "There is no set of men employed by the Government that get less pay for the services rendered, than the men employed in the Life-Saving stations. And what does the Government expect of them? Why, to march and countermarch along the exposed beach through the blinding storms of rain, snow, sleet and sand, and with the thermometer at or below zero. Look for a moment at the risk they run when they launch their frail boats; the sea running high, death staring them in the face, within a half inch of eternity (for that is the thickness of the planking of their boats), and yet these brave heroic men fear no danger, and therefore, see none where duty calls."

Of course, it wasn't all gloom and doom for the lifesaving crews. Occasionally their work threw them a bouquet—sometimes more than that. This was certainly the case on June 29, 1888, when the Italian ship *Civita Carara* grounded outside Manasquan. After several attempts, the lifesaving crew finally managed to connect a breeches buoy line to the ship and rescue the thirteen crewmen. As each of the crew touched down onto the beach, he handed a gallon of gin to his rescuers. There were undoubtedly many toasts proffered that night at the lifesaving station.

Statistics backed up the popular perception of the Life-Saving Service's efficiency. From November 1, 1871, to June 30, 1877, 1,411 people were saved by Jersey Shore lifesaving crews, while only 12 lives were lost. The new emphasis on drill and preparation paid off in a big way on February 3, 1880, for the crew at Life-Saving Station No. 4 at Monmouth Beach. Nature had unleashed all its fury that terrible winter's day; snow, sleet, and rain mixed with wind clocked at eighty-four miles an hour battered the coast.

Shortly after midnight, the *E. C. Babcock* went aground one hundred yards off the beach near Station No. 4. The lifesavers rushed into action. After a two-hour battle against the elements,

Significant Rescues Attempted by the Jersey Shore Life-Saving Service

The United States Life-Saving Service saved countless lives and property during its nearly seventy-year tenure on the Jersey Shore. It would take an entire book just to chronicle all the ships and people saved by lifesaving crews. Below is a sampling of some of the more significant wrecks.

JANUARY 12, 1850	*Ayrshire* (Chadwicks)	201 saved
DECEMBER 3, 1852	*Georgia* (Long Beach Isl.)	296 saved
JANUARY 13, 1853	*Cornelius Grinnell* (Manasquan)	234 saved
OCTOBER 22, 1853	*Western World*	700 saved
JANUARY 12, 1854	*Chauncery Jerome, Jr.* (Long Branch)	100 saved
APRIL 16, 1854	*Powhattan* (Long Beach Isl.)	354 lost
NOVEMBER 11, 1854	*New Era* (Asbury Park)	163 saved, 222 lost
LATE 1854	*Underwriter* (Mantoloking)	500 saved
JANUARY 26, 1856	*New York* (Barnegat Inlet)	313 saved
JANUARY 24, 1863	*Mortimer Livingston* (Ludlam Island)	300 saved
DECEMBER 23, 1865	*Idaho* (Barnegat Inlet)	150 saved
MARCH 16, 1870	*James H. Hoyt* (Highlands)	196 lost
MARCH 20, 1876	*Maggie M. Weaver* (Sandy Hook)	6 lost
MARCH 2, 1877	*Margaret and Lucy* (Toms River)	7 lost
MARCH 17, 1877	*Rusland* (Long Branch)	204 saved
MARCH 21, 1889	*J. W. Wendt* (Barnegat)	28 saved
FEBRUARY 1891	*Howard Williams* (Cape May)	all lost
FEBRUARY 6, 1893	*Alice* (Long Beach Isl.)	12 saved, 4 lost
APRIL 12, 1894	*Kate Markee* (Spermacetti Cove)	7 lost
MAY 23, 1901	*Bianca Aspasia* (Ship Bottom)	15 saved
JANUARY 20, 1902	*Abiel Abott* (Ship Bottom)	4 saved, 4–5 lost

(*continued*)

~~~~~~

Significant Rescues Attempted by the Jersey Shore Life-Saving Service *(continued)*

AUGUST 20, 1903	*Chloris* (Absecon)	2 saved
FEBRUARY 22, 1904	*Olive T. Whittier* (Long Branch)	7 saved
APRIL 8, 1904	*Rival* (Long Branch)	18 saved
DECEMBER 18, 1904	*Lizzie H. Brayton* (Point Pleasant)	9 saved
JUNE 28, 1905	*Standish* (Brigantine)	29 saved
JANUARY 12, 1906	*Cherokee* (Brigantine)	56 saved
JUNE 6, 1908	*Viva* (Atlantic City)	4 people, 1 dog saved
APRIL 15, 1914	*Charles K. Buckley* (Long Branch)	7 lost
DATE UNKNOWN	*Oklahoma* (Barnegat)	30 lost

all eight people on board the ship were rescued. But no sooner had the exhausted crew gotten the passengers back to the station and packed away the lifesaving equipment than the Spanish ship *Augustina* was driven to the beach just down from the site of the first wreck. Out raced the crew again, but their rescue efforts were misinterpreted by the Spanish sailors, several of whom jumped into the raging sea. Without hesitation the lifesavers plunged into the surf and dragged the men to safety, all the while dodging—and sometimes being hit by—cargo and debris from the *E. C. Babcock* that the storm was driving toward them.

For their courageous efforts on that dreadful night, five life-savers from Station No. 4 were awarded the Life-Saving Service Silver Medal of Honor, while the keeper received a gold medal.

For over four decades, the lifesaving crews continued to perform their heroic duties day in and day out. Eventually the service expanded onto all other U.S. coasts and the Great Lakes.

By the turn of the century, however, ships had become bigger and stronger, with more powerful engines and improved navigational systems. The number of wrecks dropped sharply. The expansion of the active season to a full twelve months made the Life-Saving Service less attractive as "part-time" work for fishermen and surfmen. These factors combined to lessen the importance of the lifesavers in the early part of the twentieth century. In 1915, an era ended when the Life-Saving Service merged with the Revenue Cutter Service to form the United States Coast Guard.

The efforts of these brave men will never be forgotten. When Coast Guard patrols today look for boaters in distress, they are continuing in the footsteps of the lifesaving crews. A granite monument laid at Asbury Park around the turn of the century commemorating the *New Era* disaster summed up what many people felt then—and still feel today—about the United States Life-Saving Service: "This monument is erected to commemorate the zeal and energy of Governor William A. Newell, of New Jersey, who as Congressman succeeded in getting a law passed establishing the United States Life Saving Service. Also to commemorate the fidelity of the Life Saving Crews whose efficiency renders such a disaster at this day almost impossible."

Dr. Newell's idea had indeed come a long, long way.

TWELVE

BEACONS
IN THE NIGHT

〰〰〰〰〰〰〰〰〰〰〰〰〰〰〰〰〰〰〰〰〰〰〰〰

For years they saved an untold number of lives and ships merely by their existence. Strung out along New Jersey's coastline like a string of shiny pearls, their powerful lights cut through the thick, black night, warning mariners not to venture too much closer. In an age before radio, when piloting a ship at night near the shoreline was one of the most difficult tasks imaginable, lighthouses were indispensable aids to navigation. Along the Jersey Shore they were also, quite literally, lifesavers.

The Jersey Shore has one of the more treacherous coastlines along the eastern United States. Sailors called the Jersey coast the Graveyard of the Sea, and for good reason: hidden shoals, shifting inlets, and sudden shallows made navigating a tricky task even when the sun was out and the sea was calm as glass. At night, especially with a choppy, storm-churned sea, it was practically impossible.

Lighthouses did more for mariners than just warn them they were approaching the shoreline. Because the characteristics of each light were unique, a navigator could take bearings from two beacons, pinpoint the ship's location, and determine whether a course change was needed. The unique appearance of each lighthouse enabled it also to serve as an important landmark during the day (think how confusing it would be if all lighthouses were the same color and shape).

But there is more to lighthouses than just functionality. Romantic, isolated, engaged in a life-and-death struggle with the sea in which there is no room for error, a lighthouse appeals to the adventurous spirit locked deep within us. Lighthouses are like time machines, summoning images of stormy seas, sailing ships, and moonlit nights when the only sound to be heard for miles around is the whispering of the wind.

◆

Incredibly the Sandy Hook Lighthouse is still standing today, even though more than two centuries have passed since it was built in 1764. Much has changed about the land called Sandy Hook in that long span of years, but, like Methuselah, the Sandy Hook Lighthouse—the nation's oldest operating lighthouse—just keeps rolling on.

The need for a beacon at Sandy Hook had been apparent long before one was built. In 1679 and 1680 the governor of New York, Sir Edmund Andros, pointed out the need for "sea marks for shipping along Sandy Point," as Sandy Hook was then known. Indeed, the narrow, curving channel that New York–bound ships had to follow past the Hook was often made even more difficult to navigate by strong tides and surging currents. According to one observer, ships had to go so close to Sandy Hook to navigate the channel that "from on board one might toss a biscuit cake on shore."

But years of agitating for a lighthouse at Sandy Hook—including pleas in newspapers like the *New York Post Boy* and the *Pennsylvania Gazette*—by businessmen, sea captains, and others, came to naught until New York merchants incurred enormous financial losses during the first three months of 1761 due to shipwrecks off Sandy Hook. In March of that year forty-three merchants petitioned Caldweller Colden, lieutenant governor of New York, to have a lighthouse built near the tip of Sandy Hook.

Colden agreed, and shortly thereafter a lottery was established to raise the 3,000 pounds thought necessary to do the job.

However, the project immediately hit several snags. The worst of these was the cost of the four acres of land on which the lighthouse was to be built. Some sources say that the Hartshorne brothers, owners of the land, were asking 1,000 pounds for the real estate. Eventually a compromise price of 750 pounds was reached, and the land was deeded to the Colony of New York in May 1762.

Construction began on the long-awaited lighthouse, but by now the money was running out, so another lottery was held in June 1763 to raise additional funds. Given the date of the second lottery, it seems logical to assume that construction of the lighthouse and keeper's quarters took place during 1763 and probably during the first part of 1764 as well. Thanks to an article in *The New York Mercury* on June 18, 1764, it is certain that the lighthouse was first lit on June 11. The article said:

> On Monday Evening last, the NEW-YORK LIGHT-HOUSE, erected at Sandy Hook, was lighted for the first Time. The House is of an Octagon Figure, having eight equal Sides; the diameter at the Base, 29 Feet; and at the Top of the Wall, 15 Feet. The Lanthorn is 7 Feet high; the Circumference 33 Feet. The whole Construction of the Lanthorn is Iron; the Top covered with Copper. There are 48 Oil Blazes. The building from the Surface is Nine Stories; the whole from Bottom to top, 103 Feet.

The builder of the New York Light (as it was initially called) was Isaac Conro of New York City. Besides being a builder and a mason, Conro was a merchant who sold fireclay, sand marble, chimney pieces, tile, and a variety of other goods. Considering that Sandy Hook was only the fifth lighthouse built in this country and that it still stands today, Conro obviously did a superb job.

It's a good thing, because a scant two years later, according to the *Mercury* of June 30, 1766, the lighthouse was "struck by Lightning, and twenty panes of the Glass Lanthorn broke to pieces; the chimney and Porch belonging to the kitchen was broke down, and some people that were in the House received a little Hurt, but are since recovered. 'Tis said the Gust was attended with a heavy shower of Hail."

Sandy Hook Lighthouse, circa 1790. (Photo courtesy Moss Archives, Sea Bright, N.J.)

A decade later the lighthouse was tested again, but this time by humanity rather than nature. With much of the action of the Revolution taking place in the vicinity of New York, the lighthouse was a prime military target, with both the colonists and the British vying for control of it.

On March 6, 1776, the New York Congress ordered Major William Malcolm to perform various acts of destruction at Sandy Hook Light—including breaking the lantern glass and removing the oil used to fire the flame—to render the lighthouse "entirely useless." Although Malcolm did his job, the British apparently repaired the damage, because on June 21 Lieutenant Colonel Benjamin Tupper and his colonial army command attacked the lighthouse. But as his artillery pounded away at the structure, Tupper found "the walls so firm I could make no Impression." Shortly thereafter warships of the main British fleet began arriving in Sandy Hook Bay, and the lighthouse remained primarily under British control for the remainder of the war. Because a band of colonists loyal to Britain called the Refugees used the lighthouse as their command post while raiding nearby towns, it became known as Lighthouse Fort or Refugees' Tower.

In 1789, after the war was over, the new federal government created the Lighthouse Service. Sandy Hook was one of twelve lighthouses built by the colonies that came under the control of the new agency. (In 1939 the Coast Guard absorbed the duties of the Lighthouse Service.)

War continued to disrupt life at Sandy Hook Lighthouse. During the War of 1812 the keeper complained of being put out of his home by the U.S. Army. In 1864 thought was given to moving the tower because the firing of big guns at nearby Fort Hancock continually shattered one of the beacon's lantern panes. This type of damage was more frequent during World War I, when the guns at Fort Hancock were bigger and the blasts more powerful.

In 1840 the Sandy Hook Lighthouse was cheated out of its place in lighthouse history by a scant few inches. It was intended that Sandy Hook be the first lighthouse in the United States to receive the new and more powerful Fresnel lens, developed in France by Augustin Fresnel. But when the lens arrived, it was too large; the keeper could not move around it to perform his duties. The lens was subsequently installed in Sandy Hook's neighbor to the immediate south, the Twin Lights Lighthouse atop the

Navesink Highlands, in 1841. Sandy Hook did get a measure of revenge in 1868, however, when the first siren fog signal in an American lighthouse was installed there.

Although the inside of the tower has been lined with brick and an iron spiral staircase was added sometime in the early 1860s, the exterior of the tower today looks remarkably similar to that which Isaac Conro constructed more than two hundred years ago. If Conro could come back and survey his handiwork, his biggest shock would undoubtedly be the lighthouse's location. When he built it, the lighthouse was just five hundred feet from the tip of Sandy Hook, close enough certainly for the early keepers to hear the sound of the waves lapping on the shore. But today, thanks to the continuous movement of coastal sand, the lighthouse is one and one-half miles from the northern end of the Hook. The sound of the waves is only a distant memory now.

But for the Sandy Hook Lighthouse, memories are enough. It has accumulated a lot of them. In 1964, on the two hundredth anniversary of its first lighting, the lighthouse was declared a National Historic Landmark. Its light continues to shine out over the dark Atlantic, and there's no reason to think it will not go on for at least another two centuries.

To set the record straight from the start, they're fraternal twins, not identical . . . but that hasn't stopped the Twin Lights from being one of the most famous lighthouses in America.

If you've ever traveled on Route 36, which runs parallel to the ocean through such towns as Monmouth Beach and Sea Bright, then you can understand why the Navesink Highlands are such a logical place for a lighthouse. Towering two hundred feet above sea level (the highest point on the eastern seaboard), the Highland hills can be seen for miles; they are easily the dominating feature of the entire region.

Recognizing that fact, sometime around 1756 New York merchants built on the site "a commodius lighthouse for the security of navigation," according to the 1765 publication *The History of New Jersey*. This structure, however, was nothing more than a tower lit by burning pots of oil that were raised high once darkness fell.

Given the Highlands' importance as a nautical navigational aid, it wasn't long before something more permanent was built there. In 1828 identical twin lighthouse towers were erected by Charles Smith of Stonington, Connecticut. Each octagonal tower rose forty-six feet into the air. The rarely used dual design (Twin Lights is one of only seven double lighthouses in the United States) was chosen to differentiate the Navesink Lighthouse from the one just a few miles away at Sandy Hook.

Twin Lights gained fame in 1841 when the first Fresnel lenses to be installed in an American lighthouse were put into both towers. Resembling huge glass beehives surrounding an illuminance, the Fresnel lens used prisms at the top and bottom to refract light toward the center, where it was intensified by a magnifying glass. The resulting narrow beam of concentrated light was equivalent to six million candlepower. It was probably this incredible beam of light—as different from what had been there previously as a searchlight is from a flashlight—that enabled Twin Lights to be considered the "best [lighthouse] on the coast of the United States" by the federal Lighthouse Board in 1841.

But the best did not last. By the mid-1850s the two towers had deteriorated to the point that saving them was out of the question. It was decided to completely rebuild Twin Lights.

As the rebuilding neared completion, it was obvious that architect Joseph Lederle had added something to make the twin towers even more unique. For reasons unknown to this day, he gave each of the towers its own personality; the south tower was square, with sixty-five steps leading to its lens, while the north tower was octagonal, with sixty-four steps. The identical twins had become fraternal.

The new towers, each 53 feet high (248 feet above sea level), were first lit on May 1, 1862. The eighteen-room keeper's building was finished the following year. It was set between the towers so that the keeper could move from one to the other without going outside. The material used in the construction—brownstone from Belleville, New Jersey—along with the design of the lighthouse gives Twin Lights the distinct appearance of a medieval fortress. With a drawbridge, a moat, and a few knights in shining armor, the lighthouse could easily have been at home in King Arthur's day.

During the next forty years Twin Lights reached the zenith of its career as a navigational aid. In 1883 both towers became the

The Twin Lights Lighthouse, showing the unique, fortresslike design. The tower in the foreground is square, the one in the background octagonal. (Photo courtesy Special Collections and Archives, Rutgers University Libraries)

initial first-order lighthouses (a first-order light was a seacoast light with five concentric wicks) in America to convert from lard oil to mineral oil (kerosene). Mineral oil had several advantages, including cleaner burning and lower cost, but the main benefit was a boost in the candlepower of the beacons from eight thousand to ten thousand.

This was just the warm-up to the main event. In 1898 the south tower at Twin Lights became the first coastal light in the United States to be fitted with an electrically powered bivalve lens (two separate lenses that made one complete lens when put together). The results of using electricity instead of oil were spectacular; candlepower increased to a mind-boggling 25 million. The light could be seen twenty-two miles out at sea, and its massive glow was reportedly visible as far as seventy miles out. (Unfortunately, the light was so bright on the landward side that it even kept cows awake on local farms. The sleepy animals refused to give milk in the morning. This cow crisis was solved by installing blackout panels on the landward side of both towers.) The north tower light was discontinued and held in reserve for emergencies.

Eventually the cost of operating this great light became too much, and in 1917 an incandescent oil vapor lamp was installed in the south tower. This cut the candlepower down to a "mere" 710,000. In 1931 the light was converted back to electricity, and at 9 million candlepower was again the most powerful light in the nation.

By this time modern technology was breathing down the neck of all American lighthouses, and Twin Lights was no exception. Radar, radio beacons, and lightships were all combining to do the job that lighthouses had done so long and so well. One by one, the faithful lights were extinguished around the country. The end came for Twin Lights in 1949, when it was decommissioned. For the first time in nearly two centuries, darkness reigned supreme over the Navesink Highlands.

But you can't keep a good lighthouse down. In 1960 Twin Lights became a New Jersey state historic site, and two years later the Coast Guard granted special permission for a one-thousand-watt bulb to glow from the north tower. Today Twin Lights is listed on both the state and national register of historic places, and it is run by New Jersey as a state park. Thousands of visitors come each year to this venerable old structure, where they trek up the sixty-four steps to the top of the north tower and gaze out over the Atlantic. Sometimes their eyes get a faraway look, and you know they're in another time and another place, when the lights in these brownstone towers meant the difference between life and death for many a mariner out at sea.

◆

Don't feel embarrassed if you're amazed that there's a lighthouse in Sea Girt. Many people who've lived at the Jersey Shore for decades and pass it every day still don't know it!

The reason that the Sea Girt Lighthouse is so easy to miss is that it sticks up out of the roof of a rambling two-story brick house on Beach Boulevard and Ocean Road; it's more like an overgrown chimney than a sentinel of the sea. This lighthouse typifies what is known as the Cape Cod style, a class of lighthouse in which the light source and the keeper's dwelling are combined.

Obviously, this lighthouse was not built to warn of a treacherous inlet or dangerous shoals, since its visibility is not nearly as great as that of Sandy Hook or Twin Lights. The story behind the Sea Girt Lighthouse is really one of circumstance.

When mariners in the late nineteenth century looked at the central Jersey shoreline, they saw a light at Barnegat, another at the Navesink Highlands—and about forty miles of darkness in between. They argued that a light was needed between the two, and Congress agreed. On October 19, 1888, it authorized the establishment of a lighthouse at Squan Inlet (now Manasquan Inlet).

But a funny thing happened on the way to building the Squan Inlet light. The site chosen was determined unacceptable. Delay followed delay as another location was scouted for the homeless lighthouse. Finally a site on the Sea Girt beach, at the intersection of Ocean and Belluvue avenues, was selected. Work began on a red brick, two-story house with a square light tower rising from the top. The new Sea Girt Lighthouse became operational on December 10, 1896.

One of the light's main functions was to mark Sea Girt Inlet, which was a major thoroughfare for ships heading in from the ocean. But by 1930 the inlet had filled so much that only boats with a two-foot draw could pass through it—and then only at high tide.

Life was quiet at Sea Girt Light; most of the activity occurred at its larger relatives to the north and south. On May 29, 1910, Harriet Yates recorded the death of her husband Abram, the keeper of the light. Mrs. Yates assumed the duties of keeper and faithfully kept the light lit until relieved two months later. Like many other women in lighthouses all over the country, Harriet Yates selflessly performed the difficult and lonely duties of lighthouse keeper, despite the pain she must have felt over her loss. The story of these unheralded female lightkeepers is a story yet to be told.

Like many New Jersey lighthouses, Sea Girt has a first to its credit. In 1921 the first radio fog beacon was installed at this small lighthouse as an aid for ships approaching New York Harbor. By crossing radio beacons from Sea Girt Light with similar signals from the Ambrose and Fire Island lightships—Sea Girt's signal was three dashes to Ambrose's one and Fire Island's two— a ship could determine its position well before reaching the harbor. The signals were operated mainly in foggy or foul weather.

But the continued filling of Sea Girt Inlet, combined with more advances in navigation, rapidly made Sea Girt Light obsolete. In 1945 the Coast Guard took the lighthouse out of service and, in August 1956, sold it to the town. There matters stood until 1981, when concerned residents formed the Sea Girt Lighthouse Citizens Committee in response to efforts to sell the graceful old structure. Through herculean fund-raising efforts the lighthouse was restored. It is used today as a community center—proof positive that old lighthouses don't fade away if you don't let them.

◆

Old Barney, as it is widely known, is probably the Jersey Shore's most famous lighthouse. For a while, after it was first built, it was probably also the Jersey Shore's most criticized lighthouse.

There had long been a need for a lighthouse on the tip of Long Beach Island. Shoals along that stretch of shoreline had doomed many a ship. Between 1830 and 1837, 125 coastal vessels met their fate on these infamous shoals from Barnegat north to Point Pleasant.

Clearly something had to be done. On October 24, 1834, the federal government paid Bornt Slaight three hundred dollars for just over five acres of land several hundred feet south of Barnegat Inlet. Construction of the lighthouse apparently started soon afterward, for the forty-five-foot-tall Barnegat Light became operational on July 20, 1835.

Quite possibly the lighthouse was built too quickly, for in less than twenty years it was literally falling apart. But shoddy workmanship wasn't the only problem with the first Barnegat Light. Mariners complained that the weak light was barely visible. "I generally steer for Barnegat, frequently passing without seeing it, owing no doubt to the low position [inferiority] of the light," said Captain William Berry. Another skipper reported that he came "very near losing my ship" because he mistook Barnegat Light for the lighthouse on Tucker's Beach farther south. To make matters worse, Barnegat Light's illumination was fixed (it did not flash), and so it was often mistaken for that of another ship.

Combined with all these shortcomings, erosion was rapidly eating away the sand in front of the lighthouse. Barnegat Inlet has been one of the most unstable on the Jersey Shore, and during the 1850s it was in one of its most active periods. In the spring of 1855, storms cut land away from the shore to within six feet of the lighthouse.

Clearly something had to be done—again. This time the government sent a U.S. Army Engineer, Lieutenant George Gordon

Barnegat Lighthouse, late nineteenth century. (Collection of Richard Steele)

Meade, to Barnegat Light. Just eight years away from commanding the Union forces in the epic Civil War battle at Gettysburg, Meade examined the crumbling lighthouse and quickly realized it wasn't worth saving. His recommendation: build a new coastal light. By mid-July 1857, the new lighthouse was under construction. Because the existing light was on such shaky ground, a temporary wooden lighthouse was built. It's a good thing, because a few years later the first Barnegat Light tumbled into the sea.

The new (and current) Barnegat Lighthouse first turned on its light on January 6, 1859. The tower was 165 feet above sea level and built of sturdy brick. Meade's new light silenced the critics who complained that the old beam was hard to see. With its powerful first-order Fresnel lens, the new lighthouse could be seen from twenty to twenty-five miles out at sea. Ships were now easily warned away from the deadly Barnegat shoals, and the number of shipwrecks dropped dramatically.

It's fortunate that Meade knew his lighthouses, because soon erosion reared its ugly head again. In 1859 Barnegat Lighthouse had been 900 feet from shore. In 1866 it was just 450 feet from shore and losing beach fast to the hungry sea. Brushwood jetties were constructed to protect the lighthouse, but storms broke them up almost as soon as they were built.

The surging sea affected more than just the lighthouse. In 1889 a magnificent two and one-half-story keeper's house was built at the base of the lighthouse at a cost of $12,000. The huge house was partitioned so that the keeper, both his assistants, and all their families could live in separate quarters. But by 1920 storms and erosion had so badly damaged the house that the Lighthouse Bureau put it up for sale at the dirt-cheap price of $160. The man who finally bought the house for a mere $126 quickly made his money back and more by stripping the house and selling off its fixtures, wood, and other parts.

Erosion continues to be a major problem for Old Barney today. Repeated attempts have been made to stem the sea's advance, including at one point the desperate efforts of local residents who raised two thousand dollars to build a small jetty. Nothing, however, seems to have much long-term effect. In the early 1990s a massive reconstruction and dredging project was undertaken in Barnegat Inlet; this seems to have bought the lighthouse a little more time, but everyone knows that nature's appetite for the shore is never sated.

For eighty-five years Barnegat Lighthouse aided mariners sailing along the difficult Long Beach Island shoreline. More than just a lighthouse, Old Barney became a rallying point and familiar sight for residents and vacationers alike. But there was no denying the march of progress. In 1927 the lighthouse's functions were taken over by an offshore lightship, and its great light was subsequently reduced in intensity. On January 1, 1944, blackness descended over Barnegat Lighthouse. Progress had done what generations of keepers had diligently tried to prevent: the extinguishing of Old Barney's light.

◆

The story of the Absecon Lighthouse is the story of one man's persistence, often in the face of overwhelming odds.

Graveyard Inlet was what mariners, mapmakers, and surveyors used to call Absecon Inlet. Shipwrecks such as the one that claimed 145 lives along with the British ship *Mermaid* on March 31, 1779, occurred in that area with frightening frequency.

The stakes were raised even further when, in the 1830s, a young doctor named Jonathan Pitney helped to found a town on the windswept, bayberry-studded stretch of beach on the south side of the inlet. First called Absecon Beach, the name of the town was changed in 1853 to Atlantic City. As people began to come to the area to live and vacation and as ship traffic increased proportionately, the need for a lighthouse at Graveyard Inlet became even more critical.

Realizing early on the necessity for a lighthouse there, Pitney began urging the federal government in the mid-1830s to build one. Little did he realize that his request, which must have seemed so eminently logical in view of all the shipwrecks, would take more twists and turns than a corkscrew over the next twenty years.

After haranguing the government for several years, Pitney must have felt close to success in the early 1840s when Congress appropriated five thousand dollars to determine the need for a lighthouse at Absecon Inlet. A naval officer named Commodore La Vallette came down, examined the area, looked over Pitney's voluminous records detailing all the shipwrecks—and recommended that a lighthouse not be built. La Vallette went back to his job, Pitney went back to pleading, and more people died. Between 1847 and 1856 more than sixty ships wrecked on Absecon Beach.

Absecon Lighthouse in 1874 showing how near it was to the water when first constructed. (Photo courtesy Atlantic County Historical Society)

Maybe these additional shipwrecks turned the tide, or possibly someone in Washington just got tired of hearing Pitney beg, but on August 3, 1854, Congress finally authorized a thirty-five thousand dollar appropriation to build a lighthouse at Absecon Inlet. Work began in June 1855 under Major Hartman Bache of the U.S. Army Corps of Topographical Engineers but was finished by Lieutenant George G. Meade (prior to his work at Barnegat Light).

When it was first lit on January 15, 1857, the Absecon Lighthouse must have been a sight to warm every mariner's heart. Towering 167 feet above sea level and fitted with a first-order Fresnel lens, the beacon could be seen for twenty miles. It was higher above sea level than any other New Jersey lighthouse except Twin Lights. But an even truer measure of Pitney's vision was that, during the first ten months of its existence, not a single wreck occurred in the former Graveyard Inlet.

But, once again, erosion began threatening a Jersey Shore lighthouse. When it was built, Absecon Light was 1,300 feet from the water's edge. In the 1870s, during northeasters, the ocean actually encircled the lighthouse and its related buildings, trapping the keeper inside. By 1876 the high-tide line had moved to within a mere 75 feet of the lighthouse. It was obvious that at the current rate the ocean would claim the lighthouse within a decade—maybe sooner.

To meet the ocean's threat, several large jetties were built out from the base of the lighthouse. Not only did these stop the erosion, they actually worked *too* well. The ocean now retreated. By the mid-1880s the jetties were covered by broad, sandy beaches. Homes and other buildings began replacing the sand dunes and trees that had once been the lighthouse's only neighbors. This is the reason that today, if you're driving down Pacific Avenue in Atlantic City, it might be quite surprising when you stumble across Absecon Lighthouse in an empty field in the middle of a residential area—a good two blocks from the ocean!

Finally, Absecon was done in by its location. The lighthouse had become so far removed from the shoreline that its beacon blended with the lights of nearby tall buildings, making it useless for ships. A new light was built atop a 70-foot-high tower on the Boardwalk, and the Absecon Lighthouse was decommissioned on July 11, 1933.

Possibly because of the popularity of Atlantic City, Absecon Lighthouse enjoyed a second career as a tourist attraction. An average of over ten thousand people yearly visited the site from around 1912 to the early 1950s. Often it was the most-visited lighthouse in the United States. (It was still popular in 1964; news of its relighting received extensive media coverage.) Although today it is solely a tourist attraction, it remains forever a monument to the tenacity and vision of one man.

♦

Tenacity also plays an important part in the story of the Hereford Inlet Lighthouse in North Wildwood—in both its birth and its resurrection.

Preceding the lighthouse along the banks of the Hereford Inlet was a lifesaving station, which was established in 1849 because of the growing use of the inlet by mariners from all over the world. Located almost directly between Great Egg Harbor to the north and Delaware Bay to the south, Hereford Inlet became well known as a convenient safe harbor for vessels running along the coast. As more and more ships used the waterway, residents and mariners began pressing for a lighthouse there. The existence of the lifesaving station, as well as the increased traffic, should have been perfect justifications for building such a structure, but as we've seen in the case of Dr. Pitney's long battle for Absecon Light, things don't always work out the way they should. It took many years—until June 10, 1872—for Congress to enact legislation to finance "a small light—say of the fourth order" at Hereford Inlet. A total of one and one-half acres were bought for $150 from Humphrey S. Cresse and his wife on July 7, 1873, and construction began shortly thereafter.

From the beginning it was always intended that Hereford Inlet be a small lighthouse, not a sky grabber like Barnegat or Absecon. But just because the light wasn't a busy coastal beacon doesn't mean that the duties were any less hazardous. Less than three months after the light became operational on May 11, 1874, keeper John Marche drowned while returning to his post in a small boat from the mainland.

Hereford Inlet was one of the most attractive lighthouses along the East Coast. Of Victorian design, with the light sticking up from the top of the roof, the structure contained five fireplaces and enough peaks and windows to make it right at home in Victorian-happy Cape May. Unfortunately, sometimes it seemed as if storms were trying to blow it straight to that town. In October of 1878 a hurricane knocked the lighthouse off its block foundation, while during an 1889 storm the structure was totally surrounded by water. In 1913 nature struck again, smashing the lighthouse so hard it had to be moved 150 feet west.

Hereford Inlet was another Jersey Shore light in which a woman carried out the duties of keeper. For two months in 1926, Laura Hedges kept the light burning after the death of her husband.

But despite the faithful service of Mrs. Hedges and many others, time and progress caught up with Hereford Inlet Light, and it was decommissioned in 1964. That might have been the end of the story—but it was really a second beginning.

Boarded up and neglected, the building soon fell into a sorry state. In a 1979 newspaper story the lighthouse was described as having caved-in walls and "gaping holes in the floor." But something about this graceful Victorian structure kept calling to the residents—something that made it seem important not to lose this part of their heritage.

The people responded to the lighthouse's silent plea by organizing a massive fund-raising and restoration drive. Good things began to happen. In 1977 the light was added to the National Register of Historic Places. In 1982 the New Jersey Department of Environmental Protection turned over stewardship of the lighthouse to the city of North Wildwood. Finally, on July 1, 1984, a portion of the restored building was reopened for use as a tourist welcome center. A landscaping project in 1986 festooned the grounds with hundreds of colorful flowers and shrubs.

Today the Hereford Inlet Lighthouse has been restored to its former glory and is a popular tourist attraction in North Wildwood. Although the lighthouse may keep the light no longer, the spirit is still alive.

◆

We come now to the lighthouse located on what is just about the end of the Jersey Shore—Cape May Point. But is this the fourth Cape May Lighthouse or the third? History has given us a mystery to ponder.

It is usually held that the first Cape May Lighthouse was built in 1823. But there is evidence of another beacon being here long before that. A deed dated September 23, 1785, confirms that land was purchased in Cape May from "Thomas Hand, 2nd, gentleman," for the purpose of "erecting thereon a beacon for the benefit of navigation." A letter confirming this transaction is dated November 12 of the same year. Furthermore, an advertisement in the *Philadelphia Aurora* in July 1801 talked about how pleasant Cape May was to visit, describing it as "just on the confluence of Delaware Bay with the ocean, in sight of the Lighthouse."

Unfortunately, there are no records to indicate that a lighthouse was ever in Cape May Point at that time. Although the circumstantial evidence is strong, solid proof is lacking. Thus to the 1823 tower goes the honor of being the first documented lighthouse in Cape May. But this seventy-foot-tall beacon didn't last long. It had been built on shifting sands, and it wasn't long before that old lighthouse bugaboo—erosion—began eating away at the beach. Finally bowing to the inevitable, federal officials discontinued the lighthouse on May 1, 1847. Its site is now underwater.

It is unclear what happened next in the Cape May Lighthouse saga. Some sources say the lighthouse was "removed" and rebuilt at a new site about four hundred feet from its first location, while others say a completely new structure was built. Either way, this

The Lightkeeper's Daytime Duties

As might be expected, lighthouse keepers were busy at night, making sure the lamp stayed lit. But when dawn brought sunlight back to the world, the keeper didn't just extinguish the lamp and go fishing. The duties performed during the day were just as important as those at night, because any mistakes could cause the lamp not to work properly the next evening. The following, quoted from the *Lightkeeper's Manual*, list the "few chores" the keepers had to do after extinguishing the lamp:

Wipe the chimney with care within and without.

Wrap the chimney in a dry cloth and place it where it will be free of dust.

Remove the lamp and, if it be a constant-level one, place it on its service-stand.

Dust the apparatus with a feather-brush, and wipe it with a soft linen cloth free of dust. If any part is spotted with oil, wash it with a little spirits of wine.

Cover the apparatus with its linen cover. Carefully wipe the glass of the lantern within and without, and, if necessary, clean it with whiting, or, if necessary, with polishing-rouge.

If the lantern is provided with curtains, hang them in place.

(continued)

second—or was it the third?—lighthouse was also not destined to last long. An 1851 inspection found it to be leaking, unpainted, rusty, damp, and unventilated. The wood inside the tower was called "rough beyond anything seen before." Worst of all, the light revolved irregularly.

Needless to say, there weren't a lot of tears shed in Cape May when a completely new lighthouse began to rise just a short distance away. Built of brick, the new structure was 167 feet above sea level. Lit for the first time on October 31, 1859, the lighthouse's beacon was visible for nineteen miles out at sea.

Much like Absecon Light years later, the new Cape May Lighthouse was a popular place to visit. An article in the January 1885 edition of the local newspaper *Star of the Cape* said: "A visit to the Cape May light house is one of great interest to

The Lightkeeper's Daytime Duties (continued)

Dust the service-table, the pedestal and the interior part of the lantern wall.

Sweep the staircase.

Take the lamp into the storeroom and weigh it to ascertain the amount of oil consumed during the night; empty the lamp and pour the oil into the strainer.

Place the oil that has fallen into the drip-cup during the night into the vessel kept for leavings, and reserve it for use.

Clean the burner with care within and without. Remove burned oil attached to the edges with a triangular scraper. Pass a bottle-brush through the interior air-tube, and wipe the outside with a linen cloth.

Carefully wipe the buttons of the lamps burning schist oil.

Wipe and clean the body of the lamp.

Fill the lamp, trim or replace the wick, and set it up again in the apparatus so that every thing may be ready for lighting up at evening.

Take care so that the spare lamp, which should be kept in the light-room, is in a serviceable condition. Two extra wick-carriers, provided with their wicks, should be ready to be placed in the lamp.

Carry a can filled with strained oil up into the lantern, or place it at the foot of the pedestal, so that it can be poured into the spare lamp if required.

most people, and one indulged in by a great many of our own people. The number of persons visiting the light house last year has not been counted up, but in 1883 over eighteen hundred were shown up the great tower, which means hundreds of trips and hundreds of explanations of the workings of the lamps by the keepers."

But the keepers might well have been grateful for the company. Their lot was often a lonely one, with no one beyond their family to break the daily routine. The keeper's primary duty was to keep the light lit no matter what; if it snowed, for instance, the keeper was expected to get out and clear the snow off the windows so that the light could be plainly seen by ships at sea. For such diligence and hard work, a keeper was usually paid a pittance. The yearly salary of the 1859 light's first keeper, William

Gregory, was $400; by May 1924 the annual wage of the last keeper, Harry H. Palmer, had risen only to $960.

The keeper's Bible was the *Lightkeeper's Manual*. It advised that the light be "visited" at least once per night from April 1 to October 1. For the remainder of the year the suggested "visitation time" was at least twice a night, or "oftener, if from any cause there may be reason to fear that the light may go out or decrease much in intensity."

To pass the time when not attending to lighthouse duties, keepers often turned to other pursuits. Palmer, for example, was a superb gardener; the lawns and gardens were always in their best shape during his tenure at Cape May Lighthouse, and his hydrangeas often won blue ribbons at the local flower show.

In 1932 people in Cape May kicked up a fuss when they learned that the Lighthouse Service might abolish the venerable light as an economy measure. The *Philadelphia Bulletin* carried an article by mariners and others singing the praises of the light. "In my opinion the Cape May Point light is . . . one of the most important on the Jersey Coast," said a local Coast Guardsman.

But although the light was saved, the keeper was not. In 1933 the lighthouse was automated, and keeper Palmer retired. During World War II the tower was used as a military observation post. Today, although its light still shines, the Cape May Lighthouse is primarily a tourist attraction, offering a breathtaking view of the sparkling blue Atlantic.

This, then, is the legacy of Jersey Shore lighthouses. Stolid, lonely, yet vitally important, they stood as silent sentinels along the shoreline for decades, even centuries. Even though modern technology has passed them by, there is still something about them that stirs the soul.

THIRTEEN

THE CHANGING COASTLINE

The next time you want a good example of the old saying "Looks can be deceiving," go to the beach.

The beach is one of the true paradoxes of nature. On the surface it seems calm and peaceful, a place where gulls glide lazily overhead, children run giddily along kicking up sand with their heels, and people seeking solitude stroll aimlessly about. Even during the summer, when crowds pack the beach and you can't walk two feet without stepping onto someone's blanket, the soothing serenity of the sand sends people to sleep like a mother's gentle lullaby.

But this pleasant appearance is only a facade. In reality, the beach is one of the most dynamic environments in the world. Natural forces like wind and water are constantly attacking the coastline—sometimes, during storms, with unbelievable violence. These assaults alter the beach to an amazing degree, taking sand away here, adding it there, moving it up or down the coast.

This happens not only during major storms but also during the most pleasant weather imaginable, when the blue sky is filled with puffy white clouds and the breeze is barely strong enough to tickle your nose. It is because of this perpetual cycle of change that a beach has been called simply a large collection of sand that is moving somewhere else.

Obviously, the Jersey Shore has felt the effects of this phenomenon. Sometimes the shoreline changes quickly and unexpectedly as the result of storms; other times the reconfiguration is more gradual, taking years to occur instead of hours. But change it does, and change it will. In the unpredictable world of the Jersey Shore, the only constant is change.

♦

Today we hear about many problems that threaten our shoreline, such as beach erosion and a rising sea level. These, however, are not uniquely modern occurrences; beaches have been eroding and the ocean has been rising since long before anyone first tossed a towel onto the sand.

Scientific data reveal that approximately 35,000 years ago sea level was about the same as it is today. However, during the last Ice Age, known as the Wisconsin age, sea level declined dramatically as ocean water became part of the giant glaciers. When the Wisconsin glaciation was at its maximum—approximately 18,000 years ago—sea level had dropped an astounding 425 feet! This meant that the New Jersey shoreline was about eighty miles farther east than it is today. Giant mastodons rambled over this newly exposed land, and possibly humans did too. (For those of you who are wondering if this means you might one day unearth the massive skull of a *Tyrannosaurus rex* while digging on the beach, forget it; this was long, long after the dinosaurs had died out.)

As the glaciers began melting and retreating to the north, the water they released flowed back into the oceans, triggering a rise in sea level. Scientific estimates indicate that from 7,000 years ago up to 2,500 years ago, the world's oceans rose at an extremely rapid rate—approximately two millimeters per year. During this time the New Jersey shoreline looked much different than it does today; it was probably just a few hundred yards wide and did not have many of the characteristics of today's coast, such as large sand dunes.

Then, for reasons still not fully understood, the rise in sea level slowed significantly, dropping to an average of about .75

millimeters per year. It was at this time—2,500 years ago—that the "modern" New Jersey shoreline began to emerge. Barrier islands began to accumulate sand and enlarge, dunes began to develop, and bays and marshland began to take on their present forms. In effect, the Jersey Shore was gaining material and building up.

About 500 years ago this "development" phase ceased, and the building up process subtly shifted into reverse. The Shore began losing material; sand was transported from the beaches out to deeper water. This was the start of the erosion that is occurring today.

On top of this, the rise in sea level—which had slowed but not stopped—began to accelerate, primarily because ocean water began to expand due to a rise in its temperature caused by the greenhouse effect. (Another result of the greenhouse effect that has contributed to rising sea level is the additional melting of mountain glaciers.) Today the sea is rising at a rate of almost 4 millimeters per year (1.3 feet per century)—twice as fast as at the conclusion of the Wisconsin glaciation. Some scientists are saying that this figure might reach 8.5 millimeters per year (2.8 feet per century) by the year 2100.

Skeeter's, a Tucker's Island hunting and gunning club, circa 1910. Insert shows Tucker's Island Lighthouse. (Collection of Richard Steele)

What the rising sea will do to the Jersey Shore is currently a matter of speculation. History has proved that the ocean is a powerful, unpredictable force—as it demonstrated in the case of Tucker's Island.

Once located off the southern end of Long Beach Island, this small spit of land (approximately five miles long and a mile wide) took its name from Reuben Tucker, who bought it in 1765.

Soon Quakers from Philadelphia were coming to Tucker's Island, ostensibly because it was a good place to hold their five-day camp meetings during the summer. It was pure coincidence that the island also provided excellent fishing and hunting, along with wonderfully cool seashore breezes.

Before long the island was enjoying a brisk business entertaining sportsmen and other visitors. In 1848 a lighthouse was built on the north end of the island, and a Life-Saving Station began operation in 1869. Gradually a little community began to develop.

Life on Tucker's Island seemed like a page out of *Tom Sawyer*. When not attending the one-room schoolhouse, children of the men who served at the Life-Saving Station romped through the tall grass and fished to their hearts' content, while on the ocean magnificent sailing ships swept by, their great sails flapping in the wind. Even though summer visitors stopped coming to the island once the railroad funneled everyone to Beach Haven on Long Beach Island, life on Tucker's Island was good.

But the ocean had other plans.

Nature had seemingly never been happy with the island. Like an artist who can't decide how to finish a painting, nature would periodically join Tucker's Island to the southern tip of Long Beach Island, then separate it again by running an inlet through the connecting sand. In 1874 the inlet closed, and the island became part of Long Beach Island. Finally, on February 4, 1920, nature made up its mind what to do with Tucker's Island—and this time the decision was irrevocable.

On that night a howling snowstorm pounded the Jersey Shore. The storm tore open the inlet—the Beach Haven Inlet—again. But this time powerful ocean currents began moving quickly southward, eating away at the coastline—including Tucker's Island. Over the next several years residents were forced to flee as

Tucker's Island Lighthouse falling into the sea in 1927. (Collection of Richard Steele)

the ocean consumed more and more of the island. Soon structures began toppling into the sea. In 1927 the lighthouse went
down, followed eight years later by the Coast Guard station. But
by then it didn't matter. On November 8, 1932, Tucker's Island
was taken off the tax assessment roles of Long Beach Township
because it had been "practically washed away by the ocean."
Today all that's left of the once-thriving resort is a shoal—a reminder of the sea's relentless appetite.

◆

Parcels of land like Tucker's Island aren't all that have vanished from the Jersey Shore's changing coastline. Inlets—those
convenient channels of water that enable boats to move from the
ocean into bays and other inland waterways—have also pulled
their share of disappearing acts throughout the centuries. Inlets
are usually formed in the aftermath of a storm, when high tides
retreat and bottled-up masses of water in the bays, pushed there
by the storm, break through the land and reach the ocean. Although today there are thirteen inlets along the Jersey Shore,
nearly two dozen others have existed and subsequently closed
during the 350-year recorded history of New Jersey's coastline.

Like beaches, inlets can be extremely active and volatile environments. One of the most fluid inlets on the entire Jersey Shore
is Barnegat Inlet, which is constantly attempting to migrate
southward, and over time has succeeded; it has moved approximately one mile since an 1812 survey.

This activity poses a continual threat to the lighthouse built
there to help guide mariners through the unpredictable channel.
Erosion claimed the first lighthouse built at Barnegat Inlet, and
it has been trying for decades to take down the current light, Old
Barney, as well. It is almost certain that the lighthouse has been
spared up to this time only by a series of dredging and shore protection projects; without human intervention the inlet might well
be much farther south than it is today, and the lighthouse would
likely be long gone.

The perpetual movement of Barnegat Inlet has long been recognized. Edwin Salter, in his 1890 book *A History of Monmouth
and Ocean Counties*, says that "Barnegat Inlet is continually
slowly shifting and changing, and always has been from our earliest accounts."

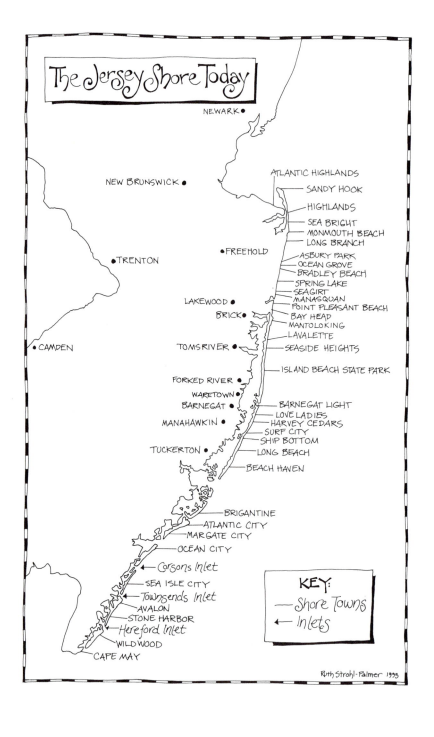

Existing and Extinct Inlets Along the Jersey Shore

Throughout the years, inlets at the Jersey Shore have opened and closed more often than the lid of a cookie jar in a house full of children. The following is a list of both existing and extinct inlets along the Jersey Shore during the past 250 years.

Absecon Inlet. Open

Barnegat Inlet. Open

Beach Haven–Little Egg inlet system. Open

Brigantine Inlet. Open (has been stable since about 1840)

Brigantine Island Breach. Closed (a breach approximately 1.5 miles north of Absecon that occurred in 1870)

Brook. (no other name recorded) Closed (near Deal)

Cape May Inlet. Open

Corsons Inlet. Open

Cranberry Inlet. Closed

Deal Lake Inlet. Closed (temporarily connected Deal Lake in Asbury Park to the sea)

Dry Inlet. Closed (a shallow inlet that temporarily cut Absecon Island approximately in half)

Duck Creek Inlet. Closed (near Bradley Beach)

Elberon Pond Inlet. Closed (at Elberon)

Fresh Pond Inlet. Closed (in Spring Lake)

Goose Pond Inlet. Closed (near Bradley Beach)

Great Egg Harbor Inlet. Open

Hereford Inlet. Open

Kettle Creek Inlet. Closed (between Mantoloking and Lavallette)

Manasquan Inlet. Open

Metedeconk River Inlet. Closed (just above Mantoloking, across from the Metedeconk River)

Navesink River Inlet. Closed

Newberry Pond Inlet. Closed (just above the current Manasquan Inlet)

Sea Girt Inlet. Closed (at Sea Girt)

Shark River Inlet. Open

Shrewsbury River Inlet. Closed

Silver Lake Inlet. Closed (just below Shark River Inlet)

Sunset Pond Inlet. Closed (in Asbury Park)

Temporary inlet at Harvey Cedars. Closed (broke through during March 1962 storm)

(continued)

Existing and Extinct Inlets Along the Jersey Shore *(continued)*

Temporary inlet at Holgate. Closed (broke through during March 1962 storm)
Three Corner Pond Inlet. Closed (between Shark River and Manasquan River inlets)
Townsend Inlet. Open
Turtle Gut Inlet. Closed (just below Wildwood Crest)
Wesley Inlet. Closed (in Asbury Park)
Whale Pond Inlet. Closed (just below Long Branch)
Wreck Inlet. Closed (just above Brigantine Inlet)

Another waterway that never seems satisfied to stay in the same place is the Beach Haven–Little Egg inlet system between Long Beach Island and Pullen Island to the south. Maps and charts from as far back as 1685 show that these two inlets have periodically merged and then split apart again. In 1743 Beach Haven Inlet was several thousand feet south of its recorded position in 1685. By 1903 both the southern tip of Long Beach Island and the adjacent Beach Haven Inlet had migrated over twenty thousand feet to the south of where they had been reported in an 1840 coastal survey. In 1903 the Beach Haven and Little Egg inlets joined to form one inlet, which was called New Inlet. But this configuration didn't last long either. The February 4, 1920, snowstorm that marked the beginning of the end for Tucker's Island again split the Beach Haven and Little Egg inlets. It was the movement of the Beach Haven Inlet south that eventually destroyed Tucker's Island.

Today these two inlets are still separate: Beach Haven Inlet provides a passage around the southern tip of Long Beach Island into Little Egg Harbor, and Little Egg Inlet allows access into Great Bay. But given the history of this notoriously unstable inlet system, who knows how long this situation will last?

Barnegat Inlet and Beach Haven Inlet, along with Great Egg Inlet, are the big movers along the Jersey Shore. One possible reason for this is that these inlets did not have a deep channel carved out for them during the Ice Age, so in effect they are free to slide back and forth. Absecon Inlet, on the other hand, did have such a channel made for it, and thus has not moved much at all—maybe a grand total of fifteen hundred feet—over the centuries.

Inlets can be the cause of adverse changes to the coastline, such as when the opening of Beach Haven Inlet eventually caused Tucker's Island's demise. Often, however, inlets have a beneficial effect: the shortcuts they provide for inland boats heading out to the ocean (and vice versa) translate into considerable savings in time and money for shipowners and captains. When inlets close, they produce not only inconvenience but also financial hardship. This was the case with Cranberry Inlet.

Cranberry Inlet was located near the mouth of the Toms River, just about in the middle of what is today known as Barnegat Beach Island (actually a twenty-two-mile-long peninsula stretching from Point Pleasant to Island Beach). The inlet, which received its name from the cranberries that grew wild near the channel's mouth, reportedly opened about 1750; it first appeared on coastal maps in 1755. Edwin Salter's *Old Times in Old Monmouth* reports that Cranberry Inlet was first discovered by young David Mapes, a Quaker who tended cattle on the beach. According to Salter, "He [Mapes] slept in a cabin, and one morning on awakening was surprised to see that the sea had broken across the beach during the night."

Holding about fifteen feet of water and approximately fifteen hundred feet wide, the new inlet quickly became economically important to the many ships that sailed in and out of the entire northern Barnegat Bay area. Instead of being forced to sail twelve miles farther south to tumultuous Barnegat Inlet, ship captains heading out to sea could use Cranberry Inlet instead. Large and small ships were apparently able to use the channel without much difficulty. Salter reported that the inlet "must have been equal to the best inlets on our coast, as we find loaded square-rigged vessels occasionally entered it." One of the reasons that Toms River became a hotbed of privateer activity during the Revolution was that colonial ships could easily slip through Cranberry Inlet into the ocean, attack an enemy ship, then dash back to port.

But nature had not intended for Cranberry Inlet to be a permanent part of the Jersey Shore. In 1812, after years of steadily increasing shoals, the inlet closed. Sea captains, merchants, and many others in the Toms River area who had grown used to the inlet were immediately at a disadvantage. The hue and cry raised about the loss of this convenient outlet to the sea was so great that in 1821 a man named Michael Ortley attempted to re-open the inlet. For several years he worked at the job off and on, investing, according to Salter, "considerable money in the under-taking." Finally, with the help of a "large company of men," Ort-ley finished the job. Then, according to Salter: "In the evening, after finishing it, Mr. Ortley and his friends had quite a merry time in celebrating the completion of the work. But great was their disappointment the following morning to find that the run-ning of the tide, which they had supposed would work the inlet deeper, had, on the contrary, raised a bulkhead of sand suffi-ciently large to close it up, and the result was the inlet was closed much more expeditiously than it was opened."

Having the work of years wiped out in one night should have been proof enough that nature did not want to give back Cran-berry Inlet, but some people still didn't get the message. In the 1840s another attempt was made to resurrect the inlet, this time under the direction of Anthony Ivens, Jr. The job was finished on July 4, 1847, but this too was doomed to failure. As Salter crisply put it: "this enterprise . . . filled up about as soon as Ortley's." The die was cast; Cranberry Inlet was destined to stay closed, and remains so to this day.

Often when inlets close, the result is a radical change in the coastal configuration. The closing of Cranberry Inlet produced one continuous strip of shoreline from Manasquan Inlet south to Barnegat Inlet. On the northern Jersey Shore, the opening and closing of the Shrewsbury and Sandy Hook inlets throughout the centuries has caused Sandy Hook to switch back and forth from an island to a peninsula.

A study of coastal maps for the past three hundred years re-veals a cyclical pattern in the geographical configuration of the two inlets and Sandy Hook. Historian George Moss, in his book *Another Look at Nauvoo to the Hook*, essentially breaks down the cycle in this manner: Stage one finds Sandy Hook connected to the Highlands of Navesink, while Shrewsbury Inlet allows direct access to both the Shrewsbury and Navesink rivers from the ocean. In stage two a new inlet (called the Sandy Hook Inlet) is cut through at the base of Sandy Hook, thus severing the Hook from the Highlands and making it a true island. Stage three finds yet a third inlet cut through the barrier beach several miles south of Sandy Hook, in effect making two islands—Sandy Hook and the land south of it (which would be roughly equivalent to the areas of Sea Bright and Monmouth Beach today). In stage four this new inlet closes, although Sandy Hook remains an island. In stage five, the final stage, Shrewsbury Inlet closes, which causes Sandy Hook to become part of the barrier beach—which is how the geography of this area appears today.

Since the end of the nineteenth century, human interference—through the use of seawalls, jetties, and other devices—has kept Sandy Hook tenuously linked to the barrier beach. Nature, however, hasn't given up trying to continue the five-stage cycle. Storms in 1962, 1974, and 1988 caused severe flooding and damage in the areas where inlets have previously opened. Only the massive sea wall that lines this part of the coast has kept the ocean from reforming the Shrewsbury and Sandy Hook inlets once again.

The battle for Sandy Hook is not over. Although humans have the technology, nature has sheer power, stubbornness, and time on its side. It remains to be seen who will win.

◆

Storms are often the cause of changes to the Jersey Shore either by creating or filling inlets, or by eroding great quantities of sand from the beaches. A storm in the early part of the nineteenth century did none of these things, yet it changed the Shore environment forever.

Great Swamp was an anomaly for a barrier island. Located on Long Beach Island, where the northern portion of Surf City is today, Great Swamp was a freshwater paradise within shouting distance of the Atlantic Ocean. The water came from the same gigantic, crystal-clear aquifer that lies under the sandy soil of the New Jersey Pinelands, and it helped to nourish Great Swamp's most distinguishing feature: tall white cedar trees. These huge trees provided a shady home for many varieties of birds and animals. Finding this junglelike area, teeming with animal life and vegetation, on a sandy barrier island was akin to finding an oasis in the barren desert.

But Great Swamp would not survive. On September 3, 1821, a fierce hurricane came up the coast and struck Long Beach Island with all its fury. Saltwater carried by massive ocean waves

flooded Great Swamp, turning it into marshland. What the howling winds did not destroy the saltwater did, and soon the majestic
cedar trees—along with the rest of Great Swamp's freshwater
vegetation—were no more. The Jersey Shore had been changed
yet again.

The story of Great Swamp, however, is atypical of how a storm
changes the Shore. Normally we associate storms with destruction, such as the terrible storm of March 6–8, 1962, that killed
twenty-one people, destroyed two thousand buildings, and caused
$103.5 million worth of damage (in 1962 dollars) along the Jersey
Shore. Nobody who lived on Long Beach Island during this storm

*A ravaged Ocean City during the March 1962 storm. In the foreground
four homes are shown burning along Central Avenue at Forty-first Street.
(Photo courtesy Urban Archives, Temple University, Philadelphia,
Pa./*Philadelphia Evening Bulletin*)*

and saw water from the ocean and bays breach the island in several places will ever forget the sight of those giant waves rolling relentlessly in from the raging Atlantic.

Waves generated by storms often cause much of the coastline to change by altering the configuration of the beach. Waves are mighty movers of sand; tests have shown that waves can move sand pebbles as much as one-half mile in a single day.

Waves usually approach a beach at an angle. Near the shore they become distorted by friction as they drag along the bottom. This causes the lower part of the wave to slow down; the top part then falls forward, producing the breakers so common to the Jersey Shore.

Breaking waves hit the beach with jackhammer force, as anybody who has ever been caught beneath one knows. These waves transport large amounts of sediment from the shoreline. Some of this material is deposited higher up on the beach, while the rest is carried offshore. However, because the wave hits the beach at a slight angle, the sediment that is taken offshore washes back to a place slightly removed from where it began its journey. This is essentially how waves move sand along a beach, although other factors come into play.

Fair-weather waves along the Jersey Shore usually vary in height from one to four feet, and they strike the shore about every five to ten seconds. During a storm, however, waves as much as ten feet high can strike the beach every eleven seconds or so. Thus it is easy to see why and how storm waves can move so much sand so quickly, and why beaches can be transformed—or destroyed—literally overnight.

Usually when we think of sand moving, we think of beach erosion, and great quantities of sand are indeed being removed from some of the Jersey Shore's beaches. In the 1977 book *The Geology and Landscapes of New Jersey*, Peter E. Wolfe says that 400,000 cubic yards of sand are moving south each year from Atlantic City, while Ocean City is losing 50,000 cubic yards of sand per year.

There is ample historical evidence of beach erosion. It might be hard today to imagine that the virtually vanished beaches of Sea Bright and Monmouth Beach used to be large enough for the fishing villages of Nauvoo and Galilee to exist on them, or that the now badly eroded Cape May beaches used to be wide enough for Henry Ford and others to race automobiles along them. Long

Branch, during the time when it was entertaining presidents and society's leading lights, was famous for its bluffs, which were small, steep hills that one had to climb down to reach the beach below. Today the Long Branch beach is as flat as any at the Jersey Shore.

As one of the earliest resorts, Cape May was one of the earliest victims of beach erosion. Estimates are that Cape May lost 169 feet of beach between 1804 and 1822. As shocking as this rapid loss of sand was, sometimes it proved even worse. In 1804 Commodore Stephen Decatur measured the beach at a particular area in Cape May at 334 feet; a mere twenty-five years later this same beach was almost entirely gone.

No matter in what century you look, you can find evidence of Jersey Shore erosion. Deeds still exist from the seventeenth century for parcels of land that today are almost a mile off the coast, underwater. A 1923 study by the New Jersey Board of Commerce and Navigation revealed the state had suffered a net loss of 2,496 acres of beachfront land in a century.

Unfortunately, humans have often helped erosion do its work. During the rush to establish resorts along the Shore in the second half of the nineteenth century, town founders frequently decided to remove unwanted obstructions from the beach such as sand dunes and vegetation. Typical of what happened to Shore beaches at this time is the example of Atlantic City, as cited in *Butler's Book of the Boardwalk*: "Not only was the beach sand deep and difficult to traverse, but it stood in great hills in places between the surf and the built-up parts of the city. Some of these hills, or dunes, were 50 feet high, built by the action of wind and wave and held together by wiry grasses and bushes. The first move to make an attractive and useful beach was to level these dunes and clear away the thick growth of trees, bushes, long grasses and scrub pines and cedars." (Atlantic City quickly learned the error of its ways. In 1870 seven thousand people signed a petition beseeching Congress to provide money to halt a severe loss of beachfront.)

Today, of course, the governing bodies of most Shore towns would do double backflips all the way from Sandy Hook to Cape May for the opportunity to have fifty-foot-high sand dunes firmly anchored by grass and bushes. Because they not only protect inland properties but also provide a reservoir of sand that can replenish beach material lost to erosion, dunes are considered an integral part of the strategy for preserving the precious shoreline. We have come a long way from the time when beachfront property was considered so worthless that a young man in 1700 sold all of Five Mile Beach and Two Mile Beach (which is today the Wildwoods) for nine pounds so he could buy his wife a dress.

Sometimes, the movement of sand builds up a beach. Anyone who has visited Wildwood recently knows that you practically have to take a taxi from the boardwalk to the ocean because the beach is so wide. The beach is expanding because jetties at Cape May Inlet are trapping much of the sand that would normally be moving south onto Cape May's beaches.

Sandy Hook is another place along the Jersey Shore that has been altered by a buildup of sand (known as accretion). The northern end of the Hook has been continuously growing at the expense of the south end. This buildup can be clearly seen in relation to Sandy Hook Lighthouse. In 1764, when it was built, the lighthouse stood just five hundred feet from the tip of the Hook. One hundred years later it was four thousand feet from the tip, and today it is one and one-half miles away.

The movement of sand at Sandy Hook is prodigious. In the 1986 book *Jersey Perspective: Selected Topics in Earth Science*, Joe Gasior cites 1966 estimates that show the net effect was an accumulation at the tip of 493,000 cubic yards of sand each year. This is equivalent to a ten-ton dump truck filled with sand arriving every eight minutes around the clock.

Beaches, of course, are the Shore areas most visible to us, and thus the places where we most often see firsthand evidence of the changing coastline. As noted before, even on the calmest days the dynamics of a beach are hard at work. Beaches even change in response to the seasons. During the summer, beaches tend to be fuller and contain more sand, because the waves are longer and lower. Winter waves, however, are often shorter and higher, moving sand from the upper beach or backshore (the part that we use for recreation) to the lower beach or offshore, which runs out to a depth of approximately thirty feet. During the summer, most—but not all—of this sand is returned.

Besides erosion and a rising sea level, another thing affecting our beaches—and consequently the shape of the coastline—is the lack of new sand arriving from inland sources. To maintain themselves, beaches must have at least as much sand deposited on them as is taken away by wind and water. However, this is not now the case in New Jersey.

Throughout the world, rivers are the major source of sand for beaches. Unfortunately, no rivers in New Jersey discharge directly into the ocean. The only way to get new material onto Jersey Shore beaches is to pump it there from someplace else. This is called beach replenishment or beach nourishment.

This is the situation in which we find ourselves today. The sea is rising, the shoreline is eroding, and there is no natural way for the beaches to replenish themselves. Historically, this situation has existed for quite some time, but it has only been since people discovered what a pleasant place the Jersey Shore is to live in and visit that this wholesale migration of real estate has become a serious problem. (A basic principle of coastal geology is that beach erosion is a common, natural event, and there is no erosion problem until a "permanent" structure is built that the eroding shoreline can then threaten.)

In short, natural forces have caused much to happen to the New Jersey coastline over the past few centuries. Much will undoubtedly happen to it in the future. If a wand could be waved and all the structures along the Shore be made to disappear, it is fairly certain that a person from one hundred years ago who was familiar with the geography of the Shore then would not recognize it today. If we could come back one hundred years from now, would we recognize the Jersey Shore?

BIBLIOGRAPHY

GENERAL

Alexander, Robert Crozer. *Ho! For Cape Island.* Robert Crozer Alexander, 1956.

Beitel, Herbert M., and Vance C. Enck. *Cape May County.* Norfolk, Va.: The Donning Company, 1988.

Boucher, Jack E. *Absegami Yesteryear.* Atlantic County Historical Society, 1963.

Boyer, George F., and J. Pearson Cunningham. *Cape May County Story.* The Laureate Press, 1975.

Butler, Frank M. *Butler's Book of the Boardwalk.* The 1954 Association, 1952.

Cain, Tim. *Peck's Beach.* Down the Shore Publishing, 1988.

Cunningham, John T. *The New Jersey Sampler: Historic Tales of Old New Jersey.* The New Jersey Almanac, 1964.

———. *The New Jersey Shore.* New Brunswick, N.J.: Rutgers University Press, 1958.

Davis, Ed. *Atlantic City Diary.* Atlantic Sunrise Publishing Company, 1980.

Dorsey, Leslie, and Janice Devine. *Fare Thee Well.* New York: Crown, 1964.

Ellis, Franklin. *History of Monmouth County, New Jersey.* R. T. Peck & Co., 1885.

Federal Writers' Project of the Works Progress Administration for the State of New Jersey. *Stories of New Jersey.* New York: M. Barrows and Company, 1938.

Fleming, Thomas. *New Jersey.* New York: W. W. Norton & Company, 1977.

Funnell, Charles E. *By the Beautiful Sea.* New Brunswick, N.J.: Rutgers University Press, 1983.

Hand Book of the Lower Delaware River. Philadelphia Maritime Exchange, 1895.

Hoagland, Stewart. *New Jersey Historical Profiles: Revolutionary Times.* Somerset Press, 1973.

Jahn, Robert. *Down Barnegat Bay.* Beachcomber Press, 1980.

Kobbe, Gustav. *The Jersey Coast and Pines.* Gustav Kobbe, 1889.

Leonard, Thomas Henry. *From Indian Trail to Electric Rail.* The Atlantic Highlands Journal, 1923.

Levi, Vicki Gold, and Lee Eisenberg. *Atlantic City: 125 Years of Ocean Madness.* New York: Clarkson N. Potter, 1979.

Lloyd, John Bailey. *Eighteen Miles of History on Long Beach Island.* Down the Shore Publishing, 1986.

———. *Six Miles At Sea.* Down the Shore Publishing, 1990.

McMahon, T. J. *The Golden Age of the Monmouth County Shore.* Self-published, 1964.

McMahon, William. *South Jersey Towns, History and Legend.* New Brunswick, N.J.: Rutgers University Press, 1984.

———. *So Young . . . So Gay!* Atlantic City Press, 1970.

Methot, June. *Up and down the Beach.* Whip Publishers, 1988.

Moss, George H., Jr. *Another Look at Nauvoo to the Hook.* Seabright, N.J.: Ploughshare Press, 1990.

———. *Nauvoo to the Hook.* Jersey Close Press, 1964.

Nelson, William. *The New Jersey Coast in Three Centuries.* The Lewis Publishing Co., 1902.

Rose, T. F., H. C. Woolman, and T. T. Price, M.D. *Historical and Biographical Atlas of the New Jersey Coast.* Woolman & Rose, 1878.

Salter, Edwin. *A History of Ocean and Monmouth Counties.* E. Gardner & Sons, 1890.

———. *Old Times in Old Monmouth.* James S. Yard, 1887.

Webster's American Biographies. Springfield, Mass.: G & C Merriam Co., 1974.

Wilson, Harold F., Ph.D. *The Jersey Shore: A Social and Economic History of the Counties of Atlantic, Cape May, Monmouth and Ocean.* Lewis Historical Publishing Company, 1953.

———. *The Story of the Jersey Shore.* Princeton, N.J.: D. Van Nostrand Company, 1964.

Who's Who in America. 46th edition. New York: Macmillan, 1990.

Who Was Who in America. 1607–1896.

Who Was Who in America. 1950–1960.

1. SHORE TOWN STORIES

Adams, Arthur, and Sarah A. Risley. *A Genealogy of the Lake Family.* Privately published, 1915.

AxellLute, Paul. *Lakewood-in-the-Pines.* Self-published, 1986.

Colton, Ray C. *The Civil War in the Western Territories.* Norman, Okla.: University of Oklahoma Press, 1959.

Jabers, Ron. "The Last Resort." *Philadelphia Magazine,* August 1980.

"James A. Bradley and Asbury Park, 1921." The Bradley Memorial Committee by Associated Reporters.

Lake, S. Wesley. Diary. Courtesy of Ocean City Historical Society.

Lee, Harold. *A History of Ocean City.* Friends of the Ocean City Historical Museum, 1965.

Ocean City Annual Reports. First Annual Report, Third Annual Report, Fifth Annual Report.

Rush, Mary Townsend. *Guide Book of Ocean City.* Ocean City, N.J., 1882.

Voss, J. Ellis. *Ocean City: An Ecological Analysis of a Satellite Community.* Philadelphia: University of Pennsylvania, 1941.

"What the Lights Reveal." *The Police Gazette,* August 1891.

Woolley, Adolph, and George Heffernan. *A Pictorial Album of Island Heights, N.J.* Ocean County Historical Society, 1971.

2. BY RAIL OR BY SEA

Alexander, Robert Crozer. *Steamboat for Cape May.* Robert Crozer Alexander, 1967.

Anderson, Elaine. *The Central Railroad of New Jersey's First 100 Years: A Historical Survey.* Center for Canal History and Technology, 1984.

Andrew, Russell M. *Railroading in Atlantic County, New Jersey.* Atlantic County Historical Society, 1981.

A Book of Cape May Point. The Albert Hand Co., 1937.

Gladulich, Richard M. *By Rail to the Boardwalk*. Trans-Anglo Books, 1986.

Kramer, Frederick A. *Pennsylvania-Reading Seashore Lines*. Crusader Press, 1980.

Moss, George H., Jr. *Steamboat to the Shore*. Jersey Close Press, 1966.

Reussille, Leon. *Steam Vessels Built in Old Monmouth 1841–1894*. Self-published, printed by J. I. Farley Printing Service, 1975.

Towle, Charles L. "History of the Camden and Atlantic Railroad and Associated Railroads, 1852–1897." Unpublished manuscript, the Atlantic County Library.

West Jersey Rails. The West Jersey Chapter of the National Railway Historical Society, 1983.

3. FAMOUS VISITORS AND RESIDENTS

Bauer, W. John, ed. *William Carlos Williams—Stephen Crane—Philip Freneau: Papers and Poems Celebrating New Jersey's Literary Heritage*. New Jersey Historical Commission, 1989.

Boulton, Agnes. *Part of a Long Story*. Garden City, N.Y.: Doubleday, 1958.

Bradley, Hugh. *Such Was Saratoga*. Garden City, N.Y.: Doubleday, Doran and Company, 1975.

Hoffman, Jeffrey. *Joe Louis: My Life*. New York: Harcourt Brace Jovanovich, 1978.

Nevins, Allan. *Grover Cleveland: A Study in Courage*. New York: Dodd, Mead & Company, 1932.

New Jersey Writer's Project. *Entertaining a Nation: The Career of Long Branch*. The Jersey Printing Co., 1940.

Sheaffer, Louis. *O'Neill: Son and Playwright*. Boston: Little, Brown & Co., 1968.

Thornbrough, Emma Lou. *T. Thomas Fortune: Militant Journalist*. Chicago: University of Chicago Press, 1970.

Uminowicz, Glenn. "Sport in a Middle-Class Utopia: Asbury Park, New Jersey, 1871–1895." *Journal of Sport History* (Spring 1984).

4. THERE SHE WAS . . . MISS AMERICA?

Bivans, Ann-Marie. *Miss America: In Pursuit of the Crown*. MasterMedia Limited, 1991.

Deford, Frank. *There She Is*. New York: The Viking Press, 1971.

Miss America Yearbook. 1947.
Miss America Yearbook. 1949.

5. WOODEN WALKWAYS ALONG THE SAND

Angott, Eleanor."Seaside Boardwalk." Unpublished manuscript, Ocean
County Historical Museum.
Purdie, William S. *Design Review: The Atlantic City Boardwalk.* The At-
lantic County Department of Regional Planning and Development,
Division of Planning, July 1987.
"Seaside Heights." Unpublished manuscript, Ocean County Historical
Museum.
Seaside Park Survey. Conducted by Michael May and Candy Peck,
Ocean County Cultural and Heritage Commission.
Wortman, Byron C. *The First Fifty: A Biographical History of Seaside
Heights, New Jersey.* 1963.

6. TRADITIONAL JERSEY SHORE CRAFTS

"Barnegat Bay Class A Racing Catboats on State Register." *Shore Her-
itage Newsletter,* Ocean County Cultural and Heritage Commission,
Winter 1985.
Guthorn, Peter J. *The Sea Bright Skiff and Other Shore Boats.* Schiffer
Publishing, 1982.
"Historic A-Cats." *Shore Heritage Newsletter,* Ocean County Cultural
and Heritage Commission, Spring 1985.
Official Guide and Program. Old Time Barnegat Bay Decoy and Gunning
Show, 1990. Times Beacon Newspapers.

7. I LOVE LUCY AND HER PALS

Boucher, Jack E. *Lucy, the Margate Elephant.* Egg Harbor, 1970.
Historic Lucy, the Margate Elephant. Pamphlet.
Kent, Bill. "Lucy the Elephant." *Atlantic City Magazine,* September
1989.
McCullough, David W. *Brooklyn: And How It Got That Way."* New York:
The Dial Press, 1983.
McCullough, Edo. *Good Old Coney Island.* New York: Scribner's, 1957.
McMahon, William. *The Story of Lucy the Elephant.* The Laureate Press,
1988.

8. SPIRITS OF THE JERSEY SHORE

Beck, Horace. *Folklore and the Sea.* Middletown, Conn.: Wesleyan University Press, 1973.

Seibold, David J., and Charles J. Adams III. *Cape May Ghost Stories.* Exeter House Books, 1988.

———. *Legends of Long Beach Island.* Self-published, 1985.

———. *Shipwrecks and Legends 'Round Cape May.* Self-published, 1987.

The Spy House Museum. Pamphlet.

9. WAR AT THE SHORE

Gordon, Robert. "The Dream That Failed." *Sea Classics,* March 1988.

Hoffman, Thomas J., park historian. *Fort Hancock.* National Park Service Booklets, Sandy Hook.

Noble, Dennis L. "The Beach Patrol and Corsair Fleet." Coast Guard Historian's Office, March 1992.

Nunn, Roy M. "The Goldschmidt Wireless." Undergraduate thesis, Albright College, 1967.

The Pathfinder, October 3, 1914.

Waltzer, Jim. "Camp Boardwalk." *Atlantic City Magazine,* July 1992.

10. SCIENCE AND INVENTION

Anderson, Norman D., and Walter R. Brown. *Ferris Wheels.* New York: Pantheon Books, 1983.

Burgess, Robert F. *Ships Beneath the Sea: A History of Subs and Submersibles.* New York: McGraw-Hill Book Company, 1975.

Carrick, Robert W. *The Pictorial History of the America's Cup Races.* New York: The Viking Press, 1964.

Catton, Bruce. *The American Heritage Picture History of the Civil War.* New York: American Heritage/Bonanza Books, 1960.

Coe, Douglas. *Marconi, Pioneer of Radio.* New York: Julian Messner, 1943.

Ferris, Timothy. *The Red Limit: The Search for the Edge of the Universe.* New York: Quill Press, 1983.

Francis, Joseph. Letter to Thomas Bond. The Ocean County Historical Museum.

"The Francis Life-Car." New Jersey State Government Hand-Out Sheet.

"Jersey Born and Bred." New Jersey State Government Hand-Out Sheet.

LeKites, Charles J. *Simon Lake, 1866–1946.* Written for the Lake Family Historical Association Annual Reunion, 1985.

"Marconi." New Jersey State Government Hand-Out Sheet.

"Marconi Wireless Telegraph." New Jersey State Government Hand-Out Sheet.

Sweeney, James B. *A Pictorial History of Oceanographic Submersibles.* New York: Crown Publishers, 1970.

11. THE LIFE-SAVING SERVICE

Bennett, Robert F. *Surfboats, Rockets, and Carronades.* Washington, D.C.: U.S. Government Printing Office, 1977.

Downey, Leland Woolley. *Broken Spars.* Brick Township Historical Society, 1983.

Holmes, Richard C. "Improvements in Surf and Life-Boats." United States Department of Commerce, Patent and Trademark Office, Washington, D.C.

Merryman, J. H. *The United States Life-Saving Service.* 1880; Santa Monica, Calif.: Vistabooks, 1989.

Miller, Pauline S. *Three Centuries on Island Beach.* The Ocean County Historical Society, 1981.

Storms, F. Dean. *History of Allentown, New Jersey.* Allentown Messenger, 1965.

12. BEACONS IN THE NIGHT

Answers to Questions Visitors Ask about Sea Girt Lighthouse. Pamphlet.

Bachand, Robert G. *Northeast Lights, Lighthouses and Lightships.* Sea Sports Publications, 1989.

"The Barnegat Lighthouse." *Shore Heritage Newsletter*, Ocean County Cultural and Heritage Commission, Summer 1991.

Beaver, Patrick. *A History of Light Houses.* Secaucus, N.J.: The Citadel Press, 1971.

Boucher, Jack E. *Historic Absecon Lighthouse.* Atlantic County Historical Society, 1964.

Hereford Inlet Lighthouse. Pamphlet.

Hoffman, Thomas J. "Sandy Hook Lighthouse History Text for Site Bulletin Handout." 1988.

Holland, Francis Ross, Jr. *America's Lighthouses.* The Stephen Green Press, 1972.

————. *Great American Lighthouses.* Walnut Creek, Calif.: Preservation Press, 1989.

"Ladies of the Lights." New Jersey State Government Hand-Out Sheet.

Laverty, Tom, and Bill Vibber. "New Jersey Lighthouse Firsts." *New Jersey Outdoors*, January/February 1988.

Lopez, John. "Sandy Hook Lighthouse." *The Keeper's Log*, Winter 1986.
"The Navesink Light Station." New Jersey State Government Hand-Out Sheet.
"New Jersey's Lighthouses." New Jersey State Government Hand-Out Sheet.
"Questions Most Often Asked about Twin Lights." New Jersey State Government Hand-Out Sheet.
"Why Are Some Lighthouses . . ." New Jersey State Government Hand-Out Sheet.

13. THE CHANGING COASTLINE

Gasior, Joe. *Jersey Perspective: Selected Topics in Earth Science*. Lenape Regional High School Board of Education, 1986.
"The Geology of Sandy Hook." New Jersey State Government Hand-Out Sheet.
"The History of Sandy Hook." New Jersey State Government Hand-Out Sheet.
New Jersey Shore Protection Master Plan. Volume I. State of New Jersey, Department of Environmental Protection, Division of Coastal Resources, 1981.
Nordstrom, Karl F., Paul A. Garès, Norbert P. Psuty, Orrin H. Pilkey, Jr., William J. Neal, and Orrin H. Pilkey, Sr. *Living with the New Jersey Shore*. Durham, N.C.: Duke University Press, 1986.
"The Ocean Beach." New Jersey State Government Hand-Out Sheet.
Widmer, Kemble. *The Geology and Geography of New Jersey*. Princeton, N.J.: D. Van Nostrand Company, 1964.
Wolfe, Peter E. *The Geology and Landscapes of New Jersey*. New York: Crane, Russak & Company, 1977.

COLLECTIONS

Atlantic County Public Library, Heston Collection.
Cape May County Historical and Genealogical Society, Robert C. Alexander Collection.
Long Branch Public Library, James F. Durnell Collection.
Monmouth County Historical Association, North American Phalanx Collection; William A. Newell Collection.
Ocean City Historical Society, Boardwalk Collection.
Office of New Jersey Heritage, Division of Parks and Forestry, New Jersey Department of Environmental Protection and Energy:

Atlantic County. Absecon Lighthouse; Atlantic City Convention Hall; Lucy, the Margate Elephant.

Cape May County. Avalon Lifesaving Station; Cape May Historic District; Hereford Lighthouse.

Monmouth County. Alexander Hamilton Steamship; Asbury Park Convention Hall; Church of the Presidents; Coast Guard Station at Sandy Hook; Fort Hancock; Fort Hancock and Sandy Hook Proving Ground Historic District; Marconi Building; Monmouth Battlefield; North American Phalanx Archeological Site; Ocean Grove Camp Meeting Association District; Sandy Hook Lighthouse; Seabrook-Wilson House; T. Thomas Fortune House; Twin Lights.

Ocean County. Barnegat Lighthouse; Bat; Island Heights Historic District; Lotus; Mary Ann; U.S. Lifesaving Station Number 14.

NEWSPAPERS

Asbury Park Evening Press & Asbury Park Press
Asbury Park Journal
Atlantic City Daily Press & Atlantic City Press
Cape May Star and Wave
Herald Lantern Dispatch
Long Branch Daily Record
New Jersey Courier
New York Herald
New York Times
Ocean City Sentinel Ledger
Ocean County Observer
Philadelphia Bulletin
The Shore Press
Star of the Cape
The Weekly Journal and Monmouth Republican

PERSONAL INTERVIEWS

Lachlan Beaton. April 1992, Mantoloking, New Jersey.
Tom Beaton. April 1992, Mantoloking, New Jersey.
John Chatterton. May 1992, Millburn, New Jersey.
Jane Doherty. March 1992, telephone interview.
Fran Doran. November 1991, telephone interview.

Virginia Hammond. April 1992, telephone interview.

Charles Hankins. January 1992, Lavallette, New Jersey.

Josephine Harron. January 1992, Margate, New Jersey.

Tom Hoffman. March 1992, Sandy Hook, New Jersey.

Sam Hunt. February 1992, Waretown, New Jersey.

Marilyn Kralik. February 1992, Island Heights, New Jersey.

George Moss. January 1992, Rumson, New Jersey.

Gertrude Neidlinger. January, 1992, Port Monmouth, New Jersey.

John Petzak. April 1992, Parkertown, New Jersey.

Harry Shourds. April 1992, Seaville, New Jersey.

John Suralik. March 1992, Tuckerton, New Jersey.

Jean Thompson Weiler. May 1992, telephone interview.

Jerry Woolley. June 1992, Point Pleasant, New Jersey.

INDEX